International Political Economy Series

Series Editor

Timothy M. Shaw, Emeritus Professor, University of Massachusetts Boston and University of London, Boston, MA, USA

The global political economy is in flux as a series of cumulative crises impacts its organization and governance. The IPE series has tracked its development in both analysis and structure over the last three decades. It has always had a concentration on the global South. Now the South increasingly challenges the North as the centre of development, also reflected in a growing number of submissions and publications on indebted Eurozone economies in Southern Europe. An indispensable resource for scholars and researchers, the series examines a variety of capitalisms and connections by focusing on emerging economies, companies and sectors, debates and policies. It informs diverse policy communities as the established trans-Atlantic North declines and 'the rest', especially the BRICS, rise.

NOW INDEXED ON SCOPUS!

Larry Swatuk · Corrine Cash
Editors

The Political Economy of Urban Water Security under Climate Change

palgrave
macmillan

Editors
Larry Swatuk
Ontario, ON, Canada

Corrine Cash
Mount Allison University
Sackville, NB, Canada

ISSN 2662-2483 ISSN 2662-2491 (electronic)
International Political Economy Series
ISBN 978-3-031-08107-1 ISBN 978-3-031-08108-8 (eBook)
https://doi.org/10.1007/978-3-031-08108-8

This Palgrave Macmillan imprint is published by the registered company Springer Nature Switzerland AG
The registered company address is: Gewerbestrasse 11, 6330 Cham, Switzerland

Acknowledgements

This collection had its genesis in the 2018 Cape Town water crisis when the city approached so-called 'day zero'—a point at which there would be no publicly supplied water available for residents of the city. The march toward crisis had many contributing factors, a multi-year drought, questionable governance, political in-fighting and poor decision-making, to name but a few. In response to these pressures and issues, a creative coalition of determined actors set about to deny the seemingly inevitable outcome—and succeeded. To be sure, the drought eventually did break and the rains have since refilled the dams. But there is strong evidence that concerted social action helped the city and its region survive in the face of collective adversity.

In July 2018, a group of like-minded individuals from around the world shopped the idea of holding an international conference on 'cities facing escalating water shortages'. As this collection illustrates, cities of all shapes and sizes are facing water crises of all kinds. In the context of climate change, it seemed vitally important to come together to learn the lessons—positive and negative—of Cape Town's water crisis and to share experience from around the world. The conference was eventually held in January 2020 at the University of the Western Cape in South Africa, in collaboration with the Institute for Ecological Civilization (EcoCiv), based in California, and several South African universities. A not-for-profit organization—W12—also provided support, and participants came from around the world.

In the lead-up to the conference, Larry Swatuk was approached to develop a 'task team' (one of five) in preparation for the conference. The task teams would develop position papers to inform the meeting. These papers were extensively rewritten and published under the title *Towards the Blue Green City: Building Urban Water Resilience* (Pretoria: Water Research Commission, 2021).

Swatuk also offered to deploy his graduate class in Water and Security at the University of Waterloo to write a series of case studies in support of the conference and follow-up activities, of which there have been many. These papers comprise the content of this book. They were first presented at the International Conference on Sustainable Development held online in September 2020 and have been significantly revised and updated. The papers are pitched at a policy level, reflecting critically on governing authorities' stated intentions and actual outcomes relative to a plethora of challenges, natural and human-made. Lurking in the interstices of most of these chapters are the marginalized and dispossessed. Indeed, it is a serious gap that their voices go unheard as cities lurch from one crisis to the next, with policymakers generally preferring well-trodden—technical and financial—pathways to 'water security' rather than undertaking the more difficult task of engaging meaningfully with stakeholders particularly those for whom 'the right to the city' is more dream than reality. As the saying goes, a chain is only as strong as its weakest link.

The co-editors would like to thank their respective home departments at Mount Allison and Waterloo for their ongoing institutional support. Larry Swatuk would like to thank Corrine Cash for accepting his invitation to help him co-edit this collection. He especially thanks Mafaniso Hara of the University of the Western Cape and Bongani Ncube of the Cape Peninsula University of Technology for reaching out to him to become part of the UWC Conference. He also thanks Philip Clayton, Ellie Leaning and Jeremy Fackenthal of EcoCiv, Rene Frank of W12+, and his task team co-collaborators in the UWC Conference, from whom he has learned so much: Gregg Brill, Charon Büchner-Marais, Kirsty Carden, Ernst Conradie, Jenny Day and Joanna Fatch.

Corrine Cash would like to thank Larry Swatuk for the opportunity to work on yet another project and, on behalf of both of them, also thank Timothy M. Shaw, Anca Pusca and Hemapriya Eswanth for their encouragement and assistance in bringing this manuscript to completion.

Waterloo, ON, Canada — Larry Swatuk
Sackville, NB, Canada — Corrine Cash

Contents

Notes on Contributors

Corrine Cash holds a Ph.D. in Urban Planning from the School of Planning, University of Waterloo, Ontario, Canada. Dr. Cash is an assistant professor in the Department of Geography and Environment at Mount Allison University in Sackville, New Brunswick, Canada. Prior to joining Mt. A., she was a member of the Programme Teaching Staff at the Coady International Institute as well as an assistant professor in the Climate and Environment Programme at St. Francis Xavier University, Antigonish, Nova Scotia, Canada. She is a co-editor of and contributor to *Water, Energy, Food and People: The Nexus in an era of Climate Change* (Palgrave Macmillan).

Elena Edo holds a Master of Development Practice Degree with a specialization in climate change from the University of Waterloo, Ontario, Canada. She is committed to promoting social justice, equity and inclusive climate policy.

Nesma Hassan is a Ph.D. student in the Sustainability Management programme at the University of Waterloo. She is also the co-founder of Life from Water Canada, and a project coordinator at the Institute for Ecological Civilization.

Cassandra Hayward is a Ph.D. candidate at the University of Cambridge in Land Economy. She previously worked as a policy analyst at Innovation, Science and Economic Development Canada, a federal institution that leads the Innovation, Science and Economic Development portfolio.

Her work mainly focuses on food manufacturing, sustainability and the sustainable development goals.

Anika Tasnim Hossain holds a Master of Development Practice Degree from the University of Waterloo, Ontario, Canada and a Bachelor of Arts Degree from BRAC University. Currently, she is a mobilization coordinator at the Canadian Red Cross. From 2017–19, she worked under the International Food Policy Research Institute (IFPRI) as a researcher and a project facilitator focusing on farm communities in Bangladesh.

Mukhnaam Kaur Chattha currently works as a Mission Zero coordinator in the Office of Sustainability at Sheridan College, Toronto, Ontario, Canada. She holds a Bachelor of Environmental Studies in Geography and Environmental Management and a Master's of Climate Change Degrees from the University of Waterloo.

Christine Kitoko holds a Bachelor of Arts in International Development Studies from York University, Toronto, Canada, and a Master of Development Practice from the University of Waterloo, Canada. She has worked as a junior professional consultant for the World Food Programme and as a research analyst at the Institute for Ecological Civilization.

Kate MacMurchy is a policy analyst with the Government of Canada. She holds a Master's Degree in Development Practice from the University of Waterloo. Her research interests include urban water security, community health and nature-based solutions.

Ayesha Binte Mannan holds a Master of Business Administration Degree from North South University, Dhaka, Bangladesh and a Master of Development Practice Degree from the University of Waterloo in Canada. She is currently working for a Canadian Insurance company.

Mohamed Mohamud holds a Master's Degree in Development Practice, University of Waterloo, and is a programme coordinator, UNODC Global Maritime Crime Program (GMCP) office in Somalia.

Ivonne Morales is a Ph.D. student in sustainability management with a focus on water at the University of Waterloo. She holds a Master in Peace and Conflict Studies, a Bachelor in Environmental Studies in International Development and a Bachelor of Arts in Public Relations.

Destinee Penney is a passionate advocate for sustainable change. She currently holds an Honour's Bachelor of Business Degree in International

Development, as well as a Master's Degree in Development Practice from the University of Waterloo. Well-travelled, she has held many positions, including a team member—Latin America and Caribbean Policy Programs at World Vision Canada, a teacher with the YMCA, and has recently found new passions in environmental and organic agriculture-related projects.

Goncha Sadayeva holds a Master's Degree in Development Practice from the University of Waterloo, specializing in sustainable development. She works as a program coordinator at MacPherson Institute at McMaster University. Goncha also supports ALG Consulting Company as the project support officer in delivering their sexual harassment and gender equality-related projects.

Juhi Shah holds a Master's Degree in Development Practice and is a mobilization coordinator with the Canadian Red Cross.

Larry Swatuk is a professor in the School of Environment, Enterprise and Development at the University of Waterloo. He is also an extraordinary professor in the Institute for Water Studies at the University of the Western Cape, South Africa and an external researcher at the Bonn International Centre for Conflict Studies in Bonn, Germany. Dr. Swatuk has published widely on the political economy of freshwater governance and management with a particular focus on the Global South. He is a co-editor of and a contributor to *Towards the Blue Green City: Building Urban Water Resilience* (Pretoria: Water Research Commission).

Ana Velasquez was born in Colombia, and presently resides in Waterloo (ON) where she finished her Master's in Development Practice at the University of Waterloo. She has dedicated the last twelve years of work to sustainable development and is currently working for a Canadian NGO that supports education and gender issues in Guatemala and Ethiopia.

Zhen Wei hold a Master's Degree in Development Practice from the University of Waterloo. She currently works as a Marketing Coordinator in Royal LePage Real Estate Services Ltd.

Margot Whittington holds a Master's Degree in Development Practice from the University of Waterloo. She currently works as a climate policy analyst at The Atmospheric Fund, a regional climate agency that invests in low-carbon solutions for the Greater Toronto and Hamilton area in Ontario, Canada.

Mandie Yantha holds a Master Degree in Development Practice from the University of Waterloo and works for the Canadian Red Cross in Emergency Response and Recovery.

Acronyms

ADB	Asian Development Bank
AUD	Australian Dollars
BBMP	Bruhat Bengaluru Mahanagara Palike
BGCMA	Breede-Gouritz Catchment Management Agency
BOT	Build-Operate-Transfer
BRP	Berg River Partnership
BWSSB	Bangalore Water Supply and Sewerage Board
C-40	Cities Climate Leadership Group
CAPWO	Cairo and Alexandria Potable Water Organization
CCT	City of Cape Town
CMA	Catchment Management Agency
CMWSSB	Chennai Metropolitan Water Supply and Sewerage Board
CRC	Cooperative Research Centre (for Water Sensitive Cities)
CSAG	Climate Systems Analysis Group
CWSS	Cauvery Water Supply Scheme
DAEE	Water and Energy Agency
DEFRA	Department for Environment Food & Rural Affairs
DELWP	Department of Environment, Land, Water and Planning
DKI	*Daerah Khusus Ibukota Jakarta* (Special Capital City District of Jakarta)
DWIQ	Drinking-Water Inspectorate
DWS	Department of Water and Sanitation
EA	Environment Agency
EIA	Environmental Impact Assessment
EU	European Union
EU IPA	European Union Instrument for Pre-Accession Assistance

EWRA	Egyptian Water Regulatory Agency
GCF	Governance Capacity Framework
GDP	Gross Domestic Product
GERD	Grand Ethiopian Renaissance Dam
GHG	Greenhouse Gases
GIS	Geographical Information System
GLA	Greater London Authority
GLP	Good Laboratory Practice
HCWW	Holding Company for Water and Wastewater
IBT	Increasing Block Tariffs
ICLEI	Local Governments for Sustainability
IMC	Istanbul Master Plan Consortium
ISKI	Istanbul Water and Sewerage Administration
IUWM	Integrated Urban Resources Management
IWM	Integrated Water Management
IWRAM	Integrated Water Resources Allocation and Management
IWRM	Integrated Water Resources Management
ISKABIS	ISKI Infrastructure Data System
JWA	Japan Water Agency
JWWA	Japan Water Works Association
lpcd	Litres Per Capita Per Day
MDG	Millennium Development Goal
MHUUC	Ministry of Housing, Utilities and Urban Communities
Mld	Million Litres Per Day
MLIT	Ministry of Land, Infrastructure, Transport and Tourism
MNDP	Ministry of National Development Planning
MoFWA	Ministry of Forestry and Water Affairs
MPC	Maximum Production Capability
MRSP	Metropolitan Region of São Paulo
MWRI	Ministry of Water Resources and Irrigation
NARBO	Network of Asian River Basin Organizations
NBS	Nature-Based Solutions
NGOs	Non-For-Profit Organizations
NOPWASD	National Organisation for Potable Water and Sanitary Drainage
NWRC	National Water Resources Council
NWRMS	National Water Resource Management System
OFWAT	Office of Water Services (UK)
OPDC	Old Oak and Park Royal Development Corporation
PAM JAYA	Jakarta Municipal Waterworks
PCJ	Piracicaba-Capivari-Jundiai
PDAM	*Perusahaan Daerah Air Minum* (Water Utility)
PPP	Public-Private-Partnerships
RBCs	River Basin Committees

RCM	Regional Climate Model
RCTWS	Regional Centre for Training and Water Studies
RPJMN	National Medium-Term Development Plan
RWH	Rainwater Harvesting
SA	South Africa
SABESP	Sao Paulo State Water and Sanitation Company
SCADA	Supervisory Control and Data Acquisition
SDG	Sustainable Development Goals
SDG6	Sustainable Development Goal 6
SDSN	Sustainable Development Solutions Network
SETEG	Socio-demographic, Economic, Technological, Environmental, and Governance
SFWRM	Service Fee for Water Resource Management
SNWDP	South-North Water Diversion Project
SUEN	Turkish Water Institute
SWRCs	State Water Resources Councils
SWRIs	State Water Resources Management Institutions
THIS	Thematic, Holistic, Integrated, Spatial
TMG	Tokyo Metropolitan Government
TOKI	Turkish Housing Development Administration
TPF	Trends and Pressures Framework
TTT	Thames Tideway Tunnel
UK	United Kingdom
UN	United Nations
UNDP	United Nations Development Programme
UNEP	United Nations Environment Programme
USAID	United States Agency for International Development
WAs	Water Agencies
WCWSS	Western Cape Water Supply System
WDM	Water Demand Management
WFD	Water Framework Directive
WHO	World Health Organization
WMAs	Water Management Areas
WSCs	Water and Sanitation Companies
WSS	Water Supply and Sanitation
WUAs	Water Use Associations
WWAP	World Water Assessment Programme
WWTP	Wastewater Treatment Plants
WWTWs	Wastewater Treatment Works

List of Tables

CHAPTER 1

Avoiding 'Day Zero': Challenges and Opportunities for Securing Water for Megacities

Larry Swatuk and Corrine Cash

Introduction

Water is a non-substitutable, essential, finite and fugitive resource (Savenije, 2002). As such, there is no escaping the politics of water. It is manifest in decisions regarding reforms to governance and management. It is manifest in decisions regarding appropriate technologies. Cities, through global processes such as Agenda 2030 and forums such as ICLEI, C-40 Cities and World Water Week learn from each other. Cities

L. Swatuk (✉)
University of Waterloo, Waterloo, ON, Canada
e-mail: lswatuk@uwaterloo.ca

C. Cash
Mount Allison University, Sackville, NB, Canada
e-mail: ccash@mta.ca

L. Swatuk and C. Cash (eds.), *The Political Economy of Urban Water Security under Climate Change*, International Political Economy Series,
https://doi.org/10.1007/978-3-031-08108-8_1

are collective social spaces governed in the main by political, techno-bureaucratic and economic elites. At the same time, cities are occupied by rate-payers, companies, industries, the marginalized and dispossessed and civil society organizations who often share strategies and tactics. In the so-called 'water sector', private sector actors compete for markets and contracts, promoting patent-protected technologies. It is these groups coming together who determine who gets what water, when and where. It is the job of academics to understand the how and why, and of (academic-)activists to fight for equity of access and sustainability of use. Evidence drawn from around the world and over time consistently shows that water flows toward money and power. Outcomes are generally socially inequitable, environmentally unsustainable and economically inefficient. How to shift existing processes toward improved practices is not clear, but, as will be shown in this collection, positive outcomes do exist.

The papers in this collection focus on the challenges and possibilities of achieving water security in megacities. Case studies are presented on São Paulo, Brazil (Chapter 2), Cape Town, South Africa and London, England (Chapter 3), Jakarta, Indonesia (Chapter 4), Bangalore and Chennai, India (Chapter 5), Beijing, China (Chapter 6), Melbourne, Australia (Chapter 7), Cairo, Egypt and Istanbul, Turkey (Chapter 8), and Tokyo, Japan (Chapter 9). The inspiration for this collection was the near 'Day Zero' event in Cape Town, South Africa. As is well-known, in March 2018, following a prolonged drought, the major dams feeding the City were at 13.5% of capacity and a concentrated campaign was undertaken to reduce citizens' average daily usage to 50 litres per capita. Other world cities such as São Paulo, Chennai and Barcelona, Spain had similar experiences. These extreme events notwithstanding, water shortages are 'normal' across large swaths of the world's megacities, particularly for the poor and marginalized for whom 'day zero' is a daily experience. The Cape Town experience presents mixed results: on one hand, it highlights the willingness of people to work together in common cause when faced with an existential threat; on the other hand, it exposed pre-existing inequalities through, for example, uneven capacities to respond and adapt (see Ziervogel, 2019 for details). While a variety of important measures were introduced by the City of Cape Town, and lessons learned by all those touched by the crisis, when the rains came and the dams refilled, for many it was back to business as usual. As of 1 March 2022, Cape Town's reservoirs stood at 78.7% of total storage capacity, which is more than 10% higher than 1 March 2020 (City of Cape Town data available at: https://www.capetown.gov.za/Family%20and%20home/residential-utility-services/residential-water-and-sanitation-services/this-weeks-dam-levels).

Amid all of this doom and gloom, Tokyo stands out as a case of good water governance and management (Chapter 9). This raises a variety of questions: What criteria are necessary for urban water security? Is water security purely a function of adequate finance? Of technological capacity? Of appropriate human resources? And what of social relations? It is axiomatic in the development industry to say that nothing is possible without 'stakeholder participation'. Is this the case in Tokyo, and, if so, what sort of participation is necessary? If citizens readily pay their taxes and levies, and if they do not steal from the system, what more 'participation' is necessary? These are some of the questions that the chapters aimed to investigate in this collection. What all the cases clearly demonstrate, however, is that water allocation and management is a political process. To imagine that achieving 'some water for all forever' is a function of techno-economic/bureaucratic practices is to set one's self up for disappointment. Tony Allan (2006) encouraged planners to include an 'A' in IWRM, Integrated Water Resources *Allocation* and Management (IWRAM), for allocation is at the heart of politics.

Politics, Political Economy, Political Ecology

Politics has been described as 'the art of the possible'. In particular, it involves the authoritative allocation of scarce resources, otherwise known as who gets what, when and where. In the context of cities, we must augment these definitions by stating that urban politics involves decisions regarding what goes where. Given these definitions, it seems problematic to separate out 'politics' from either economics or ecology: decisions affecting access, allocation, use and management of water within cities are intertwined with questions of economics (e.g. how to martial the financial resources necessary to build systems of delivery?) and ecology (e.g. how does capturing for human use a fugitive resource such as water alter the character—and possibly the sustainability—of natural ecosystems?). Recognizing the interrelationship among social, economic and environmental factors, we focus our attention on decision-making in relation to questions regarding water and systems of supply:

- Whose needs are being satisfied? (the stakeholder question)
- What is the water for? (the demand question)
- Where does the water come from? (the supply question)
- How is it accessed? (the freshwater delivery question)
- What is its quality? (the treatment question)
- What happens to it after it is used? (the wastewater conveyance question)
- How is the system financed, established, managed and governed? (the governance question)
- What is the impact (social, environmental, economic) of the overall system? (the sustainability question)

Embedded in the answer to each question are trade-offs, compromises, the exercise of influence—in other words, the social relations of power. Urban water systems are organic, evolving through time as cities themselves evolve and change. Even a cursory review of available information reveals that the discourse surrounding urban water security is negative. It goes something like this: cities are growing rapidly; water availability is limited (due either to First Order Scarcity, i.e. natural limits, or Second Order Scarcity, i.e. poor management and limited human, financial and technical resource capacity, or a combination of both); the finances available for necessary infrastructure upgrades are limited; the time for action is short; and a changing climate makes planning for the future extremely difficult.

A 2018 article from the BBC listed twelve cities facing 'day zero' scenarios: Bangalore; Beijing; Cairo; Cape Town; Istanbul; Jakarta; London; Mexico City; Miami; Moscow; São Paulo and Tokyo (https://www.bbc.com/news/world-42982959). Beyond these candidates, one might list a host of others—indeed, all cities face challenges related to sustainability irrespective of their natural resource endowments, built environments and human resource capacities. These challenges are well-known and are encapsulated in government documents, intergovernmental reports and countless academic studies. The point being made here is that no city is wholly prepared to meet the interrelated challenges posed by environmental, economic and social actors, forces and factors. At the same time, despite the massive sustainability challenges faced by all cities, there are successes, best practices, emerging networks of collaboration and a shared perspective on the need to act now.

In the balance of this chapter, we focus on the following elements. Next we provide a brief overview of water in development, with a particular focus on cities. The relevance of this section lies in the general lessons to be learned through time regarding why certain things have been done at certain times in particular places. The third section focuses specifically on water for cities, highlighting the politics underlying much of the (in)action in relation to particularly household water and sanitation. Comparative data is offered for several cities facing 'day zero' scenarios. The penultimate section presents lessons learned from the preceding sections and reflects on the necessary steps to be taken in order to develop the 'political will' necessary to act in support of environmental sustainability, social equity and economic efficiency. The final section presents short summaries of the chapters contained in this collection.

Power, Politics and Development

Water is power. It drives industry. Its delivery to people wins elections, enhances authority and builds legitimacy. Historically, humans settled around water—at the mouths of rivers; in mid-stream; around lakes, springs and wetlands—moving to the resource. Over time, however, we have managed to reverse this flow, so much so that water no longer runs along its hydraulic gradient; rather, it flows toward money, people and power. Humanity's impact on the natural environment has been so dramatic that we are now said to inhabit the era of the Anthropocene. In relation to water, our determined capacity to dam, drain and divert the world's waters has firmly tied nature to the world of Enlightenment-thinking humans, creating what Linton and Budds (2014) deftly label 'the hydro-social cycle'.

Today, states such as Brazil, China and India are engaged in a sustained, state-directed hydraulic mission characterized by dam building, river training and canal building. While this 'mission' extends to many other parts of the Global South—often with the help of Chinese engineering companies—early Twenty-first-Century democracies everywhere are having a very difficult time generating either the social consensus or financial capital necessary for infrastructure maintenance, let alone new development. As the backlog of need—for refurbishment of existing infrastructure, for extension to existing systems—grows, states have abandoned this task to the private sector. 'Creative coalitions' are often not so creative: banks, developers and their sub-contractors labour for profit under the purview of more or less effective government overseers. The so-called public-private partnerships (PPPs), whether or not they serve the poor, always serve the power-political status quo (Bakker, 2013; McDonald & Ruiters, 2005; Swyngedouw, 2015). In almost every case, the society-wide benefits to be derived from these interventions—no matter the source of the funding or technical expertise—are at best inferred through the dominant development discourse of poverty alleviation, social inclusion, employment and so on. The variety of these activities are evidenced throughout the chapters. Given the challenges created by a changing climate, ensuring urban water security will require concentrated political commitment at the highest levels of government. But how to fashion such a commitment?

As Tony Allan (2006) has shown us through the metaphor of the 'hydraulic mission', our understanding of what water is, what it might be and should be for, changes as new knowledge reveals new things to us about resources and about ourselves. The complexity of water and the diversity of needs and wants ensure that decisions regarding access, use and management are highly political. In an age of democracy, climate change and highly networked globalization, arriving at consensus regarding large-scale projects is more and more difficult: Who will benefit? Who will pay? History shows us that hydraulic bureaucracies have emerged across the world, particularly in arid/semi-arid environments, to 'push rivers around' in support of grand schemes serving the most influential actors in society (Molle et al., 2009; Solomon, 2010; Worster, 1985). Cities worldwide operate as catchments of capital and resources (as well as people). Nearly forty years of neoliberal globalization has widened the gap between the haves and have-nots. Gini coefficients of income inequality partially reflect this fact, being highest in extractive economies of the Global South, and lower but far from equal everywhere else. The Gini coefficients of income inequality in the countries of study in this collection are as follows: South Africa, 63 (2014 data); Brazil, 53.9 (2019); Turkey, 41.9 (2019); China, 38.5 (2016); Indonesia, 38.2 (2019); India, 35.7 (2011); the United Kingdom, 35.1 (2017); Australia, 34.4 (2014); Japan, 32.9 (2013) and Egypt, 31.5 (2017) (World Bank data available at: https://data.worldbank.org/indicator/SI.POV.GINI). These inequalities are readily regarded in the urban environment through two contrasting images: the gated community and the walled-off favela.

Urban Challenges

Providing adequate water and sanitation for the world's urban masses is perhaps the greatest challenge of the Twenty-first Century. According to ICLEI, '[t]he world has become predominantly urban, and cities are the place where the main challenges of sustainable development are being tackled. Although only occupying 2 percent of the land, cities are responsible for 70 percent of global GDP, greenhouse gas emissions (GHG), and global waste and over 60 percent of global energy consumption' (quoting UN-Habitat, 2016). As demonstrated in the pages below, though similar conceptually, cities face very different sorts of challenges. Those that arose out of the so-called first demographic transition fostered by the industrial revolution face significant challenges related to ageing infrastructure: how to repair it, replace it and upgrade it. This is primarily a so-called First World problem. Those cities that have arisen out of the post-World War II, post-colonial second demographic transition, face the primary challenge of meeting the needs of rapidly expanding populations that have overstretched existing infrastructure and, in many cases, exist in a sort of parallel peri-urban space: part of the greater metropolitan area, but largely unacknowledged—except to be regarded as a major problem—to formal authorities. In the Global South, every tale told about a city, is actually a tale of two cities: the formal and informal, the plumbed and unplumbed.

The absolute number and percentage of people living in cities has increased dramatically over the last 60 years, with roughly half of all urban dwellers living in Asia. While Asia's urban population has dramatically risen as a percentage of total world urban population, Europe and North American percentages have fallen significantly. In addition, the size of the world's largest cities is also increasing dramatically (see basic data for our case study cities in Table 1.1).

The Rise and Rise of Slums

The post-1945 'global development' era ushered in a demographic transition never witnessed in human history. At the time of the launch of the Colombo Plan in 1951 (in support of economic development in Asia and the Pacific), the World population was estimated to be 2.5 billion. Less than ten years later, it had topped 3 billion. In 2020, the World Bank estimated total global population to be 7.76 billion. More than half of these people live in cities, of which an estimated one billion reside in

Table 1.1 Some comparative data on case studies in this volume

City	*Governance*	*Population (millions)*	*Geography*	*Precipitation*	*Water supply*	*Issues*
Bengaluru	Bengaluru Urban District is administered by the Deputy Commissioner who oversees many sections and departments; The District is the principal administrative unit directly below the State (Karnataka in this case); Water Resources are governed by the State	13.2 GMA	Inland; average elevation 920 MASL	970 mm/a; most rain falls during May–October	80% inter-basin transfer from Cauvery River; 20% from Arkavathi River system; rainwater harvesting is mandated on all new buildings	Rapid urbanization (population in 1950 was 746,000 and 4 million in 1990); Combination of topography plus intensity and duration of precipitation events makes capture very difficult; Informal settlements; Inter-state water sharing agreements/conflicts; Groundwater pollution; Unaccounted for water

City	*Governance*	*Population (millions)*	*Geography*	*Precipitation*	*Water supply*	*Issues*
Beijing	Centrally administered (province-level) municipality; Municipal government (Beijing People's Government) elected by Beijing Municipal People's Congress; Local government consists of Mayor, Vice Mayors, various Bureaus; entire system paralleled by Chinese Communist Party	22.3 GMA	Inland; 40–60 MASL; mountains to the West and plains to the East; several rivers flow through the Greater Metropolitan Area (GMA)	570 mm/a; bimodal system with mainly summer rains	Groundwater; inter-basin transfer	Land subsidence; Drought; Pollution; Technical/economic challenges of inter-basin management

(continued)

Table 1.1 (continued)

City	*Governance*	*Population (millions)*	*Geography*	*Precipitation*	*Water supply*	*Issues*
Cape Town	Mayor-Council system; Party political; Water is managed hierarchically with the municipality responsible for planning, development and management of services/systems	4.52	Coastal	515 mm/a winter rainfall (April–October)	Complex system of mainly surface water	Drought; Slums; Inter-basin transfers; Party politics impedes decision making for best practice; Tiered governance and incomplete reform delays decision making

City	*Governance*	*Population (millions)*	*Geography*	*Precipitation*	*Water supply*	*Issues*
Cairo	Mayor-Council system is appointed by the Central Government; Ministry of Water Resources and Irrigation & the Ministry of Water Supply and Sanitation Facilities are the primary bodies responsible for water management in Egypt; Numerous other statutory bodies also involved	9.5 20.5 GMA	Inland	24.7 mm/a (several months with zero precipitation)	Nile River; groundwater; 107,000 km water distribution network; 29,000 km wastewater collection network	Unaccounted for water within the City; Degradation of resources in Cairo and upstream; Slum dwellers; Pollution; Transboundary water management challenges

(continued)

Table 1.1 (continued)

City	*Governance*	*Population (millions)*	*Geography*	*Precipitation*	*Water supply*	*Issues*
Chennai	Municipal Corporation	4.64 7.09 GMA	Coastal (avg. 6.7 m above sea level (MASL)	1380 mm/a 65% in monsoon season (October–November); February–April is dry season	Surface water reservoirs; desalination plants; high groundwater table	Flood; Drought; Slums; Downstream of agriculture; 30–40% Non-revenue water
Istanbul	Mayor-Council system; party political system	15.46 GMA	Coastal (Sea of Marmara on its South; Black Sea to its North)	849.6 mm/a (October–February is wettest season)	Inter-basin transfer; 15 lakes and dams with 19,000 km supply network	Poor governance (lack of transparency, participation, dominance from Central Government); party political system impedes best practice; Population/urbanization; Land degradation in catchment areas; Slums; Pollution; Groundwater depletion
Jakarta	Special Capital Region; elected governor, 106 councillors; 5 mayors and 1 regent chosen by governor; Water supply managed by 2 private corporations	10.5 31.2 GMA	Coastal (−2 to 50 MASL; avg. 8 MASL)	1816 mm/a (November–May rainy season)	80% surface water mainly from Citarum River and Jatilukur Reservoir; balance from groundwater	Subsidence; Flooding; Slums; Low % of household connectivity; 9% green space; Sewerage covers 1.9% of total population; 4% of housing covered by WWTPs

City	*Governance*	*Population (millions)*	*Geography*	*Precipitation*	*Water supply*	*Issues*
London	Mayor-Council system; Water delivery privatized to 4 suppliers Mayor established a Water Advisory Group Numerous national level bodies involved in water governance and management (e.g. Environment Agency, Water Services Regulation Authority)	9.5 GMA	Inland (80 km from the North Sea); 11 MASL	615 mm/a spread evenly over all 12 months	Surface and groundwater; 20,920 km water supply network	Climate change, drought and sea level rise; Aging infrastructure

(continued)

Table 1.1 (continued)

City	*Governance*	*Population (millions)*	*Geography*	*Precipitation*	*Water supply*	*Issues*
Melbourne	Governed by publicly-elected City Council, including Mayor, Deputy Mayor and 9 councillors. City Council sets the strategic direction and policy Victorian Government's Department of Environment, Land, Water and Planning provides direction within the water sector Melbourne Water is managed by independent Board of Directions & Minister of Water (Victoria); water responsibility falls to state government; waste management to councils	5	Coastal	600 mm/a most rain April–October but some rain falls in all months	Elaborate surface infrastructure; 3000 km of sewerage lines; 1300 kms of delivery; AU$3.1 billion desalination plants	Drought; Low-density (sub)urbanisation

City	*Governance*	*Population (millions)*	*Geography*	*Precipitation*	*Water supply*	*Issues*
São Paulo	State-owned, publicly-traded, water and wastewater company, SABESP, provides water & sewerage services to Metropolitan São Paulo and across the state	12.18 22 in GMA	Inland; 799 MASL; 70 km from ocean	1454 mm/a (October–March but rains in all months); upper catchment forest cover	Cantareira System (1880s) provides 50% of water through surface system (6 reservoirs across 5 basins); 80% of all water from Alto Tiete Basin; 20% of water from groundwater; Iguape system being developed	31% unaccounted for water; pollution; droughts; floods; Slums (20% of population); $22 m in sediment management
Tokyo	Water managed by the Bureau of Waterworks located within Dept of Local Public Enterprises; wastewater by Bureau of Sewerage; Tokyo Metro. Assembly approves budget, revises water charges	13.4 37.5 in GMA	Coastal	1530 mm/a mostly over 4 months (2 typhoon; 2 monsoon); 1623.5 mm/a in Western mountains; 36% forest cover	Surface water (14 dams); 27,500 km of pipes	Seismic stress on infrastructure; Drought; flood

slums. This contrasts with the estimated 650 million living in slums in 1990 (UN-Habitat, 2016). The rush from the rural areas to the cities across the Global South is astounding, with huge percentages living in informal settlements. As shown in Table 1.1, aside from Egypt, percentages of total urban populations living in slums is significant. In most cases, the dramatic drop in percentage between 1990 and 2018 masks the high level of absolute numbers. For example, drawing on World Bank data, Brazil's population in 1990 was an estimated 149.0 million, of which 36% or 54.7 million lived in slums. In 2018, though the percentage of slum dwellers dropped dramatically (16.3%), the number of slum dwellers remained high, 33.8 million. This is because Brazil's population increased by about 40% to 209.7 million over that time period. The same may be said for other regions in the Global South, with India (inferred from the South Asia data in Table 1.2) being the most dramatic example. Though the percentage of slum dwellers dropped by nearly 20%, the absolute number actually increased from 496.9 million in 1990 to 508.7 million in 2018 (see World Bank data here: https://data.worldbank.org/indicator/SP.POP.TOTL?locations=1W).

It is a truism to say that access to improved water and sanitation is less about pipes and pumps and more about enabling the poor to help themselves. Put differently, non-resource specific interventions will go a long way to improve access to the water resource itself: better incomes through employment opportunities; the right to land and security of tenure; better information about citizen's rights and better organized communities able

Table 1.2 Percentage of urban population living in slums

Country	*1990*	*2018*	*Case study City*
Brazil	36.7	16.3	Sao Paulo
East Asia & Pacific	46.0	26.4	
Egypt	50.2	5.2	Cairo
Indonesia	50.8	30.6	Jakarta
Latin America & The Caribbean	35.5	20.7	
The Middle East & North Africa	22.2	24.1	
South Africa	46.2	25.6	Cape Town
South Asia	56.9	37.6	Bangalore; Chennai
Sub-Saharan Africa	67.1	53.6	
Turkey	23.4	8.6	Istanbul

Source SDG Data Tracker available at: https://sdg-tracker.org/cities

to speak with one voice are all important elements of realizing access to improved water and sanitation.

One of the primary impediments to better provision is poor state-civil society relations. A non-responsive or even repressive state is generally ignored or avoided by the very citizens it is supposed to serve. How to build trust where past practice counsels mutual suspicion is an important question in water for cities. Participatory budgeting is regarded as one means of bringing the state and the citizenry closer together, with the Porto Alegre example being most commonly known. But in many parts of the world, we are a long way away from transparent and accountable decision-making, particularly as it relates to allocating resources to improve services for the poor.

Who Will Deliver?

Poor governance combined with incompetent public utilities led the rush toward private sector providers, particularly large multinational companies based in the UK, France and elsewhere, throughout the 1990s and into the early 2000s. By and large, this 180-degree turn from public to private was an unmitigated disaster. Rare is the example where a private sector provider followed the terms as agreed to in their contract. For most of the last 10 years, the donor world has been retreating from the private sector toward a middle ground where it is recognized that only oversight and regulation by a competent state authority will be able to ensure a provider's delivery on contract. There is a burgeoning literature discussing the return to municipal systems of oversight and delivery, commonly called 'remunicipalization' (McDonald & Swyngedouw, 2019).

Increasingly, municipalities have realized that PPPs are not enough, and that communities must be directly involved as well through, for example, civil society organizations. In highly unequal societies, such as South Africa and Brazil, differential service is regarded by the poor as a continuation of neglect and disrespect. Without community involvement, then, it is not possible to achieve buy-in regarding the possibilities for expansion and delivery.

While there are many issues related to under-performing utilities, it seems clear that the state (through goal setting, subsidies, incentives and regulation) and the market (through responsiveness to consumer needs) have roles to play in ensuring that the provider or providers—be it a public or private entity—has enough incentive to deliver as per the terms of their contract. It is a delicate balancing act. When it goes wrong, it goes very wrong indeed, as the so-called ‘water wars’ in Cochabamba, Bolivia showed. Cases where water services have been privatized but the company delivering the service is wholly (City of Johannesburg) or majority (State of Sao Paulo) owned by a public entity has yielded uneven outcomes. It is interesting to note that while the City of Paris, France remunicipalized its water services in 2010, private French water companies continue to deliver services on contract around the world. Moving toward successful delivery of water and sanitation services then seems to require utility-state-civil society negotiation and improved relations.

Given the variability of settlement patterns particularly in the primate cities of the Global South, whether expansion will mean networked or non-networked systems, pre-paid meters with automatic shut-off points (or not), step-wise tariff structures and adherence to global standards that may be beyond the technical and financial ability of the city, are all issues that require an open conversation. History shows that where non-transparent decisions have been taken ‘on behalf of’ the poor, even where a desire to help is the true motivator, there will be problems. The so-called ‘toilet wars’ in Cape Town, South Africa are an excellent example of this (Robins, 2014).

Without doubt, the world is rushing headlong into a brave new social order—an urban order with a vast array of challenges, threats and opportunities. While the challenges are many, and a continued failure to act by those with the capacity to do so, a serious threat in so many ways—from ill health to social disorder and violence—the evidence shows that the new urban reality presents many opportunities, first and foremost to rethink how we design and inhabit settled social spaces, and what our relationship is to the environment around us, and to each other, as we seek to satisfy our wants and needs.

What is very clear is that people need and deserve respect. Where the poor are consulted and made partners in problem-solving, the innovations are remarkable as are the results (Cash, 2021). Where they are treated as either undisciplined children or a problem to be contained or both, whatever the state attempts to do on their behalf will be met with contempt.

Systems of Delivery

Savenije (2002) has described water for cities as 'small water'. In other words, in comparison to the massive amounts of water that goes into irrigated agriculture—i.e. some 70% of blue water—cities' demands for blue water pales in comparison. But this is not to imply that delivering water for cities is that much easier than delivering water for agriculture. To the contrary, providing water for cities is both complicated and contentious. While it is 'small water', it is required on a 24-7 basis.

On the face of it, the method of drawing water for cities is relatively straightforward: find a source of supply, collect and, if necessary, treat the water before distributing it to various consumers (households, business and industry, use in public goods such as parks and other green spaces), collect it after it has been used and treat it again before reintroducing it back to the source. We call this the system of supply. However, each step in the system of supply presents a wide variety of challenges.

Let's begin with the source of supply. What is the source of supply? Is it a surface water body such as lake? Is it groundwater, or both? Where is this source: a natural lake located upstream, groundwater directly beneath the city or a 'well field' located at some distance away? Is the source downstream? Out of the basin altogether? How much water is there? What is the flow rate of the resource? Its recharge rate? How is its quality? Each of these questions have an associated number of issues related to them.

Questions regarding source of supply reflect human settlement patterns. Where are the people? Are they at the top of the watershed? Is the city somewhere along a river's banks at mid-stream? Or is it a coastal settlement? No two cities or settings are exactly the same. Each throws up challenges expected and unexpected. Bangalore and Sao Paulo are megacities at the top of watersheds whose primary challenge stems from this location. Cape Town, Chennai, Melbourne, Tokyo and Jakarta are coastal settlements which have sprawled in all directions. London spans the Thames River, 80 km upstream of its estuary at the North Sea. Cairo sits astride the Nile River, some 1200 km from the Mediterranean Sea. What do these basic differences of geography suggest for storage options? Moreover, Cairo or London today is not Cairo or London of fifty or one hundred years ago. As the cities increase their physical footprint, they alter the natural environment, creating a hydro-social cycle quite different from that of the early days of settlement (Swyngedouw, 2015).

While Johannesburg (as a mining town) and Bangalore (as a historical settlement taken over by the British as an administrative centre during the colonial era) have modest origins, they have grown rapidly in recent years. Today, they are home to several million inhabitants, their activities, interests, needs and so on. The pace of population increase has taxed even the most creative and well-equipped urban managers in terms of keeping up with necessary services such as water, sanitation, housing, electricity, transportation and so on. As a result, and as is typical across the Global South, many of the residents of Johannesburg and Bangalore reside in poor or un-serviced slums and squatter settlements. Moreover, the Gini coefficients of income inequality in these two cities are among the highest in the world, illustrative of the fact that almost unimaginable wealth rubs spatial shoulders with equally unimaginable poverty.

So, what are the challenges facing these cities in terms of 'water in – water out'? Let's take a quick tour of each segment of the system. In order to provide water to people in a city, it must be collected from somewhere. Availability varies dramatically, as does the quality of the water available. The city of Halifax, Nova Scotia in Canada, is blessed with pristine lakes located upstream and far from any significant human settlement, industry, mine and so on. The delivery system utilizes gravity, so there are no expenses related to pumping water uphill (as there are in Bangalore, where water has to be pumped up to the plateau on which the city perches and much of it from a great distance). There are fewer water treatment costs for Halifax as well, given the initial state of the resource. This contrasts dramatically with cities such as Dhaka whose groundwater supply is tainted with naturally occurring arsenic, or other downstream cities, such as Maputo who must deal with all sorts of effluent in their water that accumulates along the resource use chain by upstream cities and other users (such as farms and mines). This situation is not limited to the Global South, of course. For example, lots of problems happen to the waters of the mighty Mississippi in the United States as it snakes its way through several states and many cities. Almost all urban water systems—even those in the deliberately constructed cities of fast-growing states such as China and Brazil—are cumulative and reactive. What this means is that the initial system was based on several assumptions such as the current and projected growth of the city.

Cities such as Johannesburg, Harare and Nairobi were deliberately laid out to reflect the contemporary political economy of settler-based colonialism. If one lived on the 'right side of the tracks', there would be every modern service imaginable. But if one lived on 'the wrong side of the track'—next to industry and so on—access to services differed dramatically. In some cases, there were no services provided at all. This was deliberately done to discourage Africans from 'settling' in these colonial centres of commerce, industry and administration. So, high density housing estates were serviced by standpipes and shared latrines, while low density housing had in-house flush toilets and running, treated water. Following the end of colonial rule, and in the South African case, apartheid rule, people have crowded into the cities looking for economic opportunity and expecting access to water and sanitation as 'their constitutional right' (Bond, 2013; Enqvist & Ziervogel, 2019).

Obviously, a system deliberately designed to serve the few continues to have a great deal of difficulty in serving the many. The same may be said for Bangalore, and pretty much any other city of the Global South, be it large or small. So, people queuing at a public standpipe in Bangalore is hardly surprising; indeed, we seem to expect that this is the best we can do under the circumstances. But is it? Which leads us to distribution. Like collection and treatment, distribution faces many of the same challenges.

Just because there was enough financial capital, political will and human resources available to construct the initial supply and treatment system—be it a dam, or a system of well-fields where the water is moved either by gravity or diesel-powered pumps to a water treatment centre where the resource is made ready for human use and consumption—does not mean that it was distributed equitably, efficiently or sustainably, not even from the start. Initially, and across the post-colonial world, systems had been constructed based on 'Western knowledge'. Leaky pipes in temperate zones where there were upwards of 300 precipitation days per year (and free winter storage in the form of snowpack) were 'good enough'. Running the same pipes through the desert or across the tops of watersheds, however, meant that a great deal of 'unaccounted-for' water was in fact wasted, meaning beyond the use possibly ever again of the people of that particular city. Some of these systems are now almost 100 years old, and in dire need of upgrading, extension and so on. But how to do this? Cities are often bankrupt or run by corrupt officials and their cronies. Where will the money come from if people are to be properly served? Where is the human resource capacity? Who can afford appropriate technology if the mistakes of the past are not going to be replicated today and tomorrow? And all of this seems to be a race against time: before the system collapses under the weight of ever-increasing demands. In Bangalore, there are some 10,000 km of water supply transmission and distribution pipelines, and another 7000 km of lateral sewers and outfall sewers. As of 2006, there were an estimated 350,000 connections and 6350 authorized public fountains (used by the poor and unserved of the city) (Bakker, 2010; Gopekumar, 2012). How to keep this in good working order? At the same time, the costs of fuel used to pump the water up from the Cauvery River to the city bleeds the city almost dry. What is to be done?

Improved water metering is regarded as one way of ensuring the cost-effectiveness of delivery. In many parts of the world, pre-paid water meters have been introduced, particularly in high density settlement areas of cities. This system is often regarded as highly controversial, impinging on people's 'human right to water'. The city of Cape Town, for example, introduced a series of pilot projects to instal meters which deliver 300 L of government-legislated 'free basic water' to poor households. Once the limit is reached, householders must purchase additional water on a user-pay, pre-paid basis. There are many people in Cape Town's townships such as Khayelitsha who view this as an infringement on their right to water. But look at it from the City's viewpoint: water falls free from the sky, but systems of delivery cost a lot of money.

Where water is delivered into parts of the city that are unable to pay for it, not only is the water lost to other prospective uses, but the loss of revenue makes it doubly difficult for the city to deliver its existing services and to extend services to the historically disadvantaged. Yet, distribution based on cost-recovery seems somehow to remain a highly contentious issue across the Global South, and in parts of the Global North as well, such as in the scattered rural and Indigenous communities across much of Canada. How to get water to these folks without going bankrupt yourself? In some cities, surveys reveal that people are happy to pay for water (and electricity and so on) if and only if the service is reliable: people want to pay for water that they can get when they need it and of good quality for those needs. They do not want to pay for erratic delivery of water that might kill them.

What happens to the water after it is used? In industry—is it treated to a quality that makes it unharmful to humans downstream? In households, is grey water separated out from black water? In slums, are people dumping their 'night soil' into the streams that feed the aquifers, rivers and lakes that hold the water for other users? We are back to the same old issues: appropriate technology, human capacity and the cost of it all. Which leads us back to the source itself. In a city such as Harare, questions regarding the shape and condition of the water supply and distribution system are even more important because you are disposing wastewater into the downstream source of your treated water. If the system draws water beyond the recharge rate, then other sources and/or use practices will have to be found or devised. Water Demand Management (WDM) has become popular in the last three decades: we can make 'more' water by using wisely the water that we have: fixing leaky pipes and ensuring that industry and households do not pollute the resource, do not add an absolute amount to the system, but it does make more water available than would have been available had it leaked away or become unusable due to pollution. At the same time, there are important considerations of who or what is downstream. Many cities simply dump their waste into their water systems and hope it floats away. Coastal cities face numerous problems because of this practice. In effect, they are destroying the very house in which they live. But those upstream often use the practice of 'out of sight out of mind' as a low-cost management strategy.

There is one more important aspect to our system: we often fail to adequately consider the water that enters the system informally, through natural processes. Most cities have decided that the best thing to do with this water, when it isn't used as green water by the city's green spaces, is to get it out of the way as fast as possible. So, while we have devised a system of delivery for use; we have devised a parallel system of stormwater management that regards this informal water as somehow problematic. This is understandable, in some ways, given where we have settled. Cities across the tropics face seasonal floods. Given that Bangladesh is a country in a floodplain, unless more than 40% of the city of Dhaka is under water, then it is not considered a state of emergency. Flooding is part of life, but, even so, it is very poorly managed there. But should it be made to run away as fast as possible? Should it not be integrated into the entire system of supply? In a country such as Bangladesh, where arsenic is naturally found in groundwater, does it not make sense to ensure that aquifers are as full as possible to dilute arsenic so that its presence is not deathly harmful? Every year during the rainy season, we channel stormwater away from cities only to find ourselves under a water advisory in the dry season. Why? Because most of our water is groundwater and we've failed to replenish the source through a combination of stormwater 'management' and an increasingly hardened environment where impermeable concrete and asphalt have helped create the 'stormwater problem' in the first place.

To create an integrated system brings us back to capacity: human resources, finances, technology and, most importantly, the political willingness to depart from the 'beaten path'. In light of extreme events, heightened variability and climate change, it is time for a revolution in urban planning (Brown et al., 2009; Newell & Cousins, 2015).

What Have We Learned?

Urban Water Security may be defined as citizens' freedom from want, i.e. having adequate amounts of water of appropriate quality for daily consumptive (household, economic) and non-consumptive (e.g. recreational, spiritual) needs; and citizens' freedom from undue risk from natural hazard and human use outcomes. To ensure urban water security for all, steps must be taken to (i) reduce risk (from external events); and (ii) reduce vulnerability (enhancing the character and strength of the people and the built environment). For example:

Reducing risk through appropriate individual and collective action

- Due to shortage (ensuring adequate supply)
- Due to pollution (ensuring fail safe systems of conveyance)
- Due to extreme events (improving the built environment)

Reducing vulnerability through appropriate individual and collective action

- Through improved management of existing systems (at different scales)
- Through better governance and systems oversight (legal and institutional arrangements)
- Through adoption of new technologies (appropriate and affordable)
- Through knowledge mobilization and effective communication (learning from others)

As demonstrated in the chapters below, there are many examples of 'best practice' across the world's cities, including, for example:

- Low impact development
- Sponge cities
- 'Pop-up' infrastructure and other community-centred approaches to service delivery
- Public-private-community partnerships
- Infrastructure upgrades

In terms of the politics of urban water security, one can glean several factors to understand how 'best practice' emerges:

- Creative coalitions (citizen-led)
- 'No opting out' due to collective effect of impending crisis
- Pressure from citizen groups
- Enlightened leadership
- Available finance
- Peer pressure (city to city; global governance systems)
- Smart partnerships

In relation to the politics of water for cities, a review of water in development and in human settlements reveals the following:

- Water use mirrors society back to itself. It is therefore unrealistic to expect equitable access to water, indispensable though it may be, in highly unequal societies.
- As cities continue to grow, there will be no substitute for supply-side solutions to scarcities and uncertainties; rather than moving away from 'Man over Nature' approaches to resource management, we continue to reinforce these high-modern, 'hydraulic mission' approaches.
- Demand-side management as well as improvements to existing systems of supply can greatly enhance the urban water endowment but these are politically sensitive, especially when asking citizens—some of whom already have limited access—to 'want less'.
- Authoritarian/Totalitarian political systems (where civil society is weak) provide equal space for misguided projects (e.g. Three Gorges Dam; Ilisu Dam) as well as creative innovation (e.g. large-scale desalination; 'sponge cities').

- Democratic political systems are prone to compromise and path dependence (e.g. urban sprawl that generates new revenue mixed with minor innovations such as green belts) due to financial limitations, social pressure and politicians' general unwillingness to take risks (that may have impacts at the ballot box).
- In the Global South, 'big infrastructure' draws together political, economic and social power, squeezing out less influential groups, in particular the poorest citizens.
- In the Global South, where the urban poor are included it is because they have forced themselves into the public space through a combination of activism and external (NGO, IGO) support.

One conclusion to be drawn from this introductory chapter is that cities are deeply divided across several socio-economic fault lines. These divisions make every water-related decision inordinately political. How then to move toward improved practices and outcomes? Since 2000, when the Prince of Orange declared the world water crisis a 'crisis of governance', there has been concentrated efforts along two fronts: improved governance (including exposing and rooting out corruption; updating water laws; developing water resource development and management strategic plans) and improved management (specifically integrated water resources management with a focus on the river basin as the geophysical unit of water use decision-making and stakeholder participation). These efforts have been coordinated by several global and regional bodies, such as UN-Water. Donor states and international financial institutions have attempted to integrate these best practices into lending policies. On several occasions, they have made very wrong turns—with privatization of urban water systems being the prime example (Bakker, 2013).

The Book

Chapters 2 through 9 present a set of case studies, focused on the challenges and opportunities for achieving water security in eleven megacities. In Chapter 2, the authors focus on the Metropolitan Region of São Paulo (MRSP). The chapter describes the challenges faced by the city as policymakers consider the ways and means of achieving water security. The State Government of São Paulo and SABESP have taken several steps in the wake of the 2014–15 water crisis: infrastructure development, encouraging conscious consumption and improving the national regulatory framework. The chapter argues that São Paulo must make better use of the water that it does have; improve coordination among water authorities and meaningfully engage all stakeholders, including slum dwellers in devising a way forward.

In Chapter 3, Morales and Swatuk comparatively examine the cities of London and Cape Town, setting the actions taken to achieve water security within the context of what Zeitoun et al. (2016) describe as reductionist and integrative approaches. The chapter shows that reductionist and integrative approaches operate side-by-side in both cities. It argues that for London and Cape Town to ensure a human security-centred approach to water management, integrative thinking must supplant the dominant, reductionist approach, although where megacities are concerned, it is unlikely that large-scale water transfer schemes will ever be fully displaced by closed-loop approaches to water access, use and management.

Chapter 4 examines water security in Jakarta, Indonesia. Research indicates that water security in Jakarta City is impacted by inadequate infrastructure, unequal use by a growing population and poor governance. Without sustained attention to these issues, Jakarta will remain ill-prepared for present and future water challenges. The improvement of integrated water resource management (IWRM), the adoption, alignment and enactment of the New Agenda and National Action Plan principles, in addition to the improvement of education, public awareness and collaboration of all stakeholders are possible ways forward.

Chapter 5 focuses on two Indian cities, Bangalore and Chennai, which are moving toward a 'Day Zero' scenario. The authors show that rapid, unregulated urbanization and a population explosion pose serious challenges to water-secure futures. Furthermore, the expansive presence of quasi-legal water economies and the colonial legacy of high-modern water management practices impact water resources and their distribution, exacerbated by the unpredictable effects of climate change. This has created a fragmented stakeholder landscape, resulting in suboptimal, disjointed efforts to achieve urban water security that do not reflect the realities on the ground. The incorporation of the Integrated Water Resources Management framework into water management is an important first step and greater collaboration between stakeholders, particularly community-level actors, is critical to avoid 'Day Zero' scenarios and build water-secure futures in Bangalore and Chennai.

Chapter 6 examines Beijing. With a population of over twenty-one million people, Beijing is one of the largest cities in the world. The centralization of such a large population has drastically impacted the availability of resources, especially water. Water insecurity is exacerbated by increasing demand, water pollution, urban flooding, climate change, over-exploited groundwater and minimal surface water access. As Beijing inches closer to day zero, the implication of running out of water on human rights, population health and socio-economic development has raised justified alarm.

The Central Chinese and Beijing municipal governments have done substantive work in the past decade to reduce water insecurity through projects such as the south-north water transfer project, utilizing wastewater and water pricing. Although these are important measures, they are not adequate to address the need for equitable distribution of water or growing demand. To ensure both conditions, a more holistic water management approach needs to be taken to avoid Beijing's day zero. Going forward, Beijing needs to expand on existing working policies by adopting integrated water resource management. Coordination and collaboration must exist between stakeholders to unify efforts to ensure a water-secure future for Beijing.

Chapter 7 centres on Melbourne, a city of nearly five million people facing multiple threats to water security, in particular, climate change and population growth. Rising temperatures and reduced rainfall are prolonging droughts and depleting storage water levels. At the same time, an increasing population is creating greater demand despite decreasing stocks. In response, authorities have adopted a strategy meant to enhance their capacity to provide water, based on the concept of 'security through diversity'. This approach, however, is neither sustainable nor a true embodiment of the principle of diversification. It is predicated on a centralized system of urban water management that is unsuited for present circumstances, and places greater importance on supply-side interventions—such as desalination—than on initiatives meant to address demand. Thus, the strategy needs to be transformed if it is to better embody the principle of diversification and ensure water security. This could be accomplished by including a broader range of relevant stakeholders, such as Indigenous and other civil society groups, to improve the city's current water management strategies and tackle its dependence on a centralized urban water management system.

In Chapter 8, Edo and colleagues comparatively examine the cases of Cairo and Istanbul. Cairo is situated in an arid environment, relying mostly on one water resource: the River Nile. The city is becoming more vulnerable with population growth, urban sprawl and political tension over the Nile. Infrastructure, governance and management of existing water systems are posing more stress. Istanbul, in contrast, is more water-rich but is expanding beyond its watershed and drawing on water within a 200 km radius. Its water demand is expected to increase with the expected population growth, haphazard urbanization and impacts of climate change on water security. The chapter reviews the key challenges and issues that these cities face and outlines possible sustainable solutions such as decentralizing the governance framework, developing city-specific water security and climate change mitigation plans, restructuring the tiered water tariff system and deploying water-sensitive urban design. Within the context of Istanbul, for decades, considerable efforts and investments have been made by the government to develop water resources. These measures should be further expanded to address the complex challenges toward achieving urban water security in these sprawling cities.

In the last chapter, Chapter 9, Kaur and co-authors look at Tokyo described as the world's largest water-stressed city. Since 1970, low rainfall years have become more frequent and observations show an increasing trend between extremely high and low rainfall events, in addition to decreased snowfall and increased early thaw events. Other issues that Tokyo is subject to are earthquakes, floods and other natural disasters, which cause damage to water supply and sewage networks, thereby disrupting water supply service provisions. The goal of dealing with water shortages is therefore at the core of water resource development in Tokyo. In response to these challenges, the government has expanded the city's water infrastructure, water efficiency and water conservation measures, in addition to promoting a water-wise culture and developing an around-the-clock emergency water services squad to handle water shortage emergencies. The Japanese government has shown its commitment to integrated water resource management by implementing policies that support coordinated expansion and management of water, land and related resources. Good governance along with access to technical capacity and capital, has helped Tokyo build urban water resilience.

Taken together, these essays present a comprehensive overview of the complex processes of governing and managing water resources in Twenty-first-Century megacities. They highlight not only the challenges faced but some of the innovative solutions pursued by different social actors at a variety of scales. Many cities are plagued by weak governance and management regimes, path-dependent practices and the deliberate exclusion of the poorest sections of society in strategy and planning. This forms a weak foundation for dealing not only with present crises but planning for a future under climate change.

There is no escaping the politics of water. It is manifest in decisions regarding reforms to governance and management. It is manifest in decisions regarding appropriate technologies. Some regard the widespread turn toward desalination to be a consequence of the fact that the endless ocean waters are not hemmed in by land tenure, communal rights and contentious trade-offs between stakeholders as are land-based (surface and ground) water resources. Yet disposal of the brine effluent has ecological consequences which will no doubt have socio-political and economic consequences as well (Swyngedouw & Williams, 2016; also, see Melbourne case below). Cities are simultaneously settled and organic, collective and contested social spaces. In the words of Cohen (2016: 286), '[S]haring water fairly and transparently would seem to be simple and obvious. But in socio-spatially segregated urban regions, whose politics of land use and housing are fused with water infrastructures, and whose dynamics structure core economic and political logics, the question of water is a question of power'.

References

Allen, J. A. (2006). IWRM: The new sanctioned discourse? In P. Mollinga, A. Dixit, & K. Athukorala (Eds.), *Integrated Water Resources Management: Global theory, emerging practice and local needs* (pp. 38–63). Sage.

Bakker, K. (2010). *Privatizing Water: Governance failure and the world's urban water crisis*. Cornell University Press.

Bakker, K. (2013). Neoliberal versus postneoliberal water: Geographies of privatization and resistance. *Annals of the Association of American Geographers, 103*(2), 253–260.

Bond, P. (2013). Water rights, commons and advocacy narratives. *South African Journal of Human Rights, 29*(1), 126–144.

Brown, R. R., Keath, N., & Wong, T. H. F. (2009). Urban water management in cities: Historical, current and future regimes. *Water Science and Technology, 59*, 847–855.

Cash, C. (2021). Creating the conditions for climate resilience: A community-based approach in Canumay East Philippines. *Urban Planning, 6*(4), 298–308.

Cohen, D. (2016). The rationed city: The politics of water, housing and land use in drought-parched Sao Paulo. *Public Culture, 22*(2), 261–289.

Enqvist, J. P., & Ziervogel, G. (2019). Water governance and justice in Cape Town: An overview. *Wiley Interdisciplinary Reviews, 6*(4), 1354.

Gopekumar, G. (2012). *Transforming urban water supplies in India*. Routledge.

Linton, J., & Budds, J. (2014). The hydrosocial cycle: Defining and mobilizing a relational-dialectical approach to water. *Geoforum, 57*, 170–180.

McDonald, D. A., & Ruiters, G. (Eds.). (2005). *The age of commodity*. Earthscan.

McDonald, D. A., & Swyngedouw, E. (2019). The new water wars: Struggles for remunicipalisation. *Water Alternatives, 12*(2), 322–333.

Molle, F., Mollinga, P. P., & Wester, P. (2009). Hydraulic bureaucracies and the hydraulic mission: Flows of water, flows of power. *Water Alternatives, 2*(3), 328–349.

Newell, J. P., & Cousins, J. J. (2015). The boundaries of urban metabolism: Towards a political-industrial ecology. *Progress in Human Geography, 39*(6), 702–728.

Robins, S. (2014). The 2011 Toilet Wars in South Africa: Justice and transition between the exceptional and the everyday after apartheid. *Development and Change, 45*(3), 479–501.

Savenije, H. H. G. (2002). Why water is not an ordinary good, or why the girl is special. *Physics and Chemistry of the Earth, 27*, 741–744.

Solomon, S. (2010). *Water: The epic struggle for wealth, power and civilization*. HarperCollins.

Swyngedouw, E. (2015). *Liquid power: Contested hydro-modernities in twentieth century Spain*. MIT Press.

Swyngedouw, E., & Williams, J. (2016). From Spain's hydro-deadlock to the desalination fix. *Water International, 41*(1), 54–73.

UN-Habitat. (2016). *Slum Almanac 2015–2016: Tracking improvements in the lives of Slum Dwellers*. UNON.

Worster, D. (1985). *Rivers of empire: Water, aridity, and the growth of the American West*. Oxford University Press.

Zeitoun, M., Lankford, B., Krueger, T., Forsyth, T., Carter, R., Hoekstra, A. Y., Taylor, R., Varis, O., Cleaver, F., Boelens, R., Swatuk, L. A., Tickner, D., Scott, C. A., Mirumachi, N., & Matthews, N. (2016). Reductionist and integrative research approaches to complex water security policy challenges. *Global Environmental Change, 39*, 143–154.

Ziervogel, G. (2019). *Unpacking the Cape Town drought: Lessons learned*. Technical Report, Cities Support Programme, Cape Town: African Centre for Cities.

CHAPTER 2

São Paulo's Water System: A Megacity's Efforts to Fight Water Scarcity

Ayesha Binte Mannan, Ana Velasquez, and Larry Swatuk

Introduction

In 2018, the United Nations identified São Paulo, Brazil as the fourth largest megacity in the world, with more than 22 million inhabitants living in its metropolitan region (UN, 2018). Rapid urbanization leads to numerous challenges such as water demand and supply management, waste disposal, adequate and affordable housing, just to name the most obvious (Braga et al., 2006; Varis, 2006). As demonstrated in this collection, São Paulo's struggles are similar to those facing million- and megacities elsewhere in the Global South: poverty, violence, crowding and, despite receiving considerable amounts of precipitation, water scarcity.

A. B. Mannan
University of Waterloo, Waterloo, ON, Canada

A. Velasquez · L. Swatuk (✉)
University of Waterloo, Waterloo, ON, Canada
e-mail: lswatuk@uwaterloo.ca

L. Swatuk and C. Cash (eds.), *The Political Economy of Urban Water Security under Climate Change*, International Political Economy Series,
https://doi.org/10.1007/978-3-031-08108-8_2

Located in the highlands of São Paulo State, the Metropolitan Region of São Paulo (MRSP) receives approximately 1,317 mm of precipitation which falls as a bimodal system with considerably more rain between September and April, and less in the other months (World Bank, 2017). Its southern region is covered by rainforest and northwest by Araucaria forest (Varis, 2006). São Paulo obtains its water from several river basins through extensive and complex inter-basin transfer schemes (Braga & Kelman, 2020).

In 2015, São Paulo faced a severe water crisis. The water level of the Cantareira reservoir—approximately only five percent of capacity—was so low that it exposed its 'dead volume' (Empinotti et al., 2019). Facing this crisis, the governor of São Paulo State and the CEO of the São Paulo State Water and Sanitation Company (SABESP), assured citizens that the city would not run out of water. However, despite the government's assurances, the citizens and businesses became habituated to water shortages from 2014 onwards. As shown below, the plans that emerged reflect conventional high-modern 'water security' interventions: economically expensive and highly technical infrastructural development designed to tap new supplies in support of current and projected future demands (domestic, industrial, agricultural) (Empinotti et al., 2019). Like most cities around the world, São Paulo demonstrates path dependence not only in terms of locked-in systems of delivery but also in terms of the commitment to outmoded understandings of how nature must be bent to the service of human interest. In this chapter, we locate São Paulo's many challenges within the context of the 'hydro-social cycle' (Linton & Budds, 2014), to open up new pathways of thinking and action for urban water security.

The hydro-social cycle can be defined 'as a socio-natural process by which water and society make and remake each other over space and time' (Linton & Budds, 2014). Stated differently, humanity's need to manage water has an essential effect on the organization of society, which in turn, affects the disposition of water, which gives rise to new forms of social organization and so on in a cyclical process. Water and society have an internal relation, which means that particular kinds of social relations produce different kinds of water, and vice versa. The physical properties of water play a defining role in the hydro-social process, sometimes constructing and rupturing social relations (Linton & Budds, 2014), for example through predicted (monsoonal systems), unpredicted (once-in-a-thousand year flood) and knowable but uncertain (El Nino, La Nina) events. Moreover, it is estimated that one-third of São Paulo's residents live in informal settlements, dramatically impacting and being impacted by natural and human-made flows of water—almost all of which have been harnessed to serve the formal residential, commercial and industrial sections of society. The hydro-social cycle therefore requires a more holistic, integrated and reflexive understanding of water security, one that moves significantly beyond cost-benefit analyses of developing and delivering new systems of supply for industry, energy, agriculture and so on. UN-Water has shifted slightly in this direction, defining water security as 'the capacity of the population to safeguard sustainable access to adequate quantities of acceptable quality water for sustaining livelihoods, human wellbeing, and socioeconomic development, for ensuring protection against water-borne pollution and water-related disasters, and for preserving ecosystems in a climate of peace and political stability' (UN-Water, 2013).

Water flows increasingly in accordance with flows of capital and political interests (Linton & Budds, 2014). In 2014 and 2015, political obstinacy along with a severe drought pushed São Paulo to the edge of a socio-ecological disaster (Cohen, 2016, 2018; Millington, 2018). Despite claims by the state government that only a minority suffered without water, the reality was quite different. Residents of the urban periphery, who number in the millions, were disproportionately impacted. People's differing experiences of water scarcity reflected a combination of existing inequities in city's water infrastructure and the differentiated—class, race, ethnicity, gender—abilities of residents to access the resource (Millington, 2018). Water is not just a resource to drive economies or a commodity to sell, but a necessary element of social sustainability. In the case of water security for São Paulo, it is important to see how water is used, who has it, who does not, how decisions are made, and to parse out the hydro-social system rather than just seek new sources of water.

Toward this end, the chapter presents a background of São Paulo, describes key water security challenges, reflects on São Paulo's current action plans and makes several recommendations for improving water security for all.

Background

São Paulo is the techno-financial capital of Brazil, and in 2019 ranked 10th in the Megacities Index (UNDESA, 2019). Located in the south-east of Brazil, 50 kilometres inland from the Atlantic Ocean, it is home to 22,043,028 inhabitants, of which one-third to one-half live in slums across the municipal region. In contrast, in 1950 the population of São Paulo was nearly ten times smaller: 2,334,038 people. The water supply systems developed over time reflect these changing circumstances. In the early Twentieth Century, the Guarapiranga reservoir was constructed to serve the growing metropolis. Some twenty years later, the Billings reservoir was built to supply electricity. Both systems lie within the Alto-Tietê basin, thus constituting classical high-modern interventions typical of Western development. Today, the Billings reservoir has shifted to water supply and flood control. In the early 1960s, the Cantareira system was initiated consisting of an elaborate series of reservoirs, pipelines, pumping stations and treatment plants that tap the headwaters of the Piracicaba-Capivari-Jundiai (PCJ) basin (Milano et al., 2018). Eight water treatment plants operated by SABESP supply nearly all the potable water for MRSP. Their joint Maximum Production Capability (MPC) is approximately 73 m^3/s (Braga & Kelman, 2016). Today, several new systems of supply are in development so reinforcing the city's, state's and indeed the country's orthodox approach to carrying out their 'hydrological mission'. Groundwater historically has contributed very little to the system of supply but is increasing as citizens tap into it. The amount of groundwater recharge and extraction is estimated at 15 m^3/s and 10 m^3/s respectively, and the latter is expected to increase (World Bank, 2012).

In 2011, average water use in São Paulo was 181 litres per capita per day (lpcd) (World Bank, 2017). Given vast socio-economic inequalities, this average hides as much as it reveals about per capita consumption. For example, according to The World Bank, 'The scarcity of potable water and the deficit of wastewater collection and treatment are more common in poor neighbourhoods, and particularly severe in slums. This is the case of São Paulo where about 54 percent of the poor live in areas of critical water deficit and 59 percent lack proper sanitation'. Despite the fact that wealthy households consume far more water than do poor households, all were negatively impacted by the drought. The average fell dramatically over the course of the years of the drought, reaching 120 lpcd in 2015.

The roots of São Paulo's water crisis extend far beyond a spatially and temporally delimited drought. Even when rainfall is abundant, the city's location on a plateau means that when rain falls it quickly flows away, facilitated too by the hardening of soils due to urban sprawl. Besides regular and increasing drought, environmental degradation, pollution of drinking water, poverty and illegal settling around the river basins, lack of water treatment and conflicts over water consumption exacerbate the crisis.

Water Governance and Management

The main stakeholders in water governance and management in MRSP are the State's government, the State's water and sanitation utility SABESP and 39 other municipal governments. A basin committee for the Alto-Tietê basin, which covers the entire area of the MRSP and supplies half of its water, brings together all stakeholders (Barbosa et al., 2017). Brazil has three administrative levels, and they are local (city councils), State and federal. In each level, there is a sectoral structure of secretariats (in states and local governments) and ministries (federal level) who are responsible for different issues, for instance, energy, water, agriculture and tourism (Braga et al., 2008). Only the state and national levels own constitutional rights for water resource management. The local authorities entirely control the water supply and sanitation companies (Barbosa et al., 2016). The National Water Resources Management System is a political and institutional mechanism that defines the form of participation of stakeholders in water policy implementation. Representation is among national, State and local governments (these three categories cover up to 50% of representation), civil society entities that act in the basin, and users of the water (these two categories cover at least 50%) (Porto & Porto, 2008). The river basin committees set concentration on water management, facilitate conflict resolution, approve the river basin plans and design and implement charging systems. These committees have periodical meetings with local authorities and SABESP, to analyse what is happening with approved projects and initiatives in the basin, as well as further project development and the needs for the future. Additionally, water agencies manage the funds from charging systems and provide technical and administrative support to the decision-making process (Barbosa et al., 2016).

The state level comprises of two major agencies: Water and Energy Agency (DAEE) and Environmental Agency (Cetesb). DAEE is currently linked to the Sanitation and Water Resources Secretary, which is responsible for quantitative water aspects, especially the issuance of water use permits. Cetesb is associated with the Environment Secretary and is responsible for qualitative aspects of water, specifically to protection and conservation (Barbosa et al., 2016). SABESP provides services to 93% of the municipalities including São Paulo city, with the other seven percent attended to by municipal companies in each locality.

Pricing and Cost Recovery

It is common knowledge that there is a massive investment gap in relation to water supply and sanitation needs worldwide (Tortajada & Biswas, 2003). It is also common knowledge that consumers are used to paying very little, if anything at all, for their water. For several decades there have been variable attempts at achieving cost recovery in the water sector (Garrick et al., 2020). 'The idea of water pricing and cost recovery was originated in the 1990s; it was understood as a silver bullet for solving problems involving the efficient allocation of water resources and reducing demand to more sustainable levels' (Berbel & Exposito, 2020: 669). MRSP follows a block tariff pricing system for piped water and sewerage, dividing consumers into several categories. There are three classes of residential consumer—with social assistance, vulnerable, normal—and five classes of industrial/commercial. Vulnerable consumers pay a flat rate of 0.94 USD for the first 10 m^3, after which the rate rises in blocks of 10 m^3 reaching a rate of 1.80 USD/m^3 beyond 50 m^3/month. Normal consumers pay 6.00 USD/month for the first 10 m^3 and the blocks increase at a rate of about five times that of vulnerable groups. Commercial entities working with people on social assistance receive a discounted rate while normal commercial and industrial entities pay about twice the rate of normal consumers. The rates vary slightly by municipality.

SABESP functions as a private company with the State government being the majority shareholder. This is similar to other large cities such as Johannesburg. In theory, the 'for profit' aspect plays a subordinate role to the 'social and environmental good' aspect. In the wake of the 2014–15 crisis, SABESP came under sustained criticism (Böhm & Flores, 2015). On its own website, SABESP states that it 'supplies 28.6 million people with water and provides sewage collection services to 24.9 million people'. It also states that '[b]etween 2022 and 2026, it plans to invest

... R$23.8 billion, focused on expanding water availability and security, without jeopardizing the improvements to sewage collection and treatment ratios' (https://ri.sabesp.com.br/en/company/profile/).

Key Issues/Challenges

The rapid growth of São Paulo over the last two decades has created many new challenges for the city and its citizens while exacerbating existing ones (Braga et al., 2006; Varis, 2006). Where water security is concerned, the most critical challenges to overcome are five: water pollution; poverty and informal settlements; state of calamity (drought and flood); conflicts of consumption; and lack of water treatment. We briefly discuss each of these in turn.

Water Pollution

The Metropolitan Region of São Paulo sources water from different basins. The system of supply has become degraded all along the route. Surface and groundwater is contaminated by a combination of solid and liquid waste, from households, farms and industry. Industrial spillover, illegal dumping of industrial residues, agricultural pesticides, fertilizers and other pollutants contaminate the water, negatively affecting its suitability for human use and consumption (Braga et al., 2006). Throughout the metropolitan area, people have settled informally along rivers and streams (World Bank, 2017). These people live under extreme poverty conditions, and their house structures lack even the most basic water and sanitation facilities. Put differently, the surface waters are their sewers.

Poverty and Illegal Settling Around the River Basins

São Paulo does not have the appropriate infrastructure to cope with the millions of inhabitants living in the metropolitan region. There is increasing correlation between urban sprawl and poverty as low-income citizens settle in the city's periphery (Formiga-Johnsson & Kemper, 2005). According to World Bank (2017), this is far more evident in the Alto-Tietê basin where investments have been scarce and only 47% of the water receives treatment (Braga et al., 2006; World Bank, 2017). The Alto-Tietê basin is composed of a complex hydraulic and hydrological system. Though the basin has an extensive network of dams and pipes, the water availability of the region is estimated to be 201 m^3/cap/yr (far below the accepted benchmark of 1600 m^3/cap/yr as recommended in Falkenmark & Rockstrom, 2005: 58). The total demand for water consumption in the Alto-Tietê River basin exceeds the basin water supply. Current public urban system supply is 63 m^3/s (serving 99% of the basin's population), irrigation consumes 2.6 m^3/s of the water supply, while industrial demand is met by both the public system (9.5 m^3/s) and by independent withdrawals and extraction of groundwater (Formiga-Johnsson & Kemper, 2005). Groundwater is being extracted at an alarming rate where industrial wells take 35% of the share, household (private homes and apartment buildings) take 25% and other services take 24%. The rate of extraction is considered 'alarming' because of a lack of monitoring and control of groundwater use (Formiga-Johnsson & Kemper, 2005). At the same time, illegal connections contribute to MRSP's high rate of unaccounted-for water. 'Most people living in the informal settlements have illegal and unpaid access to potable water through precarious and wasteful distribution systems formed by a bundle of small-diameter plastic tubes connected to the mains' (Braga & Kelman, 2020).

State of Calamity (Flooding and Drought)

The Cantareira delivery system is complex. The objective was to transfer water from the dams in the upper Tietê River basin (Edgard de Souza, Pirapora, Billings and Guarapiranga) toward the Billings reservoir by reversing its natural flow with the help of pumping stations (Braga et al., 2006). Further, water was transferred to the Pedras reservoir while generating hydroelectricity at the Henry Borden hydropower plant using a 750m hydraulic head. This innovative system increased the supply of hydroelectricity to more than 600 MW, which boosted industrialization, development and urbanization of the region (Braga et al., 2006). The rapid industrialization of the region and an inadequate plan of treating the water produced a deficient quality of the water in the upper Tietê River basin. These problems included the low Tietê River flow (average 17 m^3/km), which made flooding a significant issue in the basin (Braga et al., 2006). Floods in this basin bear a public health threat because the poor water quality in the rivers can lead to a variety of gastrointestinal ailments.

During 2013–2015, instead of the usual one or two weeks of drought, the region had an extremely dry and hot climate in summer 2014 (Milano et al., 2018). As a result, there was a significant reduction in water flows from 70% to 35% in the reservoirs, according to SABESP records, which adversely affected the water supply to the metropolitan region (Braga & Kelman, 2016). According to Braga and Kelman (2020: 280), 'in January 2015, the Cantareira system storage was less than 5% of maximum, including dead storage (technical reserve), and the water level was several metres below the intake elevation. Since May 2014, water had been pumped out of the dead storage'.

Conflicts in Water Consumption

The water supply problem also possesses a conflict between two principal regions: the MRSP and the Piracicaba River basin. A water supply inter-basin transfer scheme was implemented to transfer water from the Piracicaba River basin to the MRSP in the 1970s. This system transferred water naturally to the downward stream, from the Jaguari, Cachoeira and Atibainha Rivers into the Paiva Castro reservoir, where water is then pumped to a treatment station 120m uphill. As noted earlier, this inter-basin transfer is named the Cantareira system, facilitating a continuous transfer of 33 m^3/s of water to the MRSP (Braga et al., 2006). The Cantareira system has been a significant source of water supply for the MRSP, and its establishment was made in the timeline when the industrial development of São Paulo State was not high when compared with the MRSP. Hence, at the beginning of the 1970s, water taken from the Piracicaba River basin had a small impact on the local communities. However, in the 1980s and 1990s, this region experienced an accelerated growth with high demands for domestic and industrial water supply, irrigation and wastewater dilution (Braga et al., 2006). Water demands are growing in these basins, and conflicting situations have become critical consequently.

On the other hand, the struggle for drinking water in Greater São Paulo also came into conflict with the influential hydropower sector (Formiga-Johnsson & Kemper, 2005). Section 21-XII of the Brazilian Federal Constitution grants the federation authority to explore the hydroelectric potential of the country's water resources (Braga et al., 2006). As mentioned earlier, the Guarapiranga and Billings reservoirs were built for hydropower generation purposes in the 1920s and 1930s, respectively. Nevertheless, water treatment infrastructure in São Paulo failed to enhance at the same rate as the population, resulting in severe degradation of these rivers and, consequently, of the Billings reservoir (Formiga-Johnsson & Kemper, 2005). Even though politicians and engineers have known the importance of drinking water for decades, the priority had always been placed on hydropower generation, as was backed by the constitution.

Lack of Water Treatment

Investments in water treatment and collection network expansion commenced in the Alto-Tietê basin in the 1970s and increased significantly in the 1990s (Formiga-Johnsson & Kemper, 2005). Nevertheless, by 2005 only 65% of wastewater was collected, and of that portion, only 32% was treated (Formiga-Johnsson & Kemper, 2005). Many major municipalities have their sanitation systems, and these are exclusively underserved as SABESP is the only water company in the basin that treats sewage. SABESP's most recent forecasted figures indicate a significant increase in sewage collection, reducing the deficit in coverage from 17% in 2005 to 7% in 2020, but no figures for increases in wastewater treatment have been estimated by SABESP (Formiga-Johnsson & Kemper, 2005).

Efforts to Achieve Water Security

After the 2014–2015 drought it was clear to Brazilian authorities that the situation needed to be handled in order to prevent the event from happening again. Different measures were taken by Central and State governments and by the SABESP and NGOs in the State of São Paulo.

State government and SABESP developed a strategic plan to address urgently the possible catastrophes that could be faced under these conditions (Braga & Kelman, 2016). The plan addressed the following specific issues:

- Institutional strengthening at all levels toward sustainability and water protection;
- Development of institutional tools and technical instruments that support the measurement of all the dimensions involved in water security;

- Development of instruments for community and public participation;
- Community mobilization and environmental education;
- Rehabilitation of basin in terms of ecological recovery including natural infrastructure, residue and waste management.

These measures will increase the water security for the region, the city and their inhabitants. Let us briefly look at 5 key issues: infrastructure development; building consumer/citizen confidence; regulatory frameworks and practices; the Reagua Project and the communications campaign.

Infrastructure Development

At micro level, one example of how SABESP intervened to make sure the flows run continuously toward the city, was the installation of floating pumps and the building of channels and cofferdams, through which water was pulled upstream avoiding dead storage and contamination, especially at the Jaguari point. Braga and Kelman (2020) detail the many other infrastructural efforts undertaken to deal with the immediate crisis and better prepare the MRSP for future challenges: refurbished pumping stations; interlinked reservoirs; enhanced water treatment capacity and new storage tanks.

Building Citizen/Consumer Confidence

For more than two decades, different efforts have been made to incentivize through economic instruments the protection of the water systems and ecosystems restoration (Costanza et al., 1997; also Tortajada & Biswas, 2003 in the Latin American context). In 1997, the National Water Act was promulgated, marking a significant turn away from regarding water solely as an input into industrial production and increasingly as an entity whose condition shapes the wealth and well-being of society (Farias, 2009). This national act complemented the already existing 1991 São Paulo State statute in support of Integrated River Basin Management (Farias, 2009). The National Water Act contained the elements to protect the reservoirs and watershed, allowing SABESP and other governmental institutions to invest in their reforestation and restoration. Significant partnerships in support of ecosystem services have been formed among government, civil society and the private sector. According to the World Resources Institute, 'thousands of farmers, budding entrepreneurs, NGOs and established companies are restoring lost forests and degraded farms through the Atlantic Forest Restoration Pact' (Matsumoto et al., 2021). These measures have also motivated economic growth and created jobs along the banks of the rivers through environmental rehabilitation efforts, the reforestation and the protection of biodiversity along with supporting and enhancing environmental education on these communities.

National Regulations and Framework

In Brazil, the National Water Act (Law 9433 of 1997) established the framework of the National Resource Policy and the National Water Resource Management System (NWRMS) proposing a new strategy throughout the application of economic and planning elements (Veiga & Magrini, 2013). This framework is composed of the National Water Resources Council (NWRC), State Water Resources Councils (SWRCs), River Basin Committees (RBCs), State Water Resources Management Institutions (SWRIs) and Water Agencies (WAs). Farias (2009) and others have remarked upon the progressive, ecocentric and socially inclusive aspects of water management in Brazil today. 'The new paradigm of participatory water management directly engages citizens to engage in self-rule…River basin management allows flexibility to adapt water use patterns to local needs … The National Water Act specified tools to implement these principles, including water resources plans, water classification schemes, water use rates, and water resource information systems' (Faris, 2009: 78). However, others such as Cohen (2016), are more critical arguing that despite improved policies, laws and institutional frameworks, implementation remains problematic.

São Paulo Water Recovery Project (Reagua)

This project, supported by the World Bank, was designed to address water shortages issue by (a) increasing the volume of water recovered by reducing real water losses and promoting rational water use in public schools; and (b) improving water quality by improving wastewater systems. The project was directed by the São Paulo State Secretary for Water Resource along with other stakeholders in the region. Upon its conclusion, an estimated 97,400 inhabitants of five different critical neighbourhoods along the river basins directly benefited through activities related to reducing and controlling real water losses and promoting rational water use (World Bank, 2020). In the World Bank's (2020) final report, it is stated that approximately 45 Mm^3 of water was recovered which 'corresponds to the consumption of around 800,000 people per year. Thus its contribution to social development is relevant, given the restrictions in water availability faced by MRSP'. The vast majority of this water was recovered through leak detection and repair.

Concerning distribution, the current situation is approaching universal access with 96.1% coverage and 93.5% service. Service is the relationship between total active water savings and total serviced households. The regional authorities have implemented micrometers in unregulated areas through the Água Legal Program (SABESP, 2019). Although SABESP cannot formally take this action in irregular households, agreements with the municipalities have allowed the measurement of water consumed in these areas and the formalized connection of more than 32,000 points.

Regarding water losses, two components describe them in the water supply system: actual and estimated. Actual losses represent leaks in pipes, overflow in reservoirs and filtrations and theft. In contrast, estimated losses can be the result of fraud, under-measurement of water meters and flaws in the SABESP internal system. According to SABESP (2021), 'from December 2008 to December 2021, the rate of losses per connection reduced from 430 to 252 litres per connection per day. In the same period, the rate of real or physical losses dropped 4 percentage points, from 22.2 percent to 18.2 percent'. The goal is to reach an average of 250 litres per connection per day by December 2022 which they say is 'comparable to supply systems in developed countries'. In order to minimize losses, SABESP carries out numerous activities: reducing actual losses—fixing leaks, investigating non-visible leaks, handling distress, enforcing categorization works, enhancing infrastructure and reducing leakage. Estimated losses measures like the calibration and adequacy of water volume measurement instruments, and optimized water meter replacement, and increasing the commercial management to increase commercial registration, consumer verification and decrease frauds.

Alongside the reduction in unaccounted-for water is concentrated effort to increase wastewater reuse. Based on SABESP studies, the MRSP has a potential of 1.2 Mm^3/year of reusable water for non-potable uses to be made available in industry, agriculture and in public spaces. With the region's critical water availability situation given the size of the consumption, these practices are increasingly important. Today, according to SABESP, advances in progress refer to improving the treatment process for reuse. However, the challenge also lies in incentivizing businesses to use treated wastewater instead of sourcing from the watershed and the potable water management system.

Communication Campaigns

In the absence of extreme events—drought or flood—citizen engagement with questions of water governance and management is notoriously low (Abu Bakar et al., 2021). Moreover, the challenges of water and sanitation for the urban poor generally fall to non-governmental and community-based entities, with government a passive bystander at best. Where promises of improved delivery have been made by government actors, such pronouncements often serve as touchpoints for state-civil society conflict and, on occasion, collaboration (Bond, 2008; Robins, 2014). In MRSP, over the course of the water crisis, the government and SABESP developed different campaigns to encourage communities to build water awareness, utilizing a variety of media in support. In addition, government created a set of economic inducements to reward water saving efforts. Braga and Kelman (2020: 285) suggest that 'the combined effect of economic incentives and communication campaigns' resulted in 'per capita household water consumption [being] reduced by 20 percent'. As the communications keep being part of the local government and SABESP strategy, the results are expected to last over the years to come. Like many other water supply companies/utilities, SABESP is active today in social media, counting 37,400 followers on Twitter. In a 24 March 2022 Tweet, SABESP showed support for nature-based solutions by re-tweeting TNC Africa's initial Tweet regarding the signing of the Water and Nature Declaration at the 2022 World Water Forum in Dakar, Senegal. Whether this all adds up to improved performance in urban water governance and management is still to be determined.

Conclusion

From this review, it is clear that there are many challenges to achieve water security for the millions of inhabitants and thousands of industries in MRSP. These challenges arise from complex interrelations across the hydro-social cycle. Significant threats to the region arise from the uncertainties associated with climate change. Higher temperatures and longer dry seasons, resulting in severe droughts, may be the new norm. At the same time, precipitation, when it falls, may increase in duration and intensity. Recent Brazilian climate projections indicate a significant decrease in rainfall in the southeast, central and northeast region, coupled by average increases in temperature. The rainfall decrease could reach 20% below the historical average by 2040, and to an impressive 40% of the average by 2100 (Júnior et al., 2016). It is imperative therefore to address as fully as possible the pre-existing challenges stemming from historical practices and approaches to resource use as well as current demographic pressures.

These trends should logically drive policymakers to a more flexible approach to water use and management, as espoused by the concept of Integrated Water Resources Management (IWRM). According to UN-Water, Brazil is 63% of the way toward reaching Sustainable Development Goal target 6.5.1 regarding implementation of IWRM. At the same time, the country is 86% of the way toward SDG 6.1.1 (universal access to safely managed drinking water) and less than halfway toward SDG 6.2.1a (universal access to safely managed sanitation) (see https://sdg6data.org/country-or-area/Brazil).

Keeping these points in mind, our recommendations are as follows:

- Prioritize afforestation of all watersheds. As the chapter on Tokyo shows, judicious management of forest resources is at the heart of downstream (urban) water security. Restoring nearly 10,000 acres of the forests in the Cantareira Water Supply System's watershed could reduce sediment pollution by 36% within 30 years, which will further reduce turbidity by almost half and boost water supply (Ozment et al., 2018).
- Systematically pursue nature-based solutions (NBS) at all scales of human settlement. Plant trees, build green roofs and walls, soften surfaces by, for example, recovering brownfields through public park development (UN-Water, 2018).
- Increase engagement with civil society through 'sponge city' initiatives and NBS as described above.
- Build trust among government, civil society and the private sector through collective management efforts such as participatory GIS training and the use of citizen science.

- Engage in active transparency, with regular dissemination of data and assessments regarding municipal contexts related to sanitation components to be used in the development of new project and frameworks for future developments in infrastructure, policy and billing initiatives.
- Expand environmental education in schools and community centres, including recruitment and training of 'water champions'. Initiatives that raise awareness about sanitation would be an important starting point.
- Integrate the information systems of the City and the Metropolitan Area and other bodies involved in sanitation services, bringing greater efficiency to tasks and municipal processes; foster the integration of services in such a way that it can cover the whole metropolitan region with the appropriate services to protect from water pollution and scarcity at the same time.
- Open pathways for participatory initiatives. Establish government entry points that can enable and consolidate the assimilation of proposals or issues brought by different actors to decision-makers.
- Establish integrated solutions adapted to local conditions for structures and service provision in support of environmental sustainability.
- Restore potable water quality in water sources like reservoirs for Guarapiranga and Billings.

Even though the current water policy is based on principles of decentralization, integration and participation, the situation in practice is rather opposite (Barbosa et al., 2017; Cohen, 2018). A gap between policy and practice is observed in the São Paulo State, which limits the accomplishments of water policy objectives and policy implementation. The water policy in the State of São Paulo can be considered to align with international approaches for water resources management. In our study, it was found that the policy principles are not sufficient to guarantee good practices. To shift from principles to practice in São Paulo, several issues need to be addressed as follows:

- constructing the decision-making authority of river basin committees,
- clarifying the roles and responsibilities of agencies and
- reducing fragmentation, by facilitating integration between organizations at different government levels and sectors (Júnior et al., 2016).

For decentralization to be effective in São Paulo, there must be:

- coordination between organizations
- a balance of power between upper and lower levels of the governance arrangement; lower levels must be empowered to make decisions; upper levels must still hold the authority to drive the decision-making process.
- Systematic application of the three principles of IWRM: integration, decentralization and public participation.

We recognize that this is a long list of things that must be done with no simple or proven pathway to move forward. Reflecting on the insights of the hydro-social cycle, it appears to us that the MRSP reflects the past as much as it anticipates the future. Systems of production and consumption remain firmly implanted in the high-modern past: water for energy, for the making of things, the generation of profit before all else. For Cohen (2016), rather than engage meaningfully with fundamental reform, 'the state government and SABESP make modest adjustments to the prevailing regime, in which companies and affluent city-dwellers have easiest access to water. Conducting slow infrastructure expansion, increasing water rates, gradually expanding the sewage network—so long as at least some progress is made, the system is safe from challenge'.

Nevertheless, throughout the world, across Brazil and parts of the MRSP, there are important insights and initiatives underway and within reach regarding fundamental changes to water and related resources management, from the rebuilding of the 'green dam' at the top of the watershed to citizen-engagement and nature-based solutions in the MRSP. The problems, in truth, are so many that it presents a hopeful picture: choose an entry point and an aspect of water-sensitive urban design, find your allies and get busy. Given the society's impact on the hydrological cycle, small determined steps toward social change are possibly more meaningful, and more sustainable, than new systems of supply.

References

Abu Bakar, M. F., Wu, W., Proverbs, D., & Mavritsaki, E. (2021). Effective communication for water resilient communities: A conceptual framework. *Water, 12*, 2880.

Barbosa, M. C., Mushtaq, S., & Alam, K. (2016). Rationalising water policy and the institutional and water governance arrangements in São Paulo, Brazil. *Water Policy, 18*, 1353–1366. https://doi.org/10.2166/wp.2016.233

Barbosa, M. C., Mushtaq, S., & Alam, K. (2017). Integrated water resources management: Are river basin committees in Brazil enabling effective stakeholder interaction? *Environmental Science and Policy, 76*, 1–11.

Berbel, J., & Exposito, A. (2020). The theory and practice of water pricing and cost recovery in the Water Framework Directive. *Water Alternatives, 13*(3), 659–673.

Bohm, S., & Flores, R. K. (2015). Sao Paulo water crisis shows the failure of public-private partnerships. *The Conversation*. https://theconversation.com/sao-paulo-water-crisis-shows-the-failure-of-public-private-partnerships-39483. Accessed 25 March 2022.

Bond, P. (2008). The case of Johannesburg water: What really happened at the pre-paid "Parish Pump". *Law, Democracy and Development, 12*(1), 1–28.

Braga, B., Flecha, R., Pena, D., & Kelman, J. (2008). Federal pact and Water Management. *Estudos Avançados, 22*(63), 17–42.

Braga, B., & Kelman, J. (2016). Facing the challenge of extreme climate: The case of Metropolitan São Paulo. *Water Policy, 18*(S2), 52–69.

Braga, B., & Kelman, J. (2020). Facing the challenge of extreme climate: The case of Metropolitan São Paulo. *International Journal of Water Resources Development, 36*(2–3), 278–291.

Braga, B., Porto, M. F. A., & Silva, R. (2006). Water management in Metropolitam São Paulo. *International Journal of Water Resources, 22*(2), 337–52.

Cohen, D. A. (2016). The rationed city: The politics of water, housing and land use in drought-parched Sao Paulo. *Public Culture, 22*(2), 261–89.

Cohen, D. A. (2018). Water crisis and eco-apartheid in Sao Paulo: Beyond naive optimism about climate-linked disasters. *International Journal of Urban and Regional Research*. https://www.ijurr.org/spotlight-on/parched-cities-parched-citizens/water-crisis-and-eco-apartheid-in-sao-paulo-beyond-naive-optimism-about-climate-linked-disasters/. Accessed 25 March 2022.

Costanza, R., d'Arge, R., de Groot, R., Farber, S., Grasso, M., Hannon, B., Limburg, K., Naeem, S., O'Neill, R. V., Paruelo, J., Raskin, R. G., Sutton, P., & van den Belt, M. (1997). The value of the world's ecosystem services and natural capital. *Nature, 387*, 253–260.

Empinotti, V. L., Budds, J., & Aversa, M. (2019). Governance and water security: The role of the water institutional framework in the 2013–15 water crisis in São Paulo, Brazil. *Geoforum, 98*, 46–54.

Falkenmark, M., & Rockstrom, J. (2005). *Balancing water for humans and nature: The new approach in ecohydrology*. Earthscan.

Farias, J. L. (2009). Brazil: The evolution of the law and politics of water. In J. Dellapenna & J. Gupta (Eds.), *The evolution of the law and politics of water* (pp. 69–86). Springer.

Filho, J. G., Zuffo, A. C., & Falconi, S. (2014). Contributions to increase the availability of water supply in regions of water shortage: The case study of São Paulo, Brazil. *The Sustainable City IX, 2*, 1567–1578. https://doi.org/10.2495/SC141332

Formiga-Johnsson, R. M., & Kemper, K. E. (2005, June). *Institutional and policy analysis of river basin management—The Alto Tiete River Basin, São Paulo. Brazil* (World Bank Policy Research Working Paper 3650). The World Bank.

Garrick, D. E., Hanemann, M., & Hepburn, C. (2020). Rethinking the economics of water: An assessment. *Oxford Review of Economic Policy, 36*(1), 1–23.

Júnior, W. S., Baldwin, C., Camkin, J., Fidelman, P., Silva, O., Neto, S., & Smith, T. (2016). Water: Drought, crisis and governance in Australia and Brazil. *Water, 8*(493), 1–21. https://doi.org/10.3390/w8110493

Linton, J., & Budds, J. (2014). The hydrosocial cycle: Defining and mobilizing a relational-dialectical approach to water. *Geoforum, 57*, 170–180.

Matsumoto, M., Anderson, W., Reytar, K., & Barbosa, L. (2021). *Brazil's forests are being restored—Now we can see where*. World Resources Institute. https://www.wri.org/insights/brazils-forests-are-being-restored-now-we-can-see-where. Accessed 27 March 2022.

Milano, M., Reynald, E., Muniz-Miranda, G., & Guerrin, J. (2018). Water supply Basins of São Paulo Metropolitan Region: Hydro-Climatic characteristics of the 2013–2015 water crisis. *Water, 10*(1517), 1–19. https://doi.org/10.3390/w10111517

Millington, N. (2018). Producing water scarcity in São Paulo, Brazil: The 2014–2015 water crisis and the binding politics of infrastructure. *Political Geography, 65*, 26–34.

Ozment, S., Feltran-Barbaeri, R., Hamel, P., Gray, E., Ribeiro, J. B., Barrêto, S. R., Padovezi, A., & Valente, T. P. (2018). *Natural infrastructure in São Paulo's Water System*. World Resources Institute.

Porto, M. F., & Porto, R. (2008). Gestão de bacias hidrográficas (Management of river basins). *Estudos Avançados, 22*(63), 43–60.

Robins, S. (2014). The 2011 toilet wars in South Africa: Justice and transition between the exceptional and everyday after apartheid. *Development and Change, 45*(3), 479–501.

SABESP. (2019). *2018 Sustainability Report*. https://site.sabesp.com.br/site/uploads/file/relatorios_sustentabilidade/sabesp_rs_2018_english.pdf. Accessed 27 March 2022.

SABESP (Companhia de Saneamento Básico do Estado de São Paulo). (2021). *2020 Sustainability Report*. https://site.sabesp.com.br/site/uploads/file/relatorios_sustentabilidade/Sabesp_2020_Sustainability_Report.pdf. Accessed 27 March 2022.

Tortajada, C., & Biswas, A. K. (2003). *Water pricing and public-private partnership in the Americas*. Third World Centre for Water Management and Inter-American Development Bank.

UNDESA (United Nations, Department of Economic and Social Affairs, Population Division). (2019). *World urbanization prospects: The 2018 revision*. United Nations.

UN-Water. (2013). *Water security and the global water agenda—A UN-Water analytical brief*. UNU-INWEH.

UN-Water. (2018). *World Water Development Report 2018: Nature-based solutions for water*. UNESCO. https://unesdoc.unesco.org/ark:/48223/pf0000261424a. Accessed 27 March 2022.

Varis, O. (2006). Megacities, development and water. *International Journal of Water Resources Development, 22*(2), 199–225.

Veiga, L. B. E., & Magrini, A. (2013). The Brazilian water resources management policy: Fifteen years of success and challenges. *Water Resources Management, 27*, 2287–2302.

World Bank. (2012). *Integrated urban water management—Case Study São Paulo*. The World Bank.

World Bank. (2017). *Water management in Latin America's most dense cities: The São Paulo experience*. The World Bank.

World Bank. (2020). *Brazil—Sao Paulo Water Recovery Project (REAGUA) (English)*. World Bank Group.

CHAPTER 3

Challenges for Urban Water Security in London and Cape Town

Ivonne Morales and Larry Swatuk

Introduction

Water has been a fundamental precondition for urban development in London and Cape Town, but cities are social, economic, political and environmental spaces where water becomes contextually defined and ascribed to each particular sphere. London and Cape Town are both coastal cities and they share a common colonial past where London was the colonizer and Cape Town the colonized. Cape Town's architecture, institutions and infrastructure mimic London and reflect past relations of domination in their urbanism (Beall & Fox, 2009: 50). Today, both cities emerge in a contemporary setting with a similar challenge: To become not only water-secure cities but sustainable water-secure cities framed in the Sustainable Development Goal 6 (SDG) launched in 2015. The goal

I. Morales · L. Swatuk (✉)
University of Waterloo, Waterloo, ON, Canada
e-mail: lswatuk@uwaterloo.ca

L. Swatuk and C. Cash (eds.), *The Political Economy of Urban Water Security under Climate Change*, International Political Economy Series,
https://doi.org/10.1007/978-3-031-08108-8_3

for both cities is to 'ensure availability and sustainable management of water and sanitation for all' (UN, 2019: 34).

However, London and Cape Town have both experienced a water crisis. For Cape Town, the Spring of 2018 nearly brought the city to a potential 'Day Zero' after three years of successive drought starting in 2015 (City of Cape Town, 2019b: 26) while London has announced a water shortfall of about 100 million litres per day by 2020, and 400 million litres per day by 2040 (GLA, 2018: 14). Besides the water crises in London and Cape Town, projections of rapid population growth of ten and five million people respectively by 2035 and climate change will compound the problem (World Population Review, 2022a, 2022b).

Both cities understand and deal with water differently and their approaches to water reveal the complexity of the water security topic. Privatization dominates the water industry in London compared with a centralized monopoly in Cape Town. For London and Cape Town to fulfil their duties in becoming cities with sustainable water securities, they must rethink different ways of designing and performing more integrated water management approaches. The various interests related to water allocation and access pose distinctive challenges for each city that affect decision-making and policies. These are connected to management and governance and are important when the goal is also focused on applying principles that foster equality and conservation.

The focus of this chapter is to review the discourses of water security for the cities of London and Cape Town, based on two approaches namely, (i) the dominant conventional reductionist approach to water challenges which undoubtedly is more popular the world over, and (ii) the more pluralistic integrative approach that broadens both the scope of uncertainties and the methods by which to integrate them (Zeitoun et al., 2016). Our review is based on the theoretical frameworks of Zeitoun et al. (2016). The chapter proceeds as follows: In the next section, we conceptualize water security. This is followed by a comparison of the background of the cities of London and Cape Town covering critical issues of geography, demography, climate, political-socio-economics and so on. The chapter then turns to a discussion of key water issues and challenges following by a focus on efforts to achieve sustainable water securities before presenting its conclusions.

Conceptualizing Water Security: Reductionist and Integrated Approaches

In the last decade, the concept of water security has received increasing attention among scholars and practitioners in response to the need to understand water security within the complexities of cities. Zeitoun and colleagues (2016) advance two main approaches, namely, reductionist and integrative approaches. The reductionist approach tends to be consistently focused on calculable risk, the interconnection between GDP and hydro-climatology and an oversimplification of 'diversity and politics' (Zeitoun et al., 2016: 145). Some strong proponents of this approach include Grey and Sadoff (2007: 550) who argue that 'investments in water infrastructure and institutions are almost always needed to achieve water security'. Garrick and Hall (2014: 617) have also argued that 'the extent to which water-related hazards must be managed varies depending on hydroclimatic characteristics'. The problem with reductionist approaches are several, but the key one concerns the way macro-analyses facilitate the emergence and entrenchment of the 'iron-triangle' of water bureaucracies—states, engineers, finance capital (Molle et al., 2009)—who stand to benefit most from supply-side interventions (Reisner, 1986; Worster, 1985).

The integrative approach, on the other hand, is closely linked to critical theoretical approaches to political economy, political ecology, anthropology, resource studies, among others (Cook & Bakker, 2012; Zeitoun, et al., 2016). It is important to note that integrative approaches are not 'anti-infrastructure' or 'anti-investment'; nor do they dispute the importance of hydro-climatic chartacteristics. Rather, integrative approaches begin with the socio-ecological context, or what Linton and Budds (2014) call the hydro-social cycle (Linton & Budds, 2014), resisting the urge to operate on the basis of aggregates (e.g. total available freshwater) and averages (e.g. freshwater use per capita), and asking questions such as who has what water why? Put differently: GDP growth for whom? Interestingly, for more than two decades, the pursuit of IWRM has functioned as a meeting place for these contrasting approaches. While some have critiqued IWRM as a platform for the commodification of water (Lubell & Balazs, 2018), others have argued that 'IWRM constitutes both a discursive site and multilateral landscape where various forms of power—political, social, cultural—are exercised in the production of new social practices' (Swatuk, 2005: 874). Jonker (2007: 1262) has also stated that 'IWRM is a framework within which to manage people's activities in such a manner that it improves their livelihoods without disrupting the water cycle'. Conca (2015: 302), too, has argued that IWRM offers 'more complex and interlocking policy mechanisms to manage water more comprehensively: across different user sectors, across different scales, in a more participatory way, with greater attention to the environment, and in a more knowledge-informed manner'. We return to the question of IWRM's ability to foster urban water security below.

Background: London and Cape Town Compared

Water must be set in its socio-ecological, socio-political and socio-economic contexts (see Tables 1.1 and 3.1). Cape Town is the legislative capital and second-most populous city in South Africa (SA), and London is the capital and largest city in the United Kingdom (UK). Whereas Cape Town is located at the coastal, London is 80 km inland set on the down-stream portion of the Thames River, a tidal river. Tides can rise by as much as 7 metres and the City of London constructed the Thames Barrier in the early 1980s to protect against surges and flooding. While Cape Town presents a Mediterranean climate, with wet, cool winters and warm dry summers (Parks et al., 2019), London enjoys a near continental climate that is most pronounced in the Thames Valley region sheltered from the influence of mid-latitude depressions (London Climate Change Partner-ship, 2002: 9). In terms of government, the City of Cape Town has a Mayor-Council system. Cape Town's 231-member council is elected in a system of mixed-member proportional representation with candidates being representatives of their political party. This mirrors national and provincial politics and outcomes at municipal level are often impacted by events at higher levels of government. In contrast, the Greater London Authority (GLA) and its 25-member London Assembly, headed by a Mayor, is the regional authority to oversee London.

Furthermore, rapid urban growth has been constant for both cities. In Cape Town, the rapid growth of informal settlements has greatly impacted the city's population. Cape Town's urban population of 4,618,000 is almost half of London's population of 9,304,000 inhabitants as of 2020. Cape Town's population is projected to grow to 5,845,000 by 2035 while London's population is expected to grow to 10,556,000 by 2035 (World Population Review, 2022a). According to the 2011 Census, 21.6% of people in Cape Town were living in informal settlements (CCT, 2012)

Table 3.1 Water background comparison—Cape Town and London

Water background	*Cape Town*	*London*
Water Legislation	Water Act 36 of 1998 framed equal water for all	Water Act of 1989 introduced privatisation
Authority Responsible for water	Government Municipality—City of Cape Town	Government as regulator Water Companies—Thames Water (water supply and sewage), Veolia Water Central, Essex & Suffolk Water and Sutton & East Surrey Water
Stakeholders	National Government Department of Water and Sanitation (DWS) Catchment Management Agencies (CMAs) DWS regional City of Cape Town (CCT) Private organizations Non-for-profit organizations (NGOs) Water user associations (WUAs)	Department for Environment Food & Rural Affairs (DEFRA) The Environment Agency (EA) Municipal level, the Greater London Authority or City Ofwat Drinking-Water Inspectorate (DWI) Consumer Council for Water or CC Water Waterwise
Annual Precipitation	500 mm (19.7 inches)	583 mm (23 inches)

(continued)

Table 3.1 (continued)

Water background	*Cape Town*	*London*
Source of Water	98% water comes from 6 main dams fed by precipitation: (1) the Theewaterskloof, (2) Voevvlei; (3) Berg River, (4) Wemmershoek, and (5–6) the Steenbras Upper and Lower dams	70% of water is surface water primordially coming from Thames River and 30% is groundwater. The Thames river basin over 16,200 km^2 (over 600 km of rivers and streams, most of which are tributaries of the Thames)
Water in the Catchment Areas	2000 mm per year	739 mm per year
Water for Agriculture Use	29% (158 Mm^3)	Less than 1%
Water per person	135 litres (2018)	167 litres (2009/2010) compared to the national average of 146 litres per person per day
Water Price	\$2.04/m^3	\$1.84/m^3
Water Needed for the City per Year	540 Mm^3	949 Mm^3

such as Khayelitsha, officially home to about 400,000 people though some estimates put the number closer to one million (WEF, 2016). Economically, both cities are dominated by services industries, but they present differences in scales. For example, the Gross Domestic Product (GDP) of Cape Town accounted for 70% of Western Cape province in 2019, R436,463 million (approximately US$23 billion) (CCT, 2019a). While London's GDP in 2018 was £487,145 million (approximately US$610 billion) (ONS, 2019). London, unlike Cape Town, is expected to rank fourth in the list of global economies with an expected GDP of $1.3 trillion under the label of 'megacity' in 2035 (WEF, 2019). The UNDP (2019) Human Development Report ranks South Africa 113th among reporting countries with a high human development index (HDI 0.625) and the UK at 15th with a very high human development (HDI 0.775). Their respective Gini indexes of 63.0 and 33.2 respectively reflects vast income and wealth distribution disparity in South Africa (UNDP, 2019). The Trust for London (2022) pegs London's Gini index at 44.3, meaning that the top decile of the City's population holds 44.3% of its income. According to the World Bank (2018: 1), in South Africa 'poverty is consistently highest among black South Africans, the less educated, the unemployed, female-households, large families and children with 55.5% of the country's population, 30.3 million, living under the national poverty line'.

Water in Context

The water supply mix is quite different in each city. Ninety-eight percent of Cape Town's water comes from rain-fed dams with a collective capacity of roughly 900 million m^3 provided mostly by six large dams (CCT, 2018: 8–9). In contrast, about 70% of London's water supplies come from the River Thames and the River Lee and the remaining 30% comes from groundwater abstracted from the aquifer beneath London (GLA, 2011: 12). In Cape Town, water protection and management are regulated primarily at the national level through the Water Act 36 of 1998 that provides power over water resources to the State of South Africa embodied by the Minister of Water Affairs and the Department of Water and Sanitation (DWS) as its main regulatory body (Beck et al., 2016). The Greater Cape Town Region receives its water from sub-catchments of the Breede, Berg and Olifants Water Management Areas (WMAs) through the Western Cape Water Supply System (WCWSS). The WCWSS is made up of 14 dams, of which six are regarded as major dams and three aquifers connected by an 11,600 km pipeline network, several storage reservoirs, pumping stations and canals (The Nature Conservancy, 2018). The City of Cape Town shares its water resources with the neighbouring district and local municipalities. The current unrestricted daily demand for water in the WCWSS is 1.35 billion litres per day (1.35 Mm^3/day) shared by the City of Cape Town, agriculture and smaller neighbouring municipalities (The Nature Conservancy, 2018).

In Cape Town's case, part of the challenge for sustainable water management lies in the existing water governance framework. The 1998 Water Act establishes the National Government 'acting through the Minister' ... '[a]s the public trustee of the nation's water resources' whereby it 'has the power to regulate the use, flow and control of all water in the Republic' (Government of South Africa, 1998). The new legislation was designed as a mechanism to avoid 'discriminatory laws and practices of the past that have prevented equal access to water'—locating human rights at the centre of policy, planning and delivery and introducing a more integrated approach to water governance and management (Government of South Africa, 1998). Through the new institutional architecture, cities are intended to be but one stakeholder among many within river basins managed by a Catchment Management Agency (CMA). In practice, however, the City of Cape Town does not participate in a functioning CMA, draws most of its water from beyond its catchment boundaries and buys most of it directly from the Department of Water and Sanitation which owns the three largest dams in the Western Cape. This form of direct bulk purchase serves as a disincentive to collective management processes (see Enqvist & Ziervogel, 2019, for details).

In contrast, in the UK, the Water Act of 1989 facilitated the privatization of water and wastewater services overseen by a variety of government and non-government regulators (Macrory, 1990; Ofwat, 2006). The revised 1991 and 2014 Water Acts introduced greater scope for competition among providers. A handful of entities oversee operations: DEFRA (governmental regulation through establishing appropriate legislative and policy frameworks); OFWAT (economic regulation through price setting); DWIQ (drinking water quality regulation through establishing standards and monitoring compliance); Environmental Agency (regulating the impact on the environment through permits) and the Consumer Council for Water (representing and protecting the interests of consumers) (see https://www.affinitywater.co.uk/corporate/about/regulators).

In terms of precipitation, Cape Town averages 500 mm/a with most rain falling during winter (May–August) (Parks et al., 2019) whereas London's 583 mm/a (GLA, 2015) falls evenly throughout the year. However, in Cape Town's case, water falls intensively in its mountainous catchment areas, generally exceeding 2000 mm/a (CCT, 2018: 6). In London's case, the average rainfall for the Thames catchment area is 739 mm/a. Spanning 16,200 km^2, the basin provides 2,100 Ml/d of water in London and another 780 Ml/d for the Thames Valley in a dry year (Thames Water, 2019a: 3–4). In the year 2014/2015, water from the Western Cape Water Supply System (WCWSS) was distributed as follows: 158 Mm^3 (29%) to agriculture; 345 Mm^3 (64%) to the city of Cape Town and 37 Mm^3 (7%) to other municipalities (CCT, 2019b: 34), totalling 540 Mm^3 (540 billion litres). While in London the main difference is that out of the 2.6 billion litres per day needed by London or 949 Mm^3, agricultural water use does not feature as a driver for demand due to the relatively small volume of water that is used for this purpose within the Thames Water supply area—an estimated 0.7% (Thames Water, 2019a). The two cities have adopted the catchment-based approach; however, some catchment boundaries do not coincide with political and administrative boundaries and the effects of any decision made outside the boundaries of both cities affect their capacity to supply water.

Water use in the city of Cape Town typically divides as follows: houses (51%); flats and complexes (9%); domestic other (2%); informal settlements (5%); retail and offices (15%); industry (5%); city-owned facilities (6%); government (2%) and other (6%) (CCT, 2018: 31). London's water use profile is delineated differently: food and drink manufacturer (6.6%); transport and manufacturer of transport equipment (3.3%); other manufacturing (3.1%); education and health (17.6%); wholesale and retail (6.1%); hotels, bars and restaurants (16%); agriculture, horticulture, forestry and fishing (1.4%) and other services (45.9%) (Thames Water, 2019a). Moreover, according to the International Benchmarking Network (IBNet, 2019), water tariffs in Cape Town at 1 July 2019 were: USD 2.04/m^3 (1–15 m^3), and the price increases to discourage water consumption USD 3.21/m^3 (16–50 m^3) and USD 4.30/m^3 (51–100 m^3). For London, Thames Water tariffs at 1 April 2020 were: USD 1.84/m^3 (1–15 m^3), USD 1.75/m^3 (16–50 m^3) and USD 1.73/m^3

(51–100 m^3). The price decreased when consumption increased (IBNet, 2020).

Furthermore, in Cape Town, water use had been reduced from 330 litres per person per day in 1998 to 220 litres per person per day in 2014. In 2018, water use was restricted to below 135 litres per person per day, which was a reduction of nearly 60% compared to 1998 (CCT, 2019b: 18). Meanwhile, London water use was an average of 167 litres per person per day in 2009/10 compared to the national average of 146 litres per person per day (GLA, 2011: 34). In Cape Town, it is estimated that 99.8% of the population have access to safe water defined as households with access to piped water inside the dwelling or yard or within 200 meters from the yard. An estimated 94.3% of Cape Town's population has access to improved sanitation according to government figures (Western Cape Government, 2017: 17). By contrast, in London, 100% of the population has access to both potable water and improved sanitation. London's water companies charge in two ways. The first is unmetered and calculates a set rate that is decided upon by the homeowner's rateable value. The rateable value is based on the local authority's assessment of the rental value of one's property. The second method is metered, where one is billed for the amount of water that is used. If one's water bill is unmetered and they feel that the bills are too high, they can ask the supplier to change to a metered bill. As such one's water usage may not have much correlation with the water bill as in the case of charges with no water meter.

Climate Change

Both London and Cape Town are far from immune from the impacts of climate change. For example, according to Miranda and colleagues (2011: 9), 'the UK is already experiencing the effects of climate change in the form of increased sea-surface temperature and rising sea levels [and] if global GHG emissions continue unabated, the UK is expected to experience progressively warmer and drier summers, wetter and milder winters and more frequent extreme weather'. These scholars go further to state that London, in particular, will be vulnerable to floods and heat-waves. Insofar as Cape Town is concerned, the University of Cape Town's Climate Systems Analysis Group (CSAG) developed downscaled climate change scenarios to interpret some of the expected changes. Interpretations from these scenarios indicated that the impacts of climate change on water sources in the Cape looked unfavourable, although some of these changes were said to also provide opportunities, such as increased civic participation, responses that reduced water wastage and collaboration between government departments (Ziervogel et al., 2010: 100). Another scenario suggested that after accounting for increasing temperatures and allocations of water to meet the ecological reserve, the WCWSS would decrease dramatically. In such a scenario, supply-side interventions would have to be implemented. For example, raising dam walls, treated wastewater reuse and groundwater exploitation, as well as restrictions on water use, might need to be imposed. Another study illustrated that traditional supply-driven water management responses need to be complemented by demand-driven management (Ziervogel et al., 2010). These scenarios were all fulfilled during the 2015–2017 drought in Cape Town and raising dam walls would have been to no positive effect with drought conditions prevailing.

Main Challenges in the Twenty-First Century

At one level of abstraction—the agglomeration of people in need of services—all cities are the same. As layers of information are added, they become simultaneously more similar (e.g. transit, energy, water requirements) and more different (e.g. appropriate systems to effectively deliver transit, energy, water). Cities are also organic, so London 2022 is a far different city than London 1992. Decisions taken by city officials set in motion a train of events which alter the city in innumerable ways, some of which are not desired. The so-called first demographic transition in Europe followed an industrial revolution which brought industry to the city. Cities such as London, Manchester, Paris and Berlin were altered forever by the steady march of people and resources to the city. The so-called second demographic transition, the post-colonial march to the cities of the Global South set in motion particular dynamics leading to the slums and service shortfalls we see today. An abiding challenge for urban planners and water policymakers is to see beyond the more similar and accept that there are no 'silver bullet' solutions to today's urban challenges (Meinzen-Dick, 2007). Easy explanations are to be resisted. As Zeitoun et al. (2016) argue, it is too simplistic to say that an unfavourable climate and limited capital lie at the heart of water insecurity across the Tropics. Elements of this are true. But no amount of built infrastructure will add up to water security 'once and for all'. Here the chapter focuses on three main challenges faced by London and Cape Town. These pressing issues are not experienced in isolation but rather, interwoven with other issues reflecting the complexity of achieving sustainable, equitable and economically affordable water for all.

Cape Town

Cape Town is currently facing a dam-water dependency that challenges all actors as stakeholders—government, Departments of Water and Sanitation (DWS) national and regional, Catchment Management Areas (CMAs), regional water utilities, NGOs, water user associations and the City of Cape Town. All these are involved in managing and supervising adequate water provision. Few people are thinking about other water sources without continuing the trend of high capital-intensive solutions that started with the construction of the Woodhead Dam in 1897 (CCT, 2018: 9). The challenge for Cape Town is to shift from a history of dam projects toward alternative solutions that contribute to more balanced equality and fairness for both locals and the environment at the same time. Ninety-eight percent of the city's water supply comes from water captured in a network of fourteen dams 'trusting' that mother nature will supply abundant water (CCT, 2018: 8). However, the drought period that started in 2015 and continued for three years in a row revealed that climate cannot be relied upon. The period was considered one that had received the lowest rainfall in 90 years, proving that 'current rainfall models were unable to predict the severity, timing or duration of the drought' (Taing et al., 2019: 531). Cape Town was able to emerge from its drought event because of an improvement in a close to average rainfall in 2018, and a series of water restriction regimes in both urban and agriculture (for details see Swatuk et al., 2021).

A second pressing issue in water security is the equitable water allocation that is closely related to poverty alleviation. The Water Act of 1998 was written to transform a legacy of many years of apartheid that separated people by racial lines. Cape Town currently supplies free water to approximately half a million people living in informal settlements such as Khayelitsha, and to around one million people in formal households living in properties with a municipal value of R400,000 (US$21,000) or less (CCT, 2019a: 21). However, women and girls living in informal settlements are responsible to carry water over long distances negatively impacting their health; at the same time, public sanitation facilities put women at risk of gender-based violence if they need to use a toilet after dark. Therefore, water security is not only about distributing water more equitably but also about understanding the full complexity of water management and poverty vulnerabilities that disrupt people's livelihoods and opportunities to flourish as human beings. The important thing to note is that total usage in informal settlements, including all types of use and losses, is about 50 litres per person per day, constituting only five percent of total usage in Cape Town (CCT, 2017). Therefore, despite the noble intention of South Africa, the challenge is how it will fulfil its promise about equitable water access as stated above.

The final important pressing water security challenge faced by Cape Town concerns the role of the State as the final water-decision-making authority embroiled in elected governments and thus, making water a hierarchical and highly politicized issue. The City needs to develop mechanisms for inclusive, participatory bottom-up governance to help offset the current tendency toward expert-led techno-economic approaches to water management. Water security is an issue that concerns not only environmental experts but organizations that are well-informed and can widen the water security context and advocate for integrating better policies.

London

In the case of London, the primary challenge is to refurbish its ageing water supply and sanitation networks. This includes 32,000 km^2 of pipes that are constantly leaking and bursting, and an outdated sewage system that is more than 100 years old. Water leakage is still a pressing issue for London. For instance, while 589 Ml of water were lost per day in 2011, Thames Water (2019b) reported that 690 Ml were lost per day in 2017/2018 (GLA, 2011). The challenge for the city has been to move away from neoliberal ideas embedded in the national infrastructure decision-making governance that calls for great capital-intensive solutions coming from the private sector based on the premise of 'efficiency' and 'expertise' (Bakker, 2013: 254). However, the fragmentation of water governance in the UK presents many limits to water security efforts locally. While the four companies responsible for water supply in London have been replacing old mains in the city, large-scale decisions that will impact the city are approved by Ofwat, the economic regulator of the water sector in the UK and Wales, such as the construction of the Thames Tideway Tunnel (TTT) that will run beneath the River Thames

(GLA, 2015: 9). The project has been more expensive than estimated. Therefore, the challenge, in this case, is about water governance.

A second challenge to achieve water security is to deal with the existing tension between land use for development and green spaces that keep the Thames River basin healthy. An average of 311 reported housing developments per annum occurred on private garden land each year. On average, 500 gardens or part gardens were lost to development per year (London Wildlife Trust, 2010: 4). The big challenge is about how to provide adequate housing to more people without stressing the Thames River Basin. London has been growing faster than the local authorities had projected. The 2011 census showed that instead of an average 51,000 people increment per year since 2001, London had grown by an average of 87,000 people per year situating the city with 8.2 million people in 2011 instead of the projected 7.8 (GLA, 2016). The challenge that arises to achieve water security is how the city will accommodate 1.2 million more people expected by 2035 (World Population Review, 2022a) when there are already 1.25 million residents currently at risk from flooding in the event of 'exceptional' tidal flow in the city (London Assembly, 2014).

The third significant challenge is pollution. Water bodies in the basin are already facing pollution from sources such as physical modifications (44%); wastewater (45%); households and transportations (17%) and pollution from rural areas (27%) (Environment Agency, 2015: 10–11). In 1957, the Natural History Museum categorized the Thames as biologically dead (Mallet, 2017). While significant efforts have been undertaken to bring the river to life, the challenges remain significant. In 2021, the UK's Environmental Audit Committee revealed that 'Thames Water's Mogden wastewater treatment works at Isleworth, west London discharged enough sewage to fill 400 Olympic-sized swimming pools' in a 48-hours period in October 2020. Total discharges into the Thames River topped 3 billion litres in 2020 (BBC, 2022). Given climate change, urbanization and ageing infrastructure, keeping the basin healthy is a big challenge impacting the livelihoods of some 15 million people living within the basin (Environment Agency, 2015).

In Search of Urban Water Security

Toward IWRM?

In line with Sustainable Development Goal 6 Target 6.5.1, the UK and South Africa have taken steps toward establishing functioning systems of integrated water resources management (IWRM). With London being the country's capital, located directly on the Thames River, only fifty kilometres upstream of its estuary on the North Sea, the city has taken significant steps toward both IWRM-based and integrated urban resources management (IUWM) planning. With relation to Cape Town, whereas at national level IWRM planning and institutional design has attempted to bridge complex levels of national, provincial and municipal water authorities and build a bottom-up, stakeholder-driven approach to management, in practice there has been little progress. Catchment management partnerships have been established to actively involve communities. For instance, the Berg River Partnership (BRP) comprises more than 30 stakeholders—government and non-government working together to improve water quality along the Berg River approximately 285 km in length that forms part of the Berg River Catchment an area of approximately 8 980 km^2 and located in the Western Cape province (Locke, 2016). These catchments are also used extensively for irrigation. The Berg River is the main source of domestic water supply and agricultural crop production with approximately 600 farm units providing employment (Western Cape Government, 2012). Another initiative is the Breede-Gouritz Catchment Management Agency (BGCMA) established in 2014 by extending the boundary and area of operation of what was known as the Breede-Overberg Catchment Management Agency (BGCMA, 2018). The BGCMA features a focus on decentralization and an emphasis on stakeholder consultation in water resources management-related decision-making processes.

Within the City government, there has been deliberate focus on sustainability and water sensitive urban design (Swatuk et al., 2021). But given the City's reliance on inter-basin transfers, the ownership of dams, and the purchase of bulk water directly from the Department of Water and Sanitation, meaningful IWRM practice has proven elusive.

In the case of London, IWRM planning displays both integration and fragmentation. Integration was driven in large part by the UK's membership in the European Union and the EU's establishment of the Water Framework Directive. In the UK, commitment to IWRM is expressed in

Water Environment (Water Framework Directive) (England and Wales) Regulations 2017. The implementing authority of Water Framework Directive regulations is the Secretary of State for Environment, Food and Rural Affairs. The Environment Agency produces and updates river basin management plans in England. 'Whilst some actions (that is, policy development and national infrastructure) will be delivered nationally, local delivery plans will need to be developed collaboratively with partners' (Environment Agency, 2021). According to the UK Government reporting on SDG 60.5.1, as of 2020 the country is 80% of the way toward reaching its IWRM target concerning the following Institutions and Participation sub-indicators:

- Basin and aquifer level organizations for leading implementation if IWRM plans
- Private sector participation in water resources development, management and use at national level
- Coordination between national government authorities representing different sectors on water resources, policy, planning and management
- Developing IWRM capacity at the national level
- Public participation in water resources, policy, planning and management at local level

The UK Government also reports that they are 90% toward public participation in water resources, policy planning and management at national level, and have achieved their targets (100%) regarding national government authority capacity for leading implementation of national IWRM plans and sub-national authorities for leading IWRM implementation (see: https://sdgdata.gov.uk/6-5-1/).

In relation to creating an enabling environment for IWRM, the UK Government reports significant progress across all sub-indicators, including having in place national water resources policy (100%), sub-national water resources regulations (100%), sub-national water resources policies (90%) and national water resources law (90%) (see: https://sdgdata.gov.uk/6-5-1/).

Managing Supply and Demand

With its near 'day zero' experience firmly in mind, the City of Cape Town (2019b) launched its water strategy *Our Shared Water Future* and announced intentions to diversify supply including alternative water sources such as groundwater, desalinization and wastewater reuse (CCT, 2019b: 30). Taing and colleagues (2019: 533) suggest that for long-term transformation, the City could recycle all its treated wastewater for potable or non-potable reuse, arguing that 'the thirteen largest wastewater treatment works (WWTWs) could supply 161.8 Ml/day of effluent for reuse' while being much less expensive than desalination plants.

Cape Town is also improving water supply by removing alien vegetation affecting stream flow into the main supply dams such as Steenbras and Wemmershoek and in the mountainous catchment areas (CCT, 2018). According to the Nature Conservancy (2018: 8), 'over two-thirds of the sub-catchments supplying the WCWSS are affected by alien plant invasions, reducing the amount of water that reaches the rivers and dams that feed the region by 55 billion litres (55 Mm^3) per year'.

The City of London (GLA, 2018) released its environment strategy in 2018, wherein water scarcity and poor surface water quality are highlighted as key sustainability challenges, and improvements to green infrastructure and natural capital as key means to success. Given London's location at the heart of the Thames River basin, it is clear that sustainable development requires an integrated approach. In 2020, the UK's Environment Agency (2020) published a *National Framework for Water Resources* highlighting that by 2050, sustainable supply will depend to a significant degree on diversifying supply and managing demand. To that end, the Environment Agency emphasizes a regional approach to water management and a usage goal of achieving 110 litres per capita per day. The report states, '[t]he potential additional water required in the south east by 2050 could be as much as half the total needed nationally'. Regional water master plans are mandated for 2023. An innovative strategy for making more of existing water supplies is cross-sector use. 'Regional groups should work with local business sectors that use non-mains supplies to seek innovative, cross-sector solutions including funding arrangements' (Environment Agency, 2020: 11). To encourage innovative thinking, the government announced its intention to bring all users under regulation.

London, IWRM strategies have allowed the convergence of different groups as it is the case of housing development. For instance, for the Old Oak and Park Royal Development Corporation (OPDC), Thames Water; the Environment Agency, the boroughs of Brent, Hammersmith and Fulham, Ealing, and Kensington and Chelsea and workshops with other stakeholders were held.

Discussion

The concept of water security can be conceptualized as 'either narrow and discipline-specific, or broad and integrative' (Zeitoun et al., 2016: 143). If water challenges are framed as taken as a simple issue, the solutions that will be crafted will follow a simplistic and usually linear path of dealing with it. On the contrary, if water security is regarded as a complex regime, the ways to deal with such a situation will be likely nonlinear and multidimensional and include, at minimum, political, economic, technological and biophysical processes (Zeitoun et al., 2016).

London's historical approach to meeting its water needs reflects the general rise of the West in the global political economy: resource capture and storage, command and control, the hierarchical separation of Man over Nature, and an abiding belief that capital and technology combined with creativity and innovation will result in an ever-expanding capacity for effective problem-solving and needs satisfaction (Crosby, 1986). This is the linear approach, and it was extended to the rest of the world through colonialism and imperialism. Cape Town was founded by the Dutch and later colonized by Britain, its entire infrastructure mimicked London and other European cities (Swatuk, 2010). The colonizers imagined that they could simply build a city in Africa modelled after their Western technologies and everything will work out well regardless of the many differences between the two cities such as the weather, geography, biophysical processes, climate, culture and so on. Thus, problems such as flood and drought reflect a type of intellectual 'lock-in' and path dependency manifest in the predilection to 'push rivers around' (Worster, 1985). In consequence, present challenges partially reflect a built environment rendered inadequate for dealing with the uncertainties resulting from 'inter-woven and constantly changing geopolitical, economic, demographic, and climatic processes' (Zeitoun et al., 2016: 144).

Reductionist Approach

Zeitoun et al. (2016: 145) defined the reductionist approach as 'seeking water security through certainty'. This approach envisages the reduction of uncertainty through risk-framing and analysis. Again, science and technology often like to deal with something that can be predicted and controlled using formulas or the scientific method. In Cape Town, there is abundant evidence about the use of the reductionist approach. For example, the WCWSS runs a complex network of dams, canals, reservoirs, pipes and other infrastructure all set as risk-management strategies. Despite all the heavy investment involved in water security infrastructure, Cape Town almost ground to Day Zero in 2018 after a long drought spell. London very much exhibits the similar characteristics of using the reductionist approach in its water security strategies. Politicians and private sector actors adhere to the idea that investment in physical infrastructure directly correlates to wealth creation and water security. The promise of 'more water' is attractive to citizens and governments advertise large-scale infrastructure projects as proof of their commitment to the health of the nation, thereby winning votes. This is a very persuasive argument, yet its success is brought into question by the facts of a growing global water crisis. Indeed, the notion of the 'crisis' is used to justify the reductionist approach to water security.

Whether intentional or accidental, the reductionist approach reduces diversity and eliminates politics in society. For example, defining 'water security [as] a tolerable level of water-related risk to society' (Zeitoun et al., 2016: 147) may seem to convey inclusiveness. In Cape Town and other cities from less developed nations, the idea that every member of society bears the same risk is fallacious. The majority of the people who were hardest hit by the 2015–2017 drought in Cape Town were people from informal settlements or marginalized communities. It will always be the women, the unemployed, street kids, the marginalized or oppressed who will 'remain water insecure so long as the cultural biases and political exclusions that in large part prevent them from accessing water on equal terms with others continue to be downplayed' (Zeitoun et al., 2016: 148).

To be more exact, Cape Town imported industrialization solutions to achieve water security by building dam infrastructures promoted by scholars such as Grey and Sadoff who argue that 'poverty demands that many developing countries will need to make large investments in water management and infrastructure at all levels' (2007: 546). Garrick and Hall (2014: 611) modify this view by introducing 'institutional investment' into the equation: 'pathways to water security capture the sequence of investments in institutions and infrastructure to reduce water-related risks and manage trade-offs'. As noted by Zeitoun et al. (2016), water security is a function of the hydro-social cycle (see also Linton & Budds, 2014), characterized by some as 'water apartheid' (Jegede & Shikwambane, 2021). Across Cape Town's informal settlements, women and girls time their use of public sanitation facilities to minimize their risk of being physically harmed. Many suffer the daily physical and psychological burden of fetching and carrying water. For many people around the world, the news about Cape Town's water crisis gave the impression that it was a new thing experienced by all residents equally, yet many citizens in Khayelitsha have been battling a water crisis for decades. Put differently, 'reservoir storage and GDP … incorrectly assume a linear and equitable share of GDP for marginalized and poor people' (Zeitoun et al., 2016: 146). Therefore, dam investment under the premise of reaping benefits for all in Cape Town does not correlate with the facts of inequitable access to water and sanitation. Historically, in South Africa, these inequalities are partly 'a result of political priorities which have historically often catered to the interests of rural, commercial, white farmers' (Enqvist & Ziervogel, 2019: 9) whose ability to create wealth not only influences politics in the city, but shapes decision-makers approach in satisfying the 'hydraulic mission' (Allan, 2006). Far from progressive, the 'sanctioned discourse' of IWRM has been disproportionately influenced by reductionist thinking, where appropriate institutions are the new improved governance 'pipeline' (Allan, 2006; Lubell & Balazs, 2018; Merrey et al., 2005). A fundamental challenge, therefore, is to put integration back into IWRM.

The Integrative Approach

Zeitoun et al. (2016: 148) have defined this approach as one that tends 'to approach the complexity of the water-society challenges either by invoking more comprehensive analysis of the underlying processes or by being socially driven and adaptive in the face of a broadened set of uncertainties that are considered'. This approach closely resembles progressive approaches to IWRM that aim to move away the classic view dominated by scientists and experts. The integrative approach most notably embraces or acknowledges the complexity of water-society challenges by 'recognizing diversity in society and the environment, while maintaining focus on the most marginalized; and incorporating water resources that are less-easily controlled; as well as welcoming innovative and adaptive approaches to move beyond supply-side prescriptions' (Zeitoun et al., 2016: 148).

Using this approach entails becoming aware that water is intrinsically related to other dynamics such as politics, power, marginalization and injustice in society. Water security for the residents of London requires everyone to see water differently. For example, the fruit juices and wine they consume comes with a price for the people in Cape Town who face water scarcity since Western Cape wealth generation is dependent on the region being a net exporter of virtual water to the UK. Being water wise means more than just limiting personal consumption of piped water.

Furthermore, for Zeitoun and his colleagues, an integrated approach recognizes 'water as an intrinsically relational, political and multiple-scale issue of both water access and control' (2016: 149), thereby acknowledging the different levels of complexity in which water affects us and we affect it. To paraphrase Oliver (2007), a majority of Londoners and rich people in Cape Town suffer from water affluenza, commonly defined as an 'unsustainable addiction to overconsumption and materialism exhibited in the lifestyle of affluent consumers'. IWRM allows flexibility in water management that focuses on moving to 'learning, adapting and consumption patterns' and the recognition of shared responsibilities (Zeitoun et al., 2016: 150). The Cape Town water crisis and London's persistent problems of pollution and ageing infrastructure have pressed those groups and individuals who are most water secure toward transformational planning and some encouraging action. The tendency to look for a panacea—lately regarded as desalination—must be resisted at all costs (Meinzen-Dick, 2007).

Conclusion

London and Cape Town share a colonial background, one as colonizer and the other as the colonized. Whereas both cities' dependence on systems of command and control face significant challenges, a more forgiving hydro-climate gives London time and space to work toward an integrative approach to achieving water security. In contrast, Cape Town's climate change impacted hydro-climate has shortened time lines for transformational action. Both cities have adopted water approaches that favour the reductionist approach. We have argued in favour of the integrated approach toward water security because of its inclusive nature, its bottom-up approach and its flexibility to acknowledge the complexity of water issues. Water is not an ordinary economic good (Savenije, 2002). It is essential and irreplaceable, bulky and fugitive, finite and ever renewable. In relation to human needs and wants, water is a central concern of economics, politics, society and the environment. Decisions impact eco-systems, social justice, and shape culture. Human-environment interrelationships create hydro-social cycles (Linton & Budds, 2014). Put simply, more than dams and pipes are required.

Our struggle to use water wisely can be seen in the many attempts to conceptualize what water security means and how it can be achieved. Integrated Water Resource Management (IWRM) must be seen as an opportunity to secure the needs of the basin and our own needs grounded on respect for the environment and solidarity among us. This is particularly important for people who suffer from exclusion and are forced to live in the margins of society. Throughout human history, the river has served as a primary platform of encounter and building relationships. In Cape Town, water use decisions are made by a top-down structure that has failed to fulfil its legal water mandate of providing water for all. In London, water falls under the purview of a complex combination of different levels of authorities which tips decision-making dangerously toward seeing it only as a commodity. An imperative in achieving water security is to understand the complexity of each city and the reality faced by its dwellers—rich and poor alike. If water is our place of convergence, then water is also our place of building relationships and attempting to do something better. Yes, water costs money but the Twenty-first Century abounds in examples of our capacity to find solutions and overcome problems.

References

Allan, J. A. (2006). IWRM: The New Sanctioned Discourse? In P. Mollinga, A. Dixit, & K. Athukorala (Eds.), *Integrated Water Resources Management: Global theory, emerging practice and local needs* (pp. 38–63). Sage.

Bakker, K. (2013). Neoliberal versus post-neoliberal water: Geographies of privatization and resistance. *Annals of the Association of American Geographers, 103*(2), 253–260.

BBC. (2022, January 18). *River Thames: More than 2bn litres of raw sewage discharged over two days*. https://www.bbc.com/news/uk-england-london-60046320. Accessed 29 March 2022.

Beall, J., & Fox, S. (2009). *Cities and development*. Routledge.

Beck, T. L., Rodina, E., Luker, L., & Harris, L. (2016). *Institutional and policy mapping of the water sector in South Africa* (Policy Report). Program on Water Governance and the University of British Columbia.

BGCMA (Breede-Gouritz Catchment Management Agency). (2018). *Annual performance plan for the fiscal year 2018/2019*. http://pmg-assets.s3-website-eu-west-1.amazonaws.com/BGCMA_APP_2018-2019.pdf. Accessed 30 March 2022.

CCT (City of Cape Town). (2012). *City of Cape Town—2011 Census—Cape Town*. https://resource.capetown.gov.za/documentcentre/Documents/Maps%20and%20statistics/2011_Census_Cape_Town_Profile.pdf. Accessed 30 March 2022.

CCT (City of Cape Town). (2017). *Water services and the cape town urban water cycle*. http://resource.capetown.gov.za/documentcentre/Documents/Citypercent20researchpercent20reportspercent20andpercent20review/Waterpercent20Outlookpercent202018_Revpercent2030_31percent20Decemberpercent202018.pdf. Accessed 29 March 2022.

CCT (City of Cape Town). (2018). *Water services and the cape town urban water cycle*. https://resource.capetown.gov.za/documentcentre/Documents/Graphicspercent20andpercent20educationalpercent20material/Waterpercent20Servicespercent20andpercent20Urbanpercent20Waterpercent20Cycle.pdf. Accessed 30 March 2022.

CCT (City of Cape Town). (2019a). *Economic performance indicators for cape town: Epic 2019 quarter 3 July–September*. http://resource.capetown.gov.za/documentcentre/Documents/Citypercent20researchpercent20reportspercent20andpercent20review/CCT_EPIC_2019-Q3.pdf

CCT (City of Cape Town). (2019b). *Our shared water future: Cape town's water strategy*. http://resource.capetown.gov.za/documentcentre/Documents/Citypercent20strategiespercent2cpercent20planspercent20andpercent20frameworks/Capepercent20Townpercent20Waterpercent20Strategy.pdf. Accessed 30 March 2022.

Conca, K. (2015). Which risks get managed? Addressing climate effects in the context of evolving water governance institutions. *Water Alternatives, 8*(3), 301–316.

Cook, C., & Bakker, K. (2012). Water security: Debating an emerging paradigm. *Global Environmental Change, 22*, 94–102.

Crosby, A. W. (1986). *Ecological imperialism: The biological expansion of Europe, 900–1900*. Cambridge University Press.

Enqvist, J. P., & Ziervogel, G. (2019). Water governance and justice in Cape Town: An overview. *Wiley Interdisciplinary Reviews, 6*(4), 1354. https://doi.org/10.1002/wat2.1354

Environment Agency. (2015, December). *Part 1: Thames river basin district. River basin management plan*. Environment Agency.

Environment Agency. (2020, March 16). *Meeting our future water needs: A national framework for water resources*. Environmental Agency.

Environment Agency. (2021, October 22). *River basin planning process overview* (Policy Paper). https://www.gov.uk/government/publications/river-basin-planning-process-overview/river-basin-planning-process-overview. Accessed 30 March 2022.

Garrick, D., & Hall, J. W. (2014). Water security and society: Risks, metrics, and pathways. *Annual Review of Environment and Resources, 39*, 611–639.

GLA (Greater London Authority). (2011). *Securing London's water future: The mayor's water strategy*. GLA.

GLA (Greater London Authority). (2015). *London sustainable drainage action plan*. GLA.

GLA (Greater London Authority). (2016). *The London plan: The spatial development strategy for London consolidated with relations since 2012*. GLA.

GLA (Greater London Authority). (2018, May). *London Environment Strategy*. GLA.

Government of South Africa. (1998). *National Water Act, 1998 (Act No. 36)*. Government Gazette.

Green, C. (2011). *Case study brief—Sustainable urban water management in London*. http://www.switchurbanwater.eu/outputs/pdfs/w6-1_gen_dem_d6.1.6_case_study_-_london.pdf. Accessed 30 March 2022.

Grey, D., Sadoff, C., & Grey, D. (2007). Sink or swim? Water security for growth and development. *Water Policy, 9*(6), 545–571.

IBNet (International Benchmarking Network). (2019, July 1). *Cape Town Metro* (South Africa). https://tariffs.ib-net.org/sites/IBNET/ViewTariff?tariffId=18842&countryId=24. Accessed 30 March 2022.

IBNet (International Benchmarking Network). (2020, April 1). *Thames Water* (UK, England and Wales). https://tariffs.ib-net.org/sites/IBNET/ViewTariff?tariffId=20703&countryId=80. Accessed 30 March 2022.

Jegede, A. O., & Shikwambane, P. (2021). Water 'Apartheid' and the significance of human rights principles of affirmative action in South Africa. *Water, 13*(8). https://doi.org/10.3390/w13081104

Jonker, L. (2007). Integrated water resource management: The theory-praxis-nexus: A South African perspective. *Physics and Chemistry of the Earth, 32*(15–18), 1257–1263.

Linton, J., & Budds, J. (2014). The hydrosocial cycle: Defining and mobilizing a relational-dialectical approach to water. *Geoforum, 57*, 170–180.

Locke, K. (2016). *A study of an integrated management initiative to improve the berg river western cape, South Africa* (A Study Report). University of Cape Town.

London Assembly. (2014). *Flood risks in London: Environment committee.* https://www.london.gov.uk/sites/default/files/gla_migrate_files_destination/14-04-07-Floodpercent20riskpercent20slidepercent20packpercent20-percent20FINAL_0.pdf. Accessed 30 March 2022.

London Climate Change Partnership. (2002). *London's warming: The impacts of climate change in London* (Technical Report). http://climatelondon.org/publications/londons-warming/. Accessed 30 March 2022.

London Wildlife Trust. (2010). *London: Garden city: Investigating the changing anatomy of London's private gardens, and the scale of their loss.* http://live-twt-d8-london.pantheonsite.io/sites/default/files/2019-05/Londonpercent20Gardenpercent20Citypercent20-percent20fullpercent20reportpercent281percent29.pdf. Accessed 30 March 2022.

Lubell, M., & Balazs, C. (2018). Integrated water resources management: Core research questions for governance. In K. Conca & E. Weinthal (Eds.), *The Oxford handbook of water politics and policy* (pp. 569–593). Oxford University Press.

Macrory, R. (1990). The privatisation and regulation of the water industry. *The Modern Law Review, 53*(1), 78–87.

Mallet, V. (2017). *River of life, river of death: The Ganges and India's future.* Oxford University Press.

Meinzen-Dick, R. (2007). Beyond panaceas in water institutions. *PNAS, 104*(39), 1–6.

Merrey, D. J., Drechsel, P., Penning de Vries, P., & Sally, H. (2005). Integrating 'livelihoods' into integrated water resources management: Taking the integration paradigm to its logical next step for developing countries. *Regional and Environmental Change, 5*(4), 197–204.

Miranda, G., Greaker, M., Krasnowski, K., Schaefer, B., & Westwood, A. (2011). *Climate change, employment and local development in London, UK* (OECD Local Economic and Employment Development (LEED) Papers). OECD Publishing.

Molle, F., Mollinga, P. P., & Wester, P. (2009). Hydraulic bureaucracies and the hydraulic mission: Flows of water, flows of power. *Water Alternatives, 2*(3), 328–349.

Ofwat (The Economic Regulator of the Water Sector in England and Wales). (2006). *The development of the water industry in England and wales.* https://www.ofwat.gov.uk/publication/the-development-of-the-water-industry-in-england-and-wales/. Accessed 31 March 2022.

Oliver, J. (2007). *Affluenza.* Vermillion.

ONS (Office for National Statistics, UK). (2019). *GDP London April–June 2019*. Available at: https://www.ons.gov.uk/economy/grossdomesticproductgdp/bulletins/gdplondon/apriltojune2019. Accessed 27 June 2022.

Parks, R., Mclaren, M., Toumi, R., & Rivett, U. (2019). *Experiences and lessons in managing water from Cape Town* (Grantham Institute Briefing Paper No. 29). Imperial College.

Reisner, M. (1986). *Cadillac desert: The American West and its disappearing water*. Penguin.

Savenije, H. H. G. (2002). Why water is not an ordinary good, or why the girl is special. *Physics and Chemistry of the Earth, 27*, 741–744.

Swatuk, L. A. (2005). Political challenges to implementing IWRM in southern Africa. *Physical and Chemistry of the Earth, 30*(11–16), 872–880.

Swatuk, L. A. (2010). The state and water resources development through the lens of history: A South African case study. *Water Alternatives, 3*(3), 521–536.

Swatuk, L. A., Brill, G., Buchner-Marais, C., Carden, C., Conradie, E., Day, J., Fatch, J., Fell, J., Hara, M., & Ncube, B. (2021). *Towards the Blue-Green City: Building Urban Water Resilience*. South African Water Research Commission.

Taing, L., Chang, C. C., Pan, S., & Armitage, N. P. (2019). Towards a water-secure future: Reflections on cape town's day zero crisis. *Urban Water Journal, 16*(7), 530–536.

Thames Water. (2019a). *Revised draft water resources management plan 2019 Section 4: Current and future water supply (October 2018)*. Thames Water.

Thames Water. (2019b). *Building a better future: Annual report and performance report 2018/2019b*. Thames Water.

The Nature Conservancy. (2018). *The Greater Cape Town Water Fund: Assessing the return on investment for ecological infrastructure restoration*. https://www.nature.org/content/dam/tnc/nature/en/documents/GCTWF-Business-Case_2018-11-14_Web.pdf. Accessed 31 March 2022.

Trust for London. (2022). *The distribution of wealth*. https://www.trustforlondon.org.uk/data/wealth-distribution/. Accessed 31 March 2022.

UN. (2019). *The sustainable development goals report 2019*. United Nations.

UNDP (United Nations Development Programme). (2019). *Human Development Report 2019: Beyond income, beyond averages, beyond today: Inequalities in human development in the 21st century*. http://hdr.undp.org/sites/default/files/hdr2019.pdf. Accessed 31 March 2022.

Western Cape Government. (2012). *A Berg River Improvement Plan—2012*. https://www.westerncape.gov.za/eadp/files/atoms/files/BRIP_Final%20Report_abridged.pdf. Accessed 31 March 2022.

Western Cape Government. (2017). *Socio-Economic Profile, City of Cape Town 2017*. https://www.westerncape.gov.za/assets/departments/treasury/Documents/Socio-economic-profiles/2017/city_of_cape_town_2017_socio-economic_profile_sep-lg_-_26_january_2018.pdf. Accessed 31 March 2022.

World Bank. (2018, March). *Overcoming poverty and inequality in South Africa: An assessment of drivers, constraints and opportunities*. The World Bank.

World Economic Forum (WEF). (2016). *These are the world's five biggest slums: Global agenda: Cities and urbanization*. https://www.weforum.org/agenda/2016/10/these-are-the-worlds-five-biggest-slums/. Accessed 31 March 2022.

World Economic Forum (WEF). (2019). *These will be the most important cities by 2035*. https://www.weforum.org/agenda/2019/10/cities-in-2035/. Accessed 31 March 2022.

World Population Review. (2022a). *London, United Kingdom*. https://worldpopulationreview.com/world-cities/london-population. Accessed 30 March 2022.

World Population Review. (2022b). *Cape Town, South Africa*. https://worldpopulationreview.com/world-cities/cape-town-population. Accessed 30 March 2022.

Worster, D. (1985). *Rivers of Empire: Water, aridity, and the growth of the American West*. Oxford University Press.

Zeitoun, M., Lankford, B., Krueger, T., Forsyth, T., Carter, R., Hoekstra, A. Y., Taylor, R., Varis, O., Cleaver, F., Boelens, R., Swatuk, L. A., Tickner, D., Scott, C. A., Mirumachi, N., & Matthews, N. (2016). Reductionist and integrative research approaches to complex water security policy challenges. *Global Environmental Change, 39*, 143–154.

Ziervogel, G., Shale, M., & Du, M. (2010). Climate change adaptation in a developing country context: The case of urban water supply in cape town. *Climate and Development, 2*(2), 94–110.

CHAPTER 4

A Megacity's Hydrological Risk: An Analysis of Water Security Issues in Jakarta City, Indonesia

Destinee Penney, Mandie Yantha, and Larry Swatuk

Introduction

More than 80% of the world's municipalities are located along rivers and coasts and more than 50% of the world's population live within these municipalities, including Jakarta (IPCC, 2012). Lying south of Malaysia, west of Papua New Guinea and north of Australia, is the Republic of Indonesia, a diverse and complex country facing significant water security challenges (United Nations University, 2015). Indonesia is an archipelago made up of approximately 17,000 islands of which 6,000 are inhabited (National Disaster Management Agency, 2015). It has a population of approximately 258.7 million, with roughly 148 million people (more than 60%) living in extremely vulnerable areas (World Bank, 2018). The

D. Penney · M. Yantha · L. Swatuk (✉)
University of Waterloo, Waterloo, ON, Canada
e-mail: lswatuk@uwaterloo.ca

L. Swatuk and C. Cash (eds.), *The Political Economy of Urban Water Security under Climate Change*, International Political Economy Series,
https://doi.org/10.1007/978-3-031-08108-8_4

megacity of Jakarta is home to approximately 10,770,485 million people and there are concerns surrounding the increased demands for water and land due to a growing population, increased economic development, industrialization, intensive agriculture and climate change (Kumar et al., 2017). Water demand is accelerating while climate change-related uncertainties are on the rise (World Bank, 2018).

The world will not be able to meet the increasing demands and development challenges of the Twenty-first Century without improving how countries manage their water resources and mitigate against rising risks. Coastal megacities such as Jakarta face significant challenges both natural and human-made (See Table 1.1; WB and ADB, 2021). Although Jakarta receives on average 1816 mm of precipitation per year, many of its residents—particularly those in low-income areas—lack access to adequate amounts of potable water and reliable sanitation (Kumar et al., 2017; see also Table 1.1). Urban water security is negatively impacted by inadequate infrastructure, unequal use by a growing population and inadequate governance structures. In areas without piped water, groundwater is extracted, leading to land subsidence and the pollution of rivers, waterways and aquifers (Kumar et al., 2017). Human development, livable cities, climate change adaptation, food security and sustainable energy consumption cannot occur sustainably without effective water management. As other case studies in this collection show, Jakarta is not alone: population growth, economic development, pollution and mismanagement practices have pushed water resources, in almost all parts of the world to their limits. The effects of climate change have driven concerns for water-related threats (e.g. drought, flood) and human security risks (e.g. loss of livelihood, negatively impacted health) to an all-time high.

The UN-Water Status Report on the Application of Integrated Approaches to Water Resources Management (2012) states that by 2025, water stress will be experienced by two-thirds of all nations globally, including Indonesia. Water security has three dimensions: environmental sustainability, social equity and economic efficiency that must be achieved together with appropriate stakeholders (GWP, 2019). Achieving water security at various scales of society requires an integrated approach to governance and management (GWP, 2019). While Jakarta City and Indonesia have made progress in planning, pricing and legislation, effective implementation is lacking.

In explication of this and action that might be taken, the chapter proceeds as follows: the next section presents a background of factors affecting water availability and accessibility in Jakarta over time. Following this, the main challenges to achieving water security will be analysed and possibilities for sustainable solutions provided.

Background of Jakarta, Indonesia

Jakarta, located on the island of Java, is Indonesia's capital city. The metropolitan area occupies approximately 6,343 km^2, resulting in a population density of about 5000 people/km^2. It is the economic and cultural hub of the country and the largest city in Indonesia and in Southeast Asia (Luo et al., 2019). Administratively, Jakarta is equal in size to a province and its official name is the Special Capital City District of Jakarta or DKI Jakarta (Luo et al., 2019). The area has a population of 10,770,485 million and it is divided into 5 municipalities, 44 sub-districts and 267 villages (World Bank, 2018; Statistik Indonesia, 2019). Jakarta's five districts are known as Jakarta Central, North, East, West and South, respectively (Statistik Indonesia, 2019). Jakarta is flanked by the Java Sea and located at the estuary of the Ciliwung River on Jakarta Bay (Luo et al., 2019). Thirteen other rivers run through the area, together playing a crucial role in water security for the Jakarta Metropolitan Region (Maru et al., 2015).

Natural Physical Characteristics of Jakarta, Indonesia

The combination of high hazard exposure and high vulnerability can be found in Jakarta due to its location along the 'ring of fire' and physical characteristics (Hoekstra et al., 2018). Indonesia has a complex archipelago with several active and extinct volcanoes, continental blocks subduction complexes and both young and old basins (Asian Development Bank, 2016a). This unique landscape makes the country highly vulnerable to natural hazards and disasters including flooding, landslides, subsidence, earthquakes and volcanic eruptions (Hoekstra et al., 2018). Jakarta is prone to flooding from sea-level rise and extreme weather events, and it is made worse because of its low elevation that ranges between 2 and 50 metres, with the average elevation being eight metres above sea level (Luo et al., 2019). This elevation is rapidly reducing because within the last 30 years Jakarta has sunk by 4 metres, twice the average for other coastal megacities, due to the over-extraction of groundwater by both domestic and industrial users (World Economic Forum,

2018). Climate change will also impact Indonesia and scientists predict an average of 7.5 cm sea-level rise per decade in Indonesian shores within the next century due to global warming (IPCC, 2012). This rate of subsidence coupled with sea-level rise will create various issues for the megacity and by 2050, it is estimated that 95% of Jakarta will be underwater at this current rate of sinking (World Economic Forum, 2018). These facts and estimates have accelerated the Indonesian government's plans to create a new capital city, officially named Nusantara, on the island of Borneo. According to the Planning Minister, 'the new capital has a central function and is a symbol of the identity of the nation, as well as a new centre of economic gravity' (BBC, 2022). By removing the administrative functions from Jakarta, Indonesia follows in the footsteps of other countries whose primate cities suffered (and continue to suffer) similar woes: Nigeria (Abuja), Tanzania (Arusha), Brazil (Brasilia).

Demographic Change over Time

According to World Bank data (2022), Indonesia's urban population has increased almost exponentially since 1960, growing to an estimated 154.9 million in 2020. As noted above, Jakarta's population of more than 10 million is expected to increase to nearly 16 million by 2050 (Statistik Indonesia, 2019). Currently, there are 2,735,100 households in Jakarta and the average household size is 3.8 people (Statistik Indonesia, 2019). The average size of households as well as the region's population density varies inversely with income (Kooy et al., 2018). Many of the low-income areas in Jakarta's five districts are in the form of slums and informal settlements, called *kampungs*, a deviation from its original meaning of 'traditional village' (Alzamil, 2018). Kampungs are typically located on government-owned land along railways, waterways, rivers and reservoirs (Baker, 2012) with North Jakarta having a high concentration of low-income communities (Kooy et al., 2018). Moreover, the lowest-income households are pushed to the highest-risk areas within kampungs.

Like other Southeast Asian cities, urban planning and development in Indonesia was influenced by colonialism (Dutch) and imperialism (British, Japanese) (Setiawan, 2014). Dutch rule in Indonesia impacted urban development through European-style influence and concentrated on the infrastructure needed for exporting commodities instead of the development of urban institutions (Setiawan, 2014). Infrastructure and amenities had been built by the private sector for the benefits and use of European settlers and excluded the rest of the population (Setiawan, 2014). Apartheid spatial organization along with ethnic segregation policies were used to attract European migrants by providing superior location, infrastructure and centralized utilities. Native people, drawn to the city in search of jobs and new livelihoods were restricted to the margins, with little access to sanitation facilities and other modern utilities (Setiawan, 2014).

The so-called 'second demographic transition' (see also Chapter 3) was initiated at independence in 1949 as rural to urban migration was complemented by an infrastructure boom at the mouth of the Ciliwung River (Firman, 2009). Urbanization resulted in extensive land degradation, as forest and cultivated land gave way to hardened city surfaces (Firman, 2009). The rapid urban expansion resulted in 25 percent of agricultural land being converted into commercial and industrial uses to meet the growing urban demand (Alzamil, 2018). Rushayati et al. (2016) show how more than two-thirds of the capital region's five municipalities consist of built-up areas. Increasingly, green space is limited to outlying regions. In a tropical environment, subject to monsoon rains, this hardening of the soils creates compound problems of flash flooding and the failure to replenish groundwater.

According to Shatkin (2019), more than 3,700 deep wells were drilled during the industrial boom due to the high-quality, low-cost groundwater source availability. The large-scale land changes have decreased natural resilience and exacerbated the social divide within Jakarta, through unequal access to housing, land and urban amenities and low-income populations forced to live in high-risk flood areas (Padawangi & Douglass, 2015). Moe et al. (2017) has determined that 'Jakarta and its surrounding areas, especially the upstream region, would be fully urbanized by 2040'. It is important to mitigate the impacts of urbanization through government interventions to recover degraded lands and to maximize green space to encourage groundwater infiltration while recognizing the unequal social impacts of natural and human-made stressors.

Jakarta's Water Resources

Jakarta is in the Ciliwung-Cisadane River basin (Hatmoko et al., 2020). The Citarum River and the Jatiluhur reservoir provide Jakarta's water supply as well as groundwater, but it is a less reliable source for domestic needs due to its limited availability and use by the private sector (Luo et al., 2019). The main source of piped water is the Citarum River, but it only reaches 60% of the residents and depending where they live water is only available during certain hours of the day (Luo et al., 2019). Clean water use in Jakarta is '413 million m^3 a year, but the supply from the District Water Utility reservoirs is limited to 200 million m^3' (Kumar et al., 2017: 1), which shows that the remaining 213 million m^3 of clean water required is reliant on underground water reservoirs (Kumar et al., 2017). Groundwater's overuse presents a classic example of Hardin's 'tragedy of the commons', and based on projections given above, creative and concentrated interventions are necessary if Jakarta is to avoid a massive human tragedy in coming decades.

Ciliwung River

The Ciliwung River basin has a watershed area of 420 km^2 and is 117 km long beginning upstream at Bogor province Tugu Punack and flowing northward from Depok and Jakarta City ending at Jakarta Bay (Kumar et al., 2017). There is 75 km of the Ciliwung River that flows inside Jakarta City with an elevation of 5 to 350 m above mean sea level (Kumar et al., 2017). The vegetation around the Ciliwung River has rapidly changed to built-up areas within the last 30 years, leading to the degradation of ecosystems, land fertility and water quality. These negative effects have been exacerbated by drought and flood events during dry and wet seasons (Kumar et al., 2017).

Although it provides about 30% of Jakarta water needs, the Ciliwung River has a high amount of pollution from households and industries. The organic pollution (as measured by Biological Oxygen Demand) and chemicals (as measured by Chemical Oxygen Demand) in the water increases as it moves downstream to, and through, the City (Kumar et al., 2017). In a study done by Kumar et al. (2017), it was found that water quality deteriorated from upstream to downstream due to sewerage. Climate change and variability will increase these negative impacts due, in part, to extreme weather events.

Precipitation

Models suggest that rainfall patterns in Jakarta are changing with more precipitation during a shorter period and less precipitation during typically dry days (Kumar et al., 2017). Jakarta's Kemayoran Station recorded 2,152.10 mm of precipitation and 151 rainy days in 2018 which is quite high leading to ample amount of water available (Statistik Indonesia, 2019). Indonesia is considered to be abundant with water, 'with 3.2 trillion cubic metres of water resource potential, which is equal to 16,800 cubic metres of water supply per capita per year' (Republic of Indonesia, 2016: 55). The average monthly discharge from 2015 to 2030 at different stations along the Ciliwung River indicates high flow rates and a forecasted increased flow in May and December in 2030 (Kumar et al., 2017).

Due to climate change, Indonesia has experienced an increase in annual rainfall by 12 percent over the last 30 years and shorter and more intense rainy seasons that have led to increased flooding (IPCC, 2012). Four-year droughts are now occurring every three years, and scientists predict the temperature will increase by 0.2–0.3 °C per decade that will have a direct impact on drought events (IPCC, 2012). This already water-abundant city will need to manage severe weather events that will bring both heavy rainfall and more intense dry seasons, so creating the risks of hazard events. As shown in Yosua et al. (2019), groundwater recharge is increasingly limited to the far south of the greater Jakarta region, specifically East Jakarta (Rushayati et al., 2016) so exacerbating the challenges of meeting urban water security.

Water User Profile

The five municipalities of Jakarta have large population, households and industrial activities that require water use. Kumar et al. (2017), simulated the water demand for Jakarta City based on population growth estimates for the year 2030 and found that 1.34 billion m^3 water will be demanded in 2030, 2.5 times the demand from 2000. Socio-economic irregularity is evident in Jakarta by a gap between water supply and demand. Piped water is common in wealthy residential areas but not in slums and poorer communities (Luo et al., 2019). Poor communities have experienced water shortages for years due to the inaccessibility of piped water and the dependence on polluted lakes, wells, river water and bottled water to meet their water needs (Luo et al., 2019). The industrial estates in Jakarta account for the activities of 518 firms whose total demand for water is between 19,602 m^3 per day to 72,963 m^3 per day (Asian Development Bank, 2016a).

Water Quality

The Asian Development Bank (2016b: 23) confirms that there has been a steady decline in water quality within the past decade across Indonesia and states that while 'some reports may indicate stabilization or even small improvements, it is expected to be applicable to specific locations or substances'. The main contributors of water pollution across the country include agriculture, fish farming, mining, industry and domestic wastewater (Asian Development Bank, 2016b). In urban areas merely one percent of wastewater is collected and treated safely and only four percent of sewerage where large amounts of fecal coli, nutrients and high amounts of COD are found in surface water (Asian Development Bank, 2016b). Jakarta groundwater is polluted and a study by Fitria et al. (2018) found that 80% of the water sampled was contaminated by E. Coli and the correlations between water quality were demographic factors such as population and density (Fitria et al., 2018).

The Ministry of Environment and Forest and The Ministry of Health are responsible for monitoring drinking water quality and regulation of water standards for water supply agencies (Asian Development Bank, 2016b). The multi-level structures of Jakarta's governance systems have become more prominent recently because of the country's decentralization policies (Ward et al., 2013). The Ministry of Public Works is responsible for river systems, while Public Works offices at the provincial level are responsible for the main drainage systems and most of the local drainage works (Ward et al., 2013). The targets for water quality are established by the government and the local governments have the power to set their own targets for industrial discharge that goes into their jurisdiction's water resource (Asian Development Bank, 2016b). Indonesia has abundant water resources and its availability surpasses the demand. Clearly, water insecurity is the result of faulty or lack of infrastructure and poor governance/management (Asian Development Bank, 2016b).

Cost of Water

There are two systems within the country to charge for water resource use, the first is a service fee for water resource management (SFWRM) and the second is a fee charged for water processed for drinking by water utility (PDAM) (Asian Development Bank, 2016b). The SFWRM is applied when efforts are made to conserve water resources and 'facilitate utilization of water through the development of infrastructure, such as dams and canals, by which the dammed water can be delivered continuously to the water users' (Asian Development Bank, 2016b: 71). Customers are charged a fee when the PDAM converts the raw water into drinking water by PDAM (Asian Development Bank, 2016b).

Water utility company PAM JAYA's water tariffs are calculated based on dwelling size and water use in three volume categories: 0–10 m^3, 11–20 m^3, and > 20 m^3 (PAM JAYA, 2020). A very low-level house is charged, Rp.1.050, Rp. 1.05 and Rp. 1.575 and an above middle-class house is charged Rp. 6.825, Rp. 8.150 and Rp. 9800 (PAM JAYA, 2020). As mentioned earlier, middle- to high-income households do not primarily use piped water and this reduces the monetary gains that may be used for infrastructure development and repair (PAM JAYA, 2020).

Governance Structures

Understanding the role of governance structures in Jakarta allows for critical understanding of existing policies, current regulations in terms of water use and quality, in addition to accountabilities. Unfortunately, governance structures within the country of Indonesia, and more specifically within the Greater Jakarta remain complex and inadequate for the needs and concerns of the growing population (Ward et al., 2013). Managing a growing population and regulating fast-paced human activities within a limited spatial concentration such as Jakarta requires a very dynamic and concrete approach with considerable investment required for proper management facilities, inclusive policy reforms and appropriate regulations (Asian Development Bank, 2016a).

Over the last five decades, the water world has increasingly focused attention on institutional reform, shifting decision-making away from governments, experts and national interests toward stakeholders, knowledge communities and river basins (Conca, 2006; GWP, 2019). In Indonesia, the governing structures regarding water management remain multifaceted and complex. As one of the fastest growing nations of Asia, the most vital issue within Indonesia today includes coping with the fast-growing demand for freshwater services in both rural and urban areas, and governing for sustainable, equitable and economically efficient development (Nastiti, 2017). The objectives of providing adequate water governance and quality water supply lie beyond physical access and include efforts to protect people's health and avoid the excessive and unnecessary costs which can follow. Poor water supplies have long been associated with water-related diseases, chemical exposure and indirect health impacts resulting from poor sanitation facilities (Nastiti, 2017). These conditions are largely due to poor governance structures which have not prioritized or funded such vital systems. Challenges persist because of insufficient coordination among governing agencies due to the country's complex nature and numerous governing bodies which govern the thousands of islands within the country. In addition, there remains limited adoption and funding at the sub-national level due to differing local priorities and political cycles (UN-ESCAP, 2020). Although recent governing mandates have committed to the improvement of drinking water and sanitation facilities, as well as targets to strengthen and develop stronger governance divisions, past years exemplified poor recognition and insufficient capacities, making the progression of development within Indonesia and issues regarding national water security both slow and unprogressive (MNDP, 2020). In addition, many violent conflicts and forms of corruption have arisen within both urban and peri-urban areas due to increasing poverty concerns and issues related to water security, holding governing bodies accountable for their lack of management (Nastiti, 2017). Fortunately, population growth, economic development, extensive pollution and poor water, sanitation and mismanagement practices have pushed water resources in Jakarta to their limits, with urgent action and viable accountability being now mandatory. Recognition and adoption of a systemic structural design, involving revised policy regulations, comprehensive implementation strategies, and multi-stakeholder considerations with government support will help revitalize and rehabilitate the country's vital structures and services (UN-ESCAP, 2020).

Challenges and Main Issues

The City of Jakarta faces several challenges regarding water security, including too much water and too little water. Although the area is water-abundant, Jakarta has several challenges that obstruct the ability to achieve urban water security. The groundwater resources are heavily over-exploited, and the quality of freshwater resources is severely deteriorated (Firman, 2009). Furthermore, infrastructure shortages, service inequalities and surface water pollution are key water-specific challenges while land use deregulation has created inequalities which has had an indirect impact on water availability and use (Padawangi & Douglass, 2015). In 2010, Jakarta met the MDG target of improving water access in the City, however this achievement was dependent upon access to groundwater and not piped water sources (Kooy et al., 2018). The following section will outline the main challenges in achieving water security. Focus is placed on three factors: inadequate infrastructure, unequal use of water by different groups and poor government structures.

Inadequate Infrastructure

Climate change is not the only factor that will have an impact upon Indonesia's water security. The over-abstraction of groundwater is causing land subsidence thereby increasing flood hazards and saline intrusion that reduces water quality (Abidin et al., 2011; Hoekstra et al., 2018). In 1997, Jakarta Municipal Waterworks (PAM JAYA) was privatized and the Jakarta Water Supply Network was split into two concession areas, Jakarta East and Jakarta West (Furlong & Kooy, 2017). The piped water provided by both networks use water that is extracted from reservoirs located south of the city (Furlong & Kooy, 2017). However, groundwater is relied upon for water supply by more than 60% of the inhabitants of Jakarta and deep aquifers are used by industry, businesses and expensive neighbourhoods (Furlong & Kooy, 2017). As high-income users do not use the piped network, it impedes 'the cross subsidization upon which service extension to the lower-income areas of the city is based' (Furlong & Kooy, 2017: 888). As a result, the Urban waterscape is fragmented by the disconnect of activities that do not include network infrastructure (Furlong & Kooy, 2017).

Where piped water is accessible, it is not available all the time and/or has inadequate pressure (Furlong & Kooy, 2017). Piped water infrastructure is absent in North, East, West and South Jakarta, but concentrated in Central Jakarta (Furlong & Kooy, 2017). Bakker and Kooy (2008), conducted a GIS-mapping study to analyse land use and water network distribution and found that key economic zones (Industrial Estates, commercial districts and residential zones for the elite) had high concentration of water supply networks. Northern Jakarta has a large concentration of poor neighbourhoods and slums that have little to no water pressure because eligibility for an on-premise piped water connection requires proof of citizenship and proof of payment/receipt of land and building tax. This regulation makes it difficult for those living in slums or on illegal land for which land and building tax is not owned or paid for (Kooy et al., 2018). Jakarta also has a high prevalence of unregistered land concentrated in varying areas along waterways and in North East Jakarta where the colonial and oldest part of town has poorly maintained infrastructure (Baker, 2012).

Inadequate Wastewater Treatment and Sewerage Management

According to the World Health Organization (WHO, 2020), poor sanitation conditions cause 85–90% of diarrhoea in developing countries and causes 1.6 million deaths annually among children under the age of five. In developing countries, the simplicity and low cost of construction of basic sanitation lavatory (simple holes) without operation and maintenance, contributes to the spread of disease through groundwater contamination and flood events (Setiawati et al., 2013).

In addition, Asian megacities experience severe pollution issues from a lack of wastewater treatment from agricultural, domestic and industrial sources (Luo et al., 2019). Jakarta's sewerage covers less than two percent of the population and the majority depend upon on-site sanitation that drains into surface water due to inadequate infrastructure (Luo et al., 2019). Wastewater treatment in Jakarta is divided into on-site sanitation and off-site sewerage management systems (Luo et al., 2019). Rapid urbanization and industrialization have also influenced the already poor infrastructure.

The drainage system in Indonesia remains increasingly problematic for several reasons: (a) most of its cities are developed incrementally instead of through long-term planning; thus it is difficult to design an integrated drainage system in the existing situation; (b) drainage system planning is still based on conditions during normal climate, while extreme rain due to climate anomaly has often occurred and (c) water runoff has increased due to land use change (Luo et al., 2019). Improving Jakarta's drainage system will enhance water quality and the collection of wastewaters for sanitation purposes and disposal within the city.

Inadequate Management Systems and Poor Governance Structures

Unfortunately, the responsibility for the functioning of Jakarta's drainage system is based on a three-tier government system. The multi-level structure has become more prominent recently because of the country's decentralization policies (Ward et al., 2013). Because of this, flood management and drainage within Jakarta is politically and administratively fragmented. In previous years, there were no agencies or institutions assigned to oversee and account for risk and vulnerability assessments, to manage climate change data, or to disseminate climate-related information to the public, and therefore water and sanitation efforts regarding drainage management remained poor and inadequate (Ward et al., 2013).

Another issue that impacts the ability for Jakarta to provide water infrastructure is the amount of money the country allocates and spends in support of it. Although Indonesia's economy grew by 5.8% during the late 2000s, there was only a three percent growth in spending on infrastructure (World Bank, 2016). This may be contrasted with China, where government spends 10% of its GDP on water infrastructure (World Bank, 2016). To maintain and improve water infrastructure, money is needed and must be allocated correctly alongside adequate management and effective systems of governance.

Key Opportunities for Water Security and Sustainability

Water Law

To address water security concerns within Jakarta, the Government of Indonesia has made special considerations since the enactment of Law No. 7/2004 on water resources (Fulazzaky et al., 2014). Guided by this law, the decision-makers, managers and operators regarding the water sector must strive to implement effective strategies, programmes and activities to support water management. The law and policies governing water resources within the city are the legal provision for managing water resources from a river basin perspective. However, they have not been synchronized effectively (Fulazzaky et al., 2014). In line with global best practice, in Indonesia, the implementation of IWRM requires a participatory approach (Fulazzaky et al., 2014). The most important milestone in implementing the IWRM principles and processes is the enactment of Law

No. 7/2004 on water resources, although several other laws and regulations are in place in Indonesia to deal with water-related issues, such as the Disaster Management Law of 24/2007 and the Spatial Planning Law of 26/2007.

Programme management in terms of climate change adaptation has been very limited, resulting in a lack of agency and institutional capacity to manage climate change data and activities (Republic of Indonesia, 2018). As a result, the lack of capacity to provide the impetus needed to develop a programmatic approach, even though the need for integrative programme management is recognized by local and regional government bodies, serves to illustrate its need for adequate and improved governance structures, as well as effective policy revisions for water management practices within the country.

The Sustainable Development Goals in Indonesia (2015–2030)

Indonesia has committed to the implementation of the Sustainable Development Goals, including initiatives for the improvement of drinking water and sanitation (SDG 6), as well as targets to strengthen and develop stronger governance divisions (MNDP, 2020). Indonesia's Presidential regulation and decree No. 59/2017, the SDG Roadmap, as well as the National Action Plan concerning the implementation of the SDGs works in partnership with the Ministry of National Development Planning (MNDP) which stresses policy revisions and regulations necessary for systemic change (MNDP, 2020). The government has also integrated 118 of the 169 global SDG targets into the National Medium-Term Development Plan (RPJMN) (UN-ESCAP, 2020). However, given the complex nature and past of governance within the country, there remains concerns regarding the viable actions and accountabilities made by governing bodies for current and future considerations (MNDP, 2020). Although baselines and targets have been set with measurable indicators, challenges remain regarding the actual method of measurement for certain indicators, insufficient coordination among governing agencies, as well as the limited adoption at the sub-national level due to differing local priorities and political cycles (UN-ESCAP, 2020).

To date, Indonesia's development plans have been designed through complex, holistic approaches, with frameworks extending to Thematic, Holistic, Integrated and Spatial (THIS) (MNDP, 2020). This reflects the country's complex nature and numerous formal entities which govern the thousands of islands within the country. Achieving SDG 6—water and sanitation for all—requires a systemic structural design, involving revised policy regulations, comprehensive implementation strategies and multi-stakeholder considerations (UN-ESCAP, 2020). Some priority policy directions identified by the government include:

- enhancing good governance for the provisions of safe drinking water,
- enhancing innovation and the capacity of technology for operating capacities of Indonesia's water systems,
- accelerating infrastructure development regarding both rural, urban and peri-urban settings,
- integrating the conservation and collection of raw water sources to optimize the utilization of raw water sources and
- encouraging efficient uses of technology for water security enhancement (MNDP, 2020).

Prioritizing these policy directions may encourage the emergence of more effective regulations, institutional accountabilities and financial support (UN-ESCAP, 2020). These active guidelines must be continuously backed up with measurable data, acknowledged accountability and real progressive change.

Other Planning Initiatives

There are a plethora of plans in place that speak to urban sustainability. For example, the New Agenda on Urban Governance Framework allows for urban populations who reside in 'unconsolidated urban areas' to access urban services such as basic water and sanitation. In addition, Indonesia's proposal for the New Urban Agenda of Habitat III (2016–2036) has been developed as a framework of the long-term national development goals (2005–2025) to achieve the vision of Indonesia as an independent, advanced, prosperous and equitable country (Republic of Indonesia, 2016). A challenge toward creating sustainable development within an urban megacity like Jakarta is the need for sustainable application regarding infrastructure and technological innovation. In alignment with the National Action Plan, the enactment of Indonesia's Green Framework was created, initiated by the Green Cities Programme of the National Plan (Republic of Indonesia, 2018). The initiative toward a greener and more sustainable nation serves to enable policymakers, governing officials and community planners to take focused action at a variety of scales. The utilization of a Green Framework can also be a critical guideline regarding spatial planning and design in Jakarta.

Managing Rapid Urbanization

According to Indonesia's National Report (2016), there are three supporting factors for an increase in urbanization: (i) natural population growth; (ii) rural-urban migration and (iii) administrative reclassification. Indonesia manages its urbanization through (a) population control; (b) expansion of urban areas and (c) migration and population mobility control. To ensure ongoing management of population and urbanization, Law No.10/1992 on Population Growth and Family Welfare Development was enacted to accommodate decentralization and balance population mobility with the environmental capacity of both Indonesia, and its capita city, Jakarta (Indonesia's National Report, 2016). The ongoing implementation of family planning could help stabilize Jakarta's population concentrations, or rather provide essential welfare development for families who may need support. In addition, managing urbanization through the improvement and expansion of urban areas, like Jakarta, can help address the negative impacts of rapid urbanization, particularly in the formation of slum settlements, impoverished communities, encroaching fertile land and limiting protected zones, which can only serve to exacerbate existing risk and vulnerabilities. Expansion of urban areas can include adding more areas and/or increasing the area carrying capacity. This of course would have to be paired with adequate supporting infrastructure for the capacity of the city to be stable. Essentially, investment and prioritization within social development, long-term planning and sustainable monitoring can contribute to achieving water security at the individual and household level.

Investment in Infrastructure and Management Systems

Meeting demand with unfettered exploitation of groundwater reflects the many interrelated problems of a megacity: disintegrated resource management in practice, an inability of governing authorities to 'get ahead' of the problem, the largely empty promises of national planning pronouncements and an over-reliance on privatized approaches to company, community and individual 'water security'. At the same time, Indonesia's decision to build an entirely new capital city suggests that policymakers are out of ideas. As a result, the necessary investment in improved and adequate infrastructure within Jakarta is not forthcoming. Not all infrastructure requires massive amounts of capital and high technology. Green infrastructure provides an important opportunity for the City to partner with communities to 'soften' the built environment through recovery of brownfields, for example. In terms of improved services in kampungs, officials can meet communities halfway. Cash (2021) chronicles an important case from metro Manila, showing how it is possible for government at different levels to partner with private sector actors and local communities in support of slum upgrading. This includes development of local water, sewage and solid waste management systems, which are often non-existent in many impoverished communities. Additionally, investment within design and smart city infrastructure can also help secure Jakarta's current water security demands and minimize costs and maintenance. To meet the growing demands for both current and future considerations, governing officials, policy planners and experts need to collaborate with civil society and prioritize investment for improved city infrastructure if sustainable transformative change is to occur.

Good Governance

For governance structures to improve, states and country borders need to agree and invest in jointly water resource management structures if they are to share both the rightful costs and associated benefits. The investment within adequate infrastructure and management systems can in turn, be a crucial source for global cooperation, trust and security. This idea of water diplomacy can serve to enhance conflict resolution which bounds the needs and conflicting views of different countries and sectors together. In turn, the emergence of water diplomacy and the focus toward jointly managed water systems can become a leveraging tool for security, prosperity and the protection of the environment all in one.

In recognizing the need for change, effective solutions toward sustainable water management is key to ensuring peace, long-term stability and security. The current global water crisis is mainly an issue of poor or inadequate governance structures or the denial of the water crisis and the mismanaged investment for current and future water considerations. As a result, good governance strategies are essential for preventing water-related conflicts at every level and ensuring all individuals and stakeholders involved have equal access to quality water and management facilities (water and sanitation), for current and future projections.

Improving Integrated Water Resource Management (IWRM)

As a management framework, integrated water resources management (IWRM) is now the dominant paradigm for water management in many developing countries, including Indonesia (Lubell & Balacz, 2018). As mentioned previously, the government of Indonesia has made special efforts on IWRM since the enactment of Law No. 7/2004 on water resources; however as effective IWRM strategies account for the inclusion, cooperation and involvement of key stakeholders (i.e. policymakers, city planners, managers and engineer operators), these approaches have yet to be synchronized effectively (Fulazzaky, 2014). The Law No. 7/2004 meets the most important elements of two aspects of IWRM (i.e. enabling environment and institutional roles), however not to the level of effectiveness needed to improve the city's water security (Fulazzaky, 2014; Swatuk et al., 2021).

UN data for SDG 6 shows that, as of 2020, Indonesia was approximately two-thirds of the way toward achieving target 6.5.1 on IWRM implementation. Most progress had been made in terms of securing finance while less progress had been made in enabling institutions (see https://www.sdg6data.org/country-or-area/indonesia). The implementation of an IWRM approach within the city of Jakarta should include the following: (1) IWRM at the level of river basins; (2) the decentralization of water management; (3) participative management and planning, involving all stakeholders and the public; (4) application of the polluter-pays principle and the engagement with Jakarta's water agencies; (5) local public municipalities' responsibility for water supply and sanitation utilities; (6) monitored use and maintenance of the various methods used for managing water utilities, either managed by a public authority or by a delegated private company and (7) transparency in the operation of services and information to the users (Fulazzaky, 2014). With these acting guidelines in place, governing members, city planners, experts and individual users can collaboratively work in transparency to overcome water security challenges in a more efficient, equitable and sustainable way in coping with heightened demands.

For effective urban water management, all stakeholders' views and interests must be taken into account. This requires policymakers to acknowledge the social relations of power made manifest through inequality of access and a willingness to address the profound water insecurity experienced by the poor. Thus, the water challenges of Jakarta are socio-economic, socio-political and socio-ecological. Many violent conflicts have taken place between different ethnic groups and between governments as a result of heightened vulnerabilities and uncertainties regarding food and water security (UN Asia-Pacific Disaster Report, 2019). This further speaks to the issues between the state and civil society/citizens, and the lack of accountability and poor performance of governing officials. As a result, these conditions have put the country of Indonesia and its population at risks of exposure to extreme scarcities, concerns for accessibility and decreasing water quality (Indonesia, 2018). Climate change will exacerbate existing challenges while creating new ones, so raising the stakes for states, civil societies and private sector actors (UN Asia-Pacific Disaster Report, 2019).

Education, Public Participation and Collaboration

In the case of Jakarta, public education, awareness and community participation are crucial for effective transformative change to occur. Law No. 12/2011 on the Establishment of Law and Regulation, states that individuals within Indonesia have the rights to provide input, verbally or written, in the process of formulating law and regulation (Republic of Indonesia, 2016). Enabling participation in policymaking and planning is vital for individual water security and well-being. This includes focused public awareness and education initiatives for individuals and industry regarding the causes and consequences of environmental degradation, as well as the interrelations among users. When stakeholders, policymakers and governing officials work together toward better education, public awareness and community participation, efforts of coordination regarding inter-ministerial cooperation can build up existing city structures and enhance sustainable adaptation and mitigation solutions for long-term water security (Padawangi & Douglass, 2015; Republic of Indonesia, 2016). The goal of participatory involvement is to help identify any gaps on the local-community level and implement mechanisms that encourage both governing officials and city planners to address direct concerns and complex challenges of water faced by the city's inhabitants. An example of this can be represented in changing community behaviours through training and education workshops by local officials and NGOs, with a focus in support of water resource conservation and the provisions and benefits of safe drinking water and conserving raw water resources to optimize water collection by locals and municipal governments (MNDP, 2020).

Conclusion

Ultimately, efforts to achieve SDG 6 in Greater Jakarta will fail if appropriate sustainable management methods and practices are not addressed and implemented. The heavy reliance on groundwater to serve industrial and domestic needs for Java's large urban areas cannot continue indefinitely. The persistence of this phenomenon is indicative of a disintegrated approach by stakeholders differently empowered across widely divergent areas of society. Although the Government of Indonesia has made considerable attempts toward sustainable change, more is needed if the city of Jakarta wishes to have its water security demands met in partnership with the complex dynamics regarding climate change, urbanization and population growth.

The challenge for the present and future development of water security within Jakarta remains conflicted within education, access, governance and management concerns. In terms of management, the country of Indonesia remains to be a conflicted context regarding water, as seasonal challenges provide both an abundance and disparity of water in variable qualities, not yet properly stored or managed effectively. As a result, these conditions have put the country of Indonesia and its population at risks of exposure to extreme scarcities, concerns for accessibility and decreasing water quality, all which have been addressed and critically reviewed within this paper.

Jakarta's water system will fail and continue to be uncertain if sustainable approaches and management strategies are not put into place. To address the water security issues in Jakarta, effective and good governance strategies must be implemented within Jakarta's social, political and economic structures with the investment of adequate infrastructure and management systems. Additionally, the improvement of integrated water resource management (IWRM), the adoption, alignment and enactment of the New Agenda and National Action Plan principles, the collection and recorded measurable targets and data provided by SDG initiatives, in addition to improvement of education, public awareness and collaboration of all stakeholders must be conducted. When governance strategies further incorporate inclusive participation among stakeholders and citizens, while working with the physical limits of water, water security can be reassured for millions of citizens, a possibility which can be implemented within the City of Jakarta under the right considerations and collective cooperation. Whether the political will exists remains to be demonstrated.

References

Abidin, H. Z., Andreas, H., Gumilar, I., Fukuda, Y., Pohan, Y. E., & Deguchi, T. (2011). Land subsidence of Jakarta (Indonesia) and its relocation with urban development. *Natural Hazards, 59*(3), 1753.

Alzamil, W. S. (2018). Evaluating urban status of informal settlements in Indonesia: A comparative analysis of three case studies in North Jakarta. *Journal of Sustainable Development, 11*(4), 148.

Asian Development Bank. (2016a). *Civil Society and Regional Governance: The Asian Development Bank and the Association of Southeast Asian Nations*. Lexington Books.

Asian Development Bank. (2016b). *Indonesia: Country water assessment*. Asian Development Bank. https://www.adb.org/sites/default/files/institutional-document/183339/ino-water-assessment.pdf

Baker, J. L. (2012). *Climate change, disaster risk, and the urban poor: Cities building resilience for a changing world*. World Bank Publications. https://elibrary.worldbank.org/doi/pdf/10.1596/978-0-8213-8845-7

Bakker, K., Kooy, M., Shofiani, N. E., & Martijn, E. J. (2008). Governance failure: Rethinking the institutional dimensions of urban water supply to poor households. *World Development, 36*(10), 1891–1915.

BBC. (2022). *Indonesia names new capital that will replace Jakarta*. https://www.bbc.com/news/world-asia-60037163#:~:text=Indonesia%20has%20announced%20that%20its,was%20first%20proposed%20in%202019. Accessed 1 April 2022.

Cash, C. (2021). Creating the conditions for climate resilience: A community-based approach in Canumay East Philippines. *Urban Planning, 6*(4), 298–308.

Conca, K. (2006). *Governing water: Contentious transnational politics and global institution building*. MIT Press.

Firman, T. (2009). The continuity and change in mega-urbanization in Indonesia: A survey of Jakarta-Bandung Region (JBR) development. *Habitat International, 33*(4), 327–339.

Fitria, F., Sutjiningsih, D., & Siswantining, T. (2018). The modelling of ground water quality in urban area based on demographics factor and building coverage ratio by using geographically weighted regression approach (case study in Jakarta, Indonesia). *MATEC Web of Conferences, 192*, 02034.

Fulazzaky, M. A. (2014). Challenges of integrated water resources management in Indonesia. *Water, 6*(7), 2000–2020.

Furlong, K., & Kooy, M. (2017). Worlding water supply: Thinking beyond the network in Jakarta. *International Journal of Urban and Regional Research, 41*(6), 888–903.

Global Water Partnership (GWP). (2019). *Mobilising for a Water Secure World: Strategy 2020–2025*. GWP.

Hatmoko, W., Firmansyah, R., & Fathony, A. (2020). Water security of river basins in West Java. *IOP Conference Series: Earth and Environmental Science, 419*(1), 012140.

Hoekstra, A. Y., Buurman, J., & van Ginkel, K. C. (2018). Urban water security: A review. *Environmental Research Letters, 13*(5), 053002.

International Panel on Climate Change. (2012). *Managing the risks of extreme events and disasters to advance climate change adaptation. A special report of working groups I and II of the Intergovernmental Panel on Climate Change*. Cambridge University Press.

Kooy, M., Walter, C. T., & Prabaharyaka, I. (2018). Inclusive development of urban water services in Jakarta: The role of groundwater. *Habitat International, 73*, 109–118.

Kumar, P., Masago, Y., Mishra, B. K., Jalilov, S., Rafiei Emam, A., Kefi, M., & Fukushi, K. (2017). Current assessment and future outlook for water resources considering climate change and a population burst: A case study of Ciliwung River, Jakarta City Indonesia. *Water, 9*(6), 410.

Lubell, M., & Balazs, C. (2018). Integrated water resources management: Core research questions for governance. In K. Conca & E. Weinthal (Eds.), *The Oxford handbook of water politics and policy* (pp. 569–593). Oxford University Press.

Luo, P., Kang, S., Apip, M. Z., Lyu, J., Aisyah, S., Binaya, M., & Nover, D. (2019). Water quality trend assessment in Jakarta: A rapidly growing Asian megacity. *PLoS ONE, 14*(7), e0219009.

Maru, R., & Ahmad, S. (2015). The relationship between land use changes and the urban heat island phenomenon in Jakarta Indonesia. *Advanced Science Letters, 21*(2), 150–152.

Ministry of National Development Planning (MNDP). (2020). *Roadmap of SGDs Indonesia. A Highlight*. Indonesia Secretariat for Sustainable Development Goals. https://www.unicef.org/indonesia/media/1626/file/Roadmap%20of%20SDGs.pdf?fbclid=IwAR0K_xHPqPV_6ihUg6qL-7DAwBWZIO_On_gaRWAdFabrIBT38wdmSkDNzfE. Accessed 31 March 2022.

Moe, I. R., Kure, S., Januriyadi, N. F., Farid, M., Udo, K., Kazama, S., & Koshimura, S. (2017). Future projection of flood inundation considering land-use changes and land subsidence in Jakarta Indonesia. *Hydrological Research Letters, 11*(2), 99–105.

Nastiti, A. (2017). *Beyond Access; the Multifaceted Water Supply in Urban and Peri-Urban Areas of Bandung and Jakarta, Indonesia.* Radboud University. https://repository.ubn.ru.nl/bitstream/handle/2066/175602/175602.pdf. Accessed 1 April 2022.

National Disaster Management Agency. (2015). *Indonesia's Disaster Risk Management Baseline Country Status Report 2015.* https://www.preventionweb.net/files/50832_5083220161031indobaselinereportfina.pdf. Accessed 1 April 2022.

Padawangi, R., & Douglass, M. (2015). Water, water everywhere: Toward participatory solutions to chronic urban flooding in Jakarta. *Pacific Affairs, 88*(3), 517–550.

PAM JAYA. (2020). *Drinking water tariff.* PAM JAYA.

Republic of Indonesia. (2016). *Indonesia National Report for Habitat III.* http://habitat3.org/wp-content/uploads/National-Report_INDONESIA.pdf. Accessed 31 March 2022.

Republic of Indonesia. (2018). *Indonesia Open Government Partnership National Action Plan 2018–2020.* https://www.opengovpartnership.org/wp-content/uploads/2019/01/Indonesia_Action-Plan_2018-2020.pdf. Accessed 31 March 2022.

Rushayati, S. B., Prasetyo, L. B., Puspaningsih, N., & Rachmawati, E. (2016). Adaptation strategy toward urban heat Island at tropical urban area. *Procedia Environmental Sciences, 33*, 221–229.

Setiawan, W. (2014). Reading the urban planning in Indonesia: A journey towards sustainable development. *Sinektika: Jurnal Teknik Arsitektur, 14*(2), 257–268.

Setiawati, E., Notodarmojo, S., Soewondo, P., Effendi, A. J., & Otok, B. W. (2013). Infrastructure development strategy for sustainable wastewater system by using SEM Method (Case study Setiabudi and Tebet Districts, South Jakarta). *Procedia Environmental Sciences, 17*, 685–692.

Shatkin, G. (2019). Futures of crisis, futures of urban political theory: Flooding in Asian coastal megacities. *International Journal of Urban and Regional Research, 43*(2), 207–226.

Statistik, B. P. (2019). *Statistik Indonesia: Statistical yearbook of Indonesia 2019.* Badan Pusat Statistik.

Swatuk, L. A., Brill, G., Buchner-Marais, C., Carden, C., Conradie, E., Day, J., Fatch, J., Fell, J., Hara, M., & Ncube, B. (2021). *Towards the Blue-Green City: Building Urban Water Resilience.* South African Water Research Commission.

United Nations Economic and Social Commission for Asia and the Pacific (UN-ESCAP). (2019). *Asia-Pacific Disaster Report 2019*. https://www.unescap.org/publications/asia-pacific-disaster-report-2019. Accessed 31 March 2022.

United Nations Economic and Social Commission for Asia and the Pacific (UN-ESCAP). (2020). *Mainstreaming the Sustainable Development Goals into National Planning, Budgetary and Financing Processes: Indonesian Experience* (A Working Paper Series). https://www.unescap.org/sites/default/files/publications/WP-20-06_final_0.pdf. Accessed 31 March 2022.

United Nations University. (2015). *Overview of Jakarta water related environmental challenges*. https://collections.unu.edu/eserv/UNU:2872/WUI_WP4.pdf. Accessed 31 March 2022.

UN-Water. (2012). *Status report on the application of integrated approaches to water resources management*. United Nations Environment Programme.

Ward, R., Pauw, W., Buuren, A., & Marfai, M. (2013). Governance of flood risk management in a time of climate change: The cases of Jakarta and Rotterdam. *Environmental Politics, 22*(3), 518–536.

World Bank. (2016). *Indonesia's urban story*. https://www.worldbank.org/en/news/feature/2016/06/14/indonesia-urban-story. Accessed 1 April 2022.

World Bank. (2018). *Population, total Indonesia*. https://data.worldbank.org/indicator/SP.POP.TOTL. Accessed 1 April 2022.

World Bank. (2022). *Urban population—Indonesia*. https://data.worldbank.org/indicator/SP.URB.TOTL?locations=ID. Accessed 1 April 2022.

World Bank and Asian Development Bank (WB and ADB). (2021). *Climate risk country profile: Indonesia*. The World Bank.

World Economic Forum. (2018). *Jakarta is slowing sinking into the Earth*. https://www.weforum.org/agenda/2018/08/jakarta-world-fastest-sinking-city/. Accessed 1 April 2022.

World Health Organization. (2020). *Indonesia*. https://www.who.int/countries/idn/en/. Accessed 1 April 2022.

Yosua, H., Soeryantono, H., & Marthanty, D. R. (2019). Jakarta groundwater basin recharge—Discharge boundary area map: A preliminary study. *IOP Conf. Series: Materials Science and Engineering 690*, 012008.

CHAPTER 5

Creating Water-Secure Futures in Megacities: A Comparative Case Study of 'Day Zero' Cities—Bangalore and Chennai

Anika Tasnim Hossain, Kate MacMurchy, Juhi Shah, and Larry Swatuk

Introduction

As two-thirds of the world's population is expected to live in urban areas by 2050, states and municipalities have unique challenges ahead of them (UN, 2019). India is projected to have the highest population increase between 2020 and 2050, overtaking China to become the world's most populous country by around 2027 (UN, 2019). Massive amounts of water are required to hydrate, feed, protect and power India's

A. T. Hossain · K. MacMurchy · L. Swatuk (✉)
University of Waterloo, Waterloo, ON, Canada
e-mail: lswatuk@uwaterloo.ca

J. Shah
Canadian Red Cross, Ottawa, ON, Canada

L. Swatuk and C. Cash (eds.), *The Political Economy of Urban Water Security under Climate Change*, International Political Economy Series,
https://doi.org/10.1007/978-3-031-08108-8_5

growth, and the country is already the world's largest user of groundwater (World Bank, 2020). However, as a perceptive reporter for *The Economist* (2019) points out, Indian cities have a management problem, not a water problem.

At the national level, water has been on the political agenda since the 1980s, with the Federal Ministry of Water Resources actively circulating bills for the regulation and control of the development and management of groundwater resources (Government of Karnataka, 2011). Arguably, the two most relevant pieces of legislation concerning water security at the federal level are the National Water Policy of 1987 (reviewed and updated 2002, 2012) and the model bill to regulate and control the development of groundwater (Ministry of Water Resources, 2005). Both measures are formulated by the Ministry of Water Resources and the Government of India to govern the planning, development and utilization of water resources (Ministry of Water Resources, 2002). The National Water Policy was the first of its kind, dating back to 1987. The policy was reviewed and updated in 2002 and later in 2012. The 2012 National Water Policy attracted criticism for its emphasis on treating water as an economic good, which the Ministry of Water Resources claims is necessary to promote its efficient use and conservation through an IWRM framework (Ministry of Water Resources, 2012).

Furthermore, the policy advocates for a demand-driven approach to water efficiency and states that 'recycling and reuse of water should be the general norm and water pricing should ensure its efficient use, and reward conservation' (GCC, 2019: 42). Demand management, as opposed to source augmentation, is a key theme throughout the 2012 policy (GCC, 2019), which explains the focus on water efficiency and conservation measures, including setting water tariffs (Visakha, 2019). Many states adopted the national policy which demonstrates the recognition of the importance of federal legislation concerning water management at the state level, as the federal government has no power to make laws for states, except as provided in articles 249 and 250 of the Constitution (Central Pollution Control Board, n.d.). This would otherwise make it challenging to collaboratively address a cross-border issue, such as water, if state governments are lacking in political will. The second important piece of legislation at the federal level is the Groundwater Model Bill, put forward for the first time in 1992 in response to the tremendous increase in groundwater use in the late twentieth century, aimed at giving greater attention in law and policy terms to groundwater use and protection

(Cullet, 2012). It provides a basis for rethinking groundwater regulation and is framed as a model bill, which is a set of guidelines for states to use to develop their own groundwater acts. As such, the model bill needs to be tailored to the contexts in which it would be applied, which suits the devolved nature of the federal government and the legislative competence states hold for regulating water (Cullet, 2012).

From within this context, there are several challenges that act as obstacles to the achievement of urban water security. Across India's megacities, unplanned and unregulated urbanization expands city limits, destroys wetlands, contaminates water resources and increases the proportion of impervious surfaces, thereby hindering the absorption of monsoon rains, on which many cities depend heavily, into the groundwater table. As municipal water authorities are racing to keep up with the skyrocketing demand, they are forced to extensively extract groundwater, which is then supplied, albeit intermittently, through deteriorating colonial-era infrastructure to households or resorting to high-modern practices of source augmentation. The intermittent supply forces the more well-off households to resort to supplementing their supply with private water tankers, operating in the informal water economy, which are profiting off poor management and governance practices in both cities. These issues, unless effectively addressed through improvements in water management and governance practices, have been and will continue to be exacerbated in the context of uncertainty created by climate change.

This chapter focuses centrally on the challenges of achieving water security in two Indian megacities, Bangalore and Chennai. It begins with a contextualization of both cities through a detailed water use profile. It then lays out the key challenges and exacerbating factors hindering urban water security in both cities, followed by a comparative stakeholder analysis at the international, state, municipal and community levels. This sets the stage for a discussion into IWRM and the role of community-level stakeholders in ensuring urban water security. The chapter concludes by finding that the achievement of urban water security in Bangalore and Chennai is possible though conditional upon sufficient political will to implement context-appropriate solutions to avoid 'Day Zero' scenarios.

Table 5.1 Population change in Chennai and Bangalore

City	*2001 (pop.)*	*2011 (pop.)*	*2018 (pop.)*	*2050 (pop.)*
Bangalore	6.53	8.52	11.44	15.62
Chennai	4.34	7.08	10.46	16.27

Source Census (2011), Hoornweg and Pope (2014) and UN (2016)

Background

Bangalore

Bangalore, the capital city of Karnataka, is one of the fastest growing cities in India. With a population of over 11 million (11,440,000) (UNDESA, 2019; see Table 5.1), it is India's fifth most populated urban city. It is located in southern India, on the Deccan Plateau at an elevation of over 900 meters above sea level, which is the highest among India's major cities. The topography of Bangalore is flat except the western parts, which are slightly hilly. Most of the city lies in the Bangalore Urban district of Karnataka and the surrounding rural areas are a part of the Bangalore Rural district. Bangalore is sometimes referred to as the 'Silicon Valley of India' because of its role as the nation's leading information technology exporter.

Chennai

Chennai, the capital city of Tamil Nadu, is located on the Coromandel Coast off the Bay of Bengal. With a population of over 10 million (10,456,000), it is India's sixth most populated urban city (UNDESA, 2019). It is located on the southeastern coast of India on a flat coastal plain with an average elevation of around 6.7 meters above sea level. The city together with the adjoining regions constitutes the Chennai Metropolitan Area. With more than one-third of India's automobile industry being based in the city, it is referred to as 'Detroit of India'. Chennai is prone to floods due to its proximity to the Bay of Bengal, heavy rainfall during monsoon, heavy precipitation and low elevation above sea level.

Water Supply and Resources

Bangalore

Precipitation averages 905 mm per year in Bangalore with most of it falling during the June–September monsoon season. However, 55% of urban water supply comes from the Cauvery River, located 100 km to the south of the city. Pumping an estimated one million cubic metres per day roughly 500 meters uphill over this considerable distance makes Bangalore's water the costliest in Asia (Bharath Joshi & Sivapriyan, 2019). The remaining 45% is obtained from groundwater resources (25%) and the Thippagondanahalli and Hesaraghatta reservoirs of the Arkavathi River (a tributary of the Cauvery located 60 km northwest of the main city; 20%). With an annual population growth of approximately four percent, the city will be unable to sustain the rising demand of water. Bangalore Water Supply and Sewerage Board (BWSSB) supplies approximately 900 million litres of water to the city per day despite a municipal demand of 1.3 billion litres. The water demand per person in Bangalore is between 150 and 200 litres per capita per day (lpcd) but average consumption is about 65 lpcd (BWSSB, 2017). Many households supplement the water supplied by the BWSSB with groundwater, which is either extracted from a private borewell or purchased from private tanker companies. In terms of wastewater treatment, there are three main sewage treatment plants located in Vrishabavathy, Koramangala-Chellaghatta and Hebbal Valleys; in addition, two mini-plants have been constructed near Madiwala and Kempambudi (BWSSB, 2017).

Chennai

The average annual rainfall is 1541 mm per year in Chennai. Three major rivers flow through the city: the Cooum, Adyar and Kosasthalaiyar rivers, all of which are heavily polluted with effluents and waste from domestic and commercial sources. The city's water supply and sewage treatment are managed by the Chennai Metropolitan Water Supply and Sewerage Board (CMWSSB) which draws water from the Red Hills and Chembarambakkam Lakes (primary water reservoirs of the city). Like Bangalore, Chennai is also expected to see a huge deficit in the water demanded as compared to water supplied. The city receives about 985 million litres per day (Mld), against the estimated required amount of 1.2 billion litres per day. The city receives 530 Mld (50.7% of daily total) from Krishna River through Telugu Ganga Project. The remaining water comes from Nemmeli (10.10%) and Minjur (10.10%) desalination plants, due to its proximity to the coast, and the Cauvery River (18.2%) and its tributaries from the Veeranam Lake (Advisian, 2017; CMWSSB, 2022). Groundwater extraction is common in Chennai, though not as frequently practised as it is in Bangalore due to the proximal supply of seawater (CMWSSB, 2022). Water treatment plants are located at Kilpauk (270 Mld), Puzhal (300 Mld), Vadakuthu (Veeranam Lake source) (180 Mld) and Chembarambakkam (530 Mld) (CMWSSB, 2022).

Cauvery River

Bangalore and Chennai both depend on the Cauvery River for part of their water supply, albeit to varying degrees. The Cauvery River is an interstate river with a unique characteristic geographical layout in that its upper hilly catchment lying in the Karnataka and Kerala states is influenced by the dependable south-west monsoon during the months June to September, while its lower part lies in the plains of the Tamil Nadu State served by the less dependable north-east monsoon from October to December (Cauvery Water Disputes Tribunal, 2007). The Cauvery River has been a source of conflict between Karnataka and Tamil Nadu for many years, which is discussed in a later section.

Water Use Profile

Several factors such as climate, culture, food habits, work and working conditions, level and type of development and physiology determine the requirement of water. As per the Bureau of Indian Standards (1993), IS: 1172–1993, a minimum water supply of 200 lpcd should be provided for domestic consumption in cities with full flushing systems. Besides domestic requirements, water is also demanded for commercial, agricultural and industrial uses.

The water consumption patterns of Chennai and Bangalore are similar. Domestic water use includes bathing, drinking, cooking, flushing and washing. Rapid urban expansion, involving port development, road construction, airports, and high rises exacerbate the pressure on water resources (Hegde, 2019). Similarly, in Bangalore, the construction of the city metro line and high-rise buildings has drained water resources. The two urban cities face similar problems of unregulated urbanization combined with massive population growth resulting in a heavy reliance on groundwater resources, and the presence of expansive quasi-legal water economies as households struggle to meet their daily water requirement through intermittent, colonial-era municipal piped water connections. As the cities are rapidly urbanizing, the demand for water will continue to rise in the context of environmental uncertainty.

Challenges

Rapid Unplanned and Unregulated Urbanization

The dire predicaments of Bangalore and Chennai depict various issues and challenges that are the indicators of the broader water mismanagement within the urban water metabolism framework in India. Both cities have witnessed a population explosion in recent years, leading to the destructive expansion of unplanned, unregulated urbanization. Rapid, unplanned urbanization poses serious challenges, bringing with it a plethora of socio-ecological issues, such as changes in the micro-climate (the 'heat island effect') and the depletion of groundwater resources through a massive increase in impervious surfaces (Ramachandra & Bharath, 2017). The Greater Chennai Corporation, Chennai's municipal government, permits building over filled-in ponds and canals and other reclaimed water bodies, which further hinders the ability of water to be absorbed into the ground (Dutta, 2019). The unprecedented rapid urbanization and sprawl in the last few decades have resulted from a mismanaged concentrated developmental path from both state and municipal governments, as both cities strive for booming economic activity (Sudhira & Nagendra, 2013). The economic opportunities in Bangalore and Chennai entice migrants with the possibility of better jobs and an improved quality of life in big cities (Sudhira & Nagendra, 2013).

Surface and Groundwater Contamination

The rapid urbanization in Bangalore and Chennai has led to massive increases in surface and groundwater contamination from industrial effluent and sewage (Ramachandra et al., 2019). One of the consequences of the unplanned urbanization in Bangalore and Chennai is increased levels of toxic waste which, without adequate infrastructure to treat contamination, then seeps into surface and groundwater resources (Ramachandra et al., 2019). A report in late 2019 gathered nearly 400 samples of tap water and groundwater from across Bangalore and reported dangerous levels of water contamination that posed a threat to public health, including heavy metals, nitrate and phosphorus (Shankar, 2011). Similarly, at least 30% of the drinking water samples tested by the Greater Chennai Corporation from January to late November 2019 have failed quality tests, with about one in every five samples having some contamination from minerals, metals, salts and organic compounds from sewage (*Times of India*, 2019). Few regulations are in place to ensure toxic wastewater from industrial effluent and sewage is minimized. Activists note that many industries dump toxic waste into rivers and lakes at night despite the presence of the Karnataka and Tamil Nadu Pollution Control Boards that are intended to monitor whether industries located near water bodies comply with effluent regulations (Bharath Joshi & Sivapriyan, 2019). Critically, neither state government has implemented a clear-cut policy for effluent treatment and release (Bharath Joshi & Sivapriyan, 2019). Moreover, the infrastructure of water treatment facilities cannot keep pace with the large-scale generation of wastewater, which has resulted in the sustained inflow of untreated or partially treated sewage to surface and groundwater resources (Ramachandra et al., 2019). Many households in both cities have noted the effects of the harmful consumption of toxic waste on their families and livelihoods. This is particularly concerning due to the heavy reliance on groundwater in both states to meet the increasing demand.

Heavy Reliance on Groundwater and Remote Resources

Over 80% of the rural and urban domestic water supplies in India are served by groundwater (World Bank, 2020), with the states of Karnataka and Tamil Nadu becoming heavily reliant on groundwater to supplement their supplies (Dhillon, 2019). Part of the reason for the heavy reliance on groundwater is caused by the expansive urbanization that is taking place around the country, including in Bangalore and Chennai. As the population increases in both cities, the demand for water increases, which cannot be met by the historical modes of water storage, including tanks, wells and lakes which hold water from monsoon rains to sustain their populations' typical consumption for the year (Sudhira & Nagendra, 2013). In Bangalore, the number of tanks and lakes has dwindled due to urban development and encroachment (Bharadwaja, 2016). Rapid changes in land use have taken place around lakes and wetland areas as water bodies have been encroached upon to be converted to urban land use, resulting in the conversion of many open, 'soft' surfaces to impervious ones (Sudhira & Nagendra, 2013). This has also led to Bangalore's reliance on pumped water from the Cauvery River.

Through the Cauvery Water Supply Scheme (CWSS), the BWSSB supplies treated river water, pumped from 100 km away, to the core area and urban local bodies through four progressive stages (Visakha, 2019). This excludes the 110 villages on the periphery of the urban area, though a fifth stage of the CWSS is in progress to supply municipal water to these households (Visakha, 2019). Due to the insufficient water supply from the Cauvery River, a significant number of households (39%) rely on groundwater to meet their water needs (Ramachandra et al., 2019). Likewise, Chennai's urban growth has increased the pressure on the water sources of the city (Arunprakash et al., 2014), which are increasingly being met by high-modern source augmentation practices including desalination and damming. After a devastating flood and monsoon season in 2015, officials authorized the systematic destruction of waterbodies in and around the city, as this was thought to be an effective method of preventing floods as part of their overarching plan of mastering control of their water supply (Allan, 2003; Lakshmi & Radhakrishnan, 2019). Thamaraikeni Lake, for instance, recently shrunk in size from 152 to 26 acres as land was reclaimed to continue the urban sprawl and reduce the proportion of water bodies in the city (*The Hindu*, 2019b). In both cities, the municipal piped water supply does not meet the demand for water, due to the extensive urbanization over the last few decades, and as a result, many parts of the cities depend on remote water resources, such as the Cauvery, and on groundwater extracted from bore wells by households and private tanker companies as the municipal water supply systems cannot keep pace with the increasing demand (Sahu, 2016; Sudhira & Nagendra, 2013).

Presence of Expansive Quasi-Legal Water Economies

The increasing water demand in Bangalore and Chennai has left many households scrambling to meet their daily water requirements as municipal water delivery systems are inadequate (Visakha, 2019). This has forced a reliance on private water tankers and, as a result, the perpetuation of quasi-regulated water economies. Lacking access to formal housing and/or a municipal piped connection, many residents are forced to rely on private vendors, neighbourhood sources or illegal networks of accessing municipal water to meet their daily demand (Sudhira &

Nagendra, 2013; Visakha, 2019). In fact, it is estimated that 60% of households in Bangalore use water either supplied by private tankers or from private borewells and more than 50% of households in Chennai supplement their intermittent municipal water supply that is available just a few hours each day irrespective of the season with private tankers (GCC, 2019; Visakha, 2019). Municipal water authorities are responsible for issuing licences to private tanker companies who can then legally supply water to households, however, relatively few licences have been granted recently in either city (GCC, 2019; Government of Karnataka, 2011). As the government is unable to effectively oversee the private tanker business through licencing, they cannot guarantee water quality standards nor can they regulate groundwater extraction from borewells, which hinders the recharge ability of the water table (Shah & Van Koppen, 2016; Visakha, 2019). Nevertheless, there are licenced private tankers that operate in both cities, which makes the water economy quasi-legal, as some standards are upheld by a few companies yet illegal activity by other actors is still present. The current municipal water systems in both cities are not conducive to growing populations and current source augmentation practices are not addressing the root causes of the situation.

High-Modern Water Management Practices

Long before colonialism took hold in India, cities used relatively interconnected, community-managed systems of tanks and wells (Broto et al., 2018). However, the colonial era left a legacy of complicated, poorly planned, high-modern infrastructure that does not adequately meet the needs of citizens. More specifically, the 'progressive industrial modernity' promoted by the West assumed that Nature could be controlled by Man (Allan, 2003: 6). The legacy of this practice is demonstrated through the promotion of high-modern, technological solutions to water management through source augmentation. For instance, by 1885, Bangalore's water supply was already running low and the colonial government responded by setting up piped infrastructure to bring water from sources 30 km away to meet the rising demand (Broto et al., 2018). In both cities, civil engineers realized the fixed size of tanks and wells was insufficient in the face of population growth and, as a result, rivers were tapped and water was brought into urban areas through pipes (Gronwell, 2008). Both Bangalore and Chennai, to a lesser extent, still rely on the colonial-era pipes that are in dire need of upgrading as seen through the average of 20% of water that is wasted in Indian cities due to leaky pipes (Broto et al., 2018; Kumar-Rao, 2019; World Bank, 2021). Presently, authorities in both cities are exploring other possibilities to ensure water security through large-scale, technocratic proposals costing billions of dollars (Broto et al., 2018), pursuing a hydraulic mission that emphasizes ownership and management of water resources. This is a clear example of the high-modernist legacy left by colonialism that is imprinted in India's water management practices.

Climate Change as an Exacerbating Effect

Climate change has made effective water management challenging due to the distortion of the quantity and frequency of rainfall. Much of India, including Bangalore and Chennai, are reliant on monsoon rains to fill reservoirs, tanks, and rivers; however, the rains have become more erratic because of climate change and monsoon seasons are increasingly unpredictable (Earth Observatory, 2019). In fact, the India Meteorological Department announced that the 2019 monsoon, which started late in June, was the most delayed withdrawal in history, ending in late October (Earth Observatory, 2019). As Bangalore and Chennai do not have adequate infrastructure in place to manage excessive rainfall, their water security is challenged by the uncertainty and unusuality of monsoon seasons. Furthermore, extreme heat waves in both cities are compounded by expansive urbanization which has decimated green spaces, which have a moderating effect on air temperatures. While climate change has different effects on Bangalore and Chennai, owing to the different topographic and climatic systems, it has compounded the water security issue in both cities by drying up reservoirs, lakes and other water sources in the catchments of the important river basins (Raj, 2013).

The mechanisms behind this are decreased levels of rainfall and increased temperatures in conjunction with the rapid unplanned, unregulated urbanization and exploitative groundwater extraction. In Chennai, climate change has made the city extremely vulnerable through its dependence on variable precipitation from October to December (Gopakumar, 2009). A considerable amount of rain falls in the span of a few months; however, the inadequate water storage infrastructure, in open wells and reservoirs, and a massive increase in impervious surfaces in the city have greatly decreased the amount of water that can recharge groundwater tables and thus be harnessed for use at another point in the year

(Lakshmi & Radhakrishnan, 2019). So, both cities face challenges in ensuring urban water security, which is exacerbated by the unpredictable effects of climate change. Such an intense reliance on unpredictable rainfall to quench growing cities' thirst will only result in more cracked mud puddles and massive floods unless concerted collaboration between stakeholders occurs.

Stakeholders

International Actors

The exponential growth in groundwater extraction in Karnataka and Tamil Nadu has gained the attention of the international community. International actors' efforts have focused on improving groundwater management at the federal and state level, as this is expected to contribute to creating sustainable water security within the two states. The interventions tend to be compartmental and focus on just one aspect of water security. For instance, the Tamil Nadu government often seeks external support for the aversion of flood and cyclone impacts on the city (Roul, 2019), preferring instead to 'flood-proof' their cities, as opposed to adapting to the new reality (GCC, 2019). The World Bank and the Asian Development Bank (ADB), most notably, fund projects in both Karnataka and Tamil Nadu. The former agreed to a USD 450 million loan with the federal government to support initiatives in groundwater-dependent states that aim to halt depleting groundwater levels and strengthening groundwater institutions under the National Groundwater Management Improvement Scheme (World Bank, 2020). Community-led management measures have emerged to make users aware of consumption patterns and create the conditions necessary to introduce economic measures that will reduce groundwater consumption (World Bank, 2020). The World Bank, in conjunction with the German Development Bank, also runs a second project in Tamil Nadu wherein the two entities are funding stormwater drains and massive underground drain projects in certain river basins as flood mitigation measures (Roul, 2019). The ADB (2019), on the other hand, also operates in Karnataka and Tamil Nadu. A loan from the ADB (2019) in Karnataka aims to improve water availability through the implementation of the Karnataka Integrated Sustainable Water Resources Management and Investment Program—a programme that aims to incorporate integrated water resources management (IWRM) into the state-level water resources mandate (Water Resources Department, 2020). In Tamil Nadu, the ADB is funding stormwater drain projects while also supporting water supply and sewerage system improvement under a state-wide urban development project (Roul, 2019). While the results of these projects remain to be seen, it is not absolute that external agencies will be able to provide much-needed water security to Bangalore and Chennai.

State Governments

Both Karnataka and Tamil Nadu recognize the pressing need to improve water development and management. Shortly after the implementation of the first National Water Policy in 1987, the Tamil Nadu government and its Water Resources Department implemented the Chennai Metropolitan Area Groundwater (Regulation) Act, which is an act to regulate and control the extraction, use and transport of groundwater with the overarching objective of increasing conservation (Government of Tamil Nadu, 1987). This piece of state legislation came into fruition after the Chennai Metropolitan Water Supply and Sewerage Board (CMWSSB) reported that all other possibilities of augmenting water supply to the city were being exhausted and that it was therefore necessary to regulate and control the extraction and use of groundwater (Government of Tamil Nadu, 1987). Just over a decade later, the Karnataka government and its Water Resources Department enacted the Karnataka Ground Water (Regulation for the Protection of Sources of Drinking Water) Act, 1999 to give priority for drinking water and its sources in the state (Government of Karnataka, 2011). This act, however, did not expand on the pivotal role of groundwater in the state. As such, in 2003, both Karnataka and Tamil Nadu enacted groundwater acts that were based on the national Groundwater Model Bill (Government of Karnataka, 2011; Government of Tamil Nadu, 2003). The Tamil Nadu government repealed their Groundwater Act in 2013, as it was found to not be sufficiently 'workable' due to a variety of reasons, including poorly defined terms (Ramakrishnan, 2016). In essence, the rapid urbanization in the state led to an exploitation of groundwater by various players that was not adequately regulated by the ordinance.

In 2011, the Karnataka government passed another act, the Karnataka Ground Water (Regulation and Control of Development and Management) Act, 2011 which, most notably, established the Karnataka Groundwater Authority (Government of Karnataka, 2011). This Authority then became the body responsible for upholding the aforementioned Act and ensuring indiscriminatory exploitation of groundwater in the state is monitored and controlled (Government of Karnataka, 2011). As will be discussed in the following section, there is an overlap in responsibilities at the state and municipal levels, which has created confusion as to the appropriate authority to monitor, regulate and enforce water use. This has facilitated the illegal extraction of groundwater across Karnataka and Tamil Nadu alike and, in both states, there appears to be little political will to comprehensively address the problem (Brunner et al., 2014). In the case of both states, plummeting groundwater levels continue with little effort made at the state level to intervene. For instance, the Tamil Nadu government has been criticized by the Madras High Court for its inaction, accused of waiting passively for the arrival of monsoon season instead of proactively handling the water crisis (Dhillon, 2019), perhaps in part due to fixation on interstate water conflicts, such as the Cauvery River.

The sharing of the water of the Cauvery River has been the source of conflict between Karnataka and Tamil Nadu since the 1890s (Cauvery River Disputes Tribunal, 2007), driven by a perceived scarcity of the resource (Ghosh et al., 2018). The importance of the river arises from its course through traditional rain-fed agriculture areas in the plateau and delta regions of Karnataka (Ghosh et al., 2018). Decades of negotiations between the two parties were fruitless until the federal government constituted a tribunal in 1990 to investigate the matter (Cauvery River Disputes Tribunal, 2007). Karnataka, the upstream state, had been planning various projects, including the construction of dams across tributaries of the Cauvery, and had not obtained prior consent from the Tamil Nadu government, the downstream state, for any of the projects, particularly a dam in Mysore (Cauvery Water Disputes Tribunal, 2007). As the Cauvery is the only major river in Tamil Nadu, contributing nearly 50% of the state's surface water use, the verdict from the tribunal in February of 2007 was such that Karnataka was obligated to release water from its reservoirs to ensure approximately 5.8 billion cubic metres of water would be available in Tamil reservoirs from June to May (Cauvery Water Disputes Tribunal, 2007). The tribunal remarked that the right to use of the flowing water is *publici juris* and common to all riparian proprietors and, as such, they do not have an absolute and exclusive right to all the water flowing within their borders (Cauvery Water Disputes Tribunal, 2007). The verdict created opportunities for setting up an appropriate river basin organization as a base for integrated governance (Ghosh et al., 2018). However, the dispute did not end there, with parties deciding to file petitions seeking clarifications and a possible renegotiation of the order (Supreme Court of India, 2018). The final verdict from the Supreme Court in February 2018 reduced the allocation of water for Tamil Nadu from 5.4 billion cubic metres to 5 billion cubic metres and increased Karnataka's allocation by 417 million cubic metres, potentially paving the way for a sustainable resolution of the interstate water dispute (Ghosh et al., 2018; Supreme Court of India, 2018).

Municipal Governments

Water provision in Bangalore and Chennai is the responsibility of municipal bodies: the Bangalore Water Supply and Sewerage Board (BWSSB) and the Chennai Metropolitan Water Supply and Sewerage Board (CMWSSB), respectively. The BWSSB provides water and sewage services on a 'no-profit, no-loss' basis to the core area and urban local bodies (Visakha, 2019). Through the Cauvery Water Supply Scheme, the BWSSB spends approximately 65% of its total revenue on power charges to raise the water approximately 500 meters, then pump it to the city (Visakha, 2019). Stakeholders in Bangalore are aware of the city's heavy dependence on the Cauvery, a river that is shared between two other states. Due to the intermittent nature of the water supply during the dry season and unreliable piped connections, households often supplement their BWSSB supply with water purchased from private tankers at fluctuating rates (Bangalore Mirror, 2021). These tankers in Bangalore are largely unregulated and unlicenced (Deepika, 2017), despite requiring a permit or licence to dig wells and extract groundwater. Both the municipal government, the Bruhat Bengaluru Mahanagara Palike (BBMP), and the Karnataka Groundwater Authority are responsible for issuing licences (Government of Karnataka, 2011). This has resulted in the ineffective implementation of licencing procedures and, as a result, poor monitoring and evaluation, thereby facilitating the illegal extraction of groundwater. As one observer pointed out, if you have a borewell, you just need to buy trucks and hire drivers to start a tanker business (Bangalore Mirror, 2021).

The situation is much the same in Chennai, albeit with different external issues placing pressure upon water supplies, as discussed in a preceding section. Under the Greater Chennai Corporation, the municipal government, the Chennai Metropolitan Water Supply and Sewerage Board (CMWSSB) is the body responsible for water supply and sewerage functions within city limits (Brunner et al., 2014). While Chennai is not reliant on a distant water source, the city relies on monsoon rains, from October to December, to fill reservoirs (Natarajan & Kalloikar, 2017). As reservoirs are not being adequately filled during the rainy season, the CMWSSB is forced to draw on groundwater to meet the demand for water (Brunner et al., 2014). As with the case of Bangalore, uncertainty of supply means that people who have the means buy water at inflated prices from private tanker companies (Dhillon, 2019). Unlike in Bangalore, wherein authorities at both the state and the municipal levels have the power to issue licences or permits to extract groundwater, the authority in Chennai is the CMWSSB under the 1987 Groundwater Regulation Act (GCC, 2019). The CMWSSB attempted to crack down on unlicenced tankers in the summer of 2019; however, the Tamil Nadu Water Lorry Owners' Association planned to go on an indefinite strike, effectively stripping individuals who depended on the tanker water of a supply (*The Hindu*, 2019a). Allegedly, the strike was called off because government authorities promised to help the tankers legally source water (*The Hindu*, 2019a). Since then, monitoring and enforcement have been poor and, as in Bangalore, illegal groundwater extractors face practically no consequences (GCC, 2019).

The extensive groundwater extraction from both legal and illegal actors in both cities has resulted in inadequate opportunities for groundwater recharge (Visakha, 2019). While there is emphasis at the state level to find sources of water as an alternative to groundwater, there are a number of promising demand management initiatives at the municipal and community levels that hold potential to achieve urban water security in both cities. This is discussed in more detail below.

As mentioned previously, the legal framework of Chennai, and Tamil Nadu more generally, creates a favourable platform from which to launch urban water security initiatives. The city has proposed a draft climate action plan in February 2020, with 199 planned activities across seven key sectors, prepared in sync with Nationally Determined Contribution which India submitted under the 2015 Paris Agreement (Chaitanya, 2020). In contrast, Bangalore does not have a municipal level climate action plan, though a state-level plan exists with gaping holes that, most notably, did not encourage climate action to be the crux of development planning (Shah, 2018). Moreover, following the disastrous 2015 floods in Chennai, more attention is being paid to restoring and protecting water bodies to enhance future water supply, as demonstrated through the CMWSSB's 'Sustainable Water Security Mission' (GCC, 2019). This mission aims to meet the future demand for water not only through restoring water bodies in and around the city, but also through expanding and strengthening rainwater harvesting and the recycling and reuse of wastewater (Roul, 2019). With the Sustainable Water Security Mission in mind, the future priority of the CMWSSB is to figure out how to create a water resource matrix that includes surface, ground and reclaimed wastewaters (World Bank, 2021). Rainwater harvesting has the highest social acceptance and the least opposition among stakeholders, likely due to court judgments supporting the practice as well as it being mandatory on rooftops since 2001 (Brunner et al., 2014; Manasi & Umamani, 2013; Metro Water, 2018a). Reservoirs are also seen as relatively uncontroversial and the city plans to enlarge existing ones, as this is seen as the most economical solution to securing a dependable water supply (Brunner et al., 2014; Natarajan & Kalloikar, 2017). Desalination, however, appears to have caught the attention of officials due to the proximity of Chennai to the coast (Ramesh, 2015). There is great scepticism among citizens, as the plants are one of the costliest options, both financially and environmentally, to secure drinking water (Brunner et al., 2014). However, this infrastructure does present an immediate, albeit expensive, solution to the present water scarcity (GCC, 2019). From a demand management perspective, metering to measure water consumption and effective pricing in the form of a water tax are the most direct ways to manage demand and encourage users to conserve water (GCC, 2019). Chennai's water tax is set at a rate of seven percent of the annual rental value, which is a fixed rate set by the municipal government (Metro Water, 2018b). Consumption is measured through meters which are, unfortunately, present in just 10% of households across the city (GCC, 2019), thereby making consumption-based pricing next to impossible.

Bangalore's transition to a water-secure future has not received the same attention as that of Chennai. The city has adopted rainwater harvesting, pricing and metering, much like Chennai and, to its credit, it has achieved better consumption-based pricing outcomes. Whereas Chennai has a fixed rate for its water tax, Bangalore's tariffs increase depending on the amount consumed or water consumption slabs, as is referred to by BWSSB. For example, a household will pay seven rupees for 1000 litres if between 0 and 8,000 litres are consumed. They will pay 11 rupees per 1000 litres if between 8,000 and 25,000 litres of water is consumed (*Times of India*, 2020). Moreover, Bangalore followed the example of Chennai and has made rainwater harvesting structures mandatory on existing and proposed buildings (Menezes, 2018). This legislation was made possible by collaborative efforts at the state and municipal level between the Karnataka Groundwater Authority, the BBMP, and the BWSSB. First, the Groundwater Authority identifies recharge-worthy areas in the state for rainwater harvesting (Central Ground Water Board, 2012; Government of Karnataka, 2011). The BBMP and the BWSSB then both operationalize the Groundwater Authority's findings through a bylaw (2003) and an Amendment Act (2009 and 2011) and Regulation (2015), respectively (Biome Environmental, 2016). The BBMP bylaw applies to all properties coming under its jurisdiction and the BWSSB Act applies to all properties that have a BWSSB connection (i.e. the core urban area) (Biome Environmental, 2016). This has ensured that the many buildings in Bangalore have rainwater harvesting systems in place to supply water in times of shortage, though the enforcement of the legislation is poor and system maintenance is lacking (Biome Environmental, 2016). In addition to rainwater harvesting to meet households' water needs, the city and its citizens, as is discussed in the proceeding section, have also undertaken lake rejuvenation projects just as Chennai is doing, which includes dredging and desilting work, followed by the filling of the water body with freshwater (Akshatha, 2019). This will assist in groundwater recharge and facilitate the efficient management of available water sources. Both examples provide a fascinating glimpse into the potential such small-scale options hold for harnessing and storing water (Broto et al., 2018).

Community Initiatives

As Bangalore and Chennai are rapidly urbanizing, the number of businesses and industries is increasing dramatically. Such expansion has repercussions on the hydrological cycle, as impervious surfaces become the norm, groundwater levels drop as water demand spikes, and water contamination becomes the harsh reality, hitting communities the hardest. Collaboration between the different levels of government has not resulted in sufficient improvements in urban water security in Bangalore and Chennai. This has resulted in an increase in community initiatives that engage and mobilize citizens to work toward achieving urban water security (Kumar-Rao, 2019). Certain organizations work on the macro level, including Isha Outreach, and are making progress on achieving a water-secure future at the municipal, state and national levels. Isha Outreach is the foundation of a well-known Indian spiritual leader, Isha Sadhguru, and it works across southern India, implementing several large-scale human service projects to support individual growth, revitalize human spirit, rebuild communities and restore the environment (Isha Foundation, 2017). The organization has two ongoing initiatives, *Cauvery Calling* and *Rally for Rivers*, both of which are concerned with the Cauvery River. *Cauvery Calling* is a first of its kind campaign, setting the standard for how India's rivers can be revitalized (Isha Foundation, 2017). Through this initiative, the organization supports farmers to plant 2.42 billion trees in Cauvery basin (Isha Foundation, 2017). This will have a triple benefit effect of improving soil health by replenishing organic content in soil, reviving the river and groundwater levels by increasing water retention in Cauvery basin, and augmenting farmer income through agroforestry. *Rally for Rivers*, on the other hand, is a movement to save India's rivers. Supported by over 162 million people, it is the world's largest ecological movement today, focusing on local-level actions. It was launched in September 2017 to raise awareness about river depletion (Isha Foundation, 2017) while simultaneously generating potential to instigate government action. River depletion is a pressing issue in India wherein many urban areas, including Bangalore and Chennai, are dependent on rivers and their tributaries, as a source of water to sustain livelihoods, both in urban and rural areas.

On the micro scale, within Bangalore and Chennai, community groups are working toward meeting their daily water requirement under the broader objective of achieving urban water security. In Bangalore, community-level approaches to creating water security are taking place throughout the city, raising awareness about the importance of the issue. Some citizen groups are mapping groundwater levels with the intention of influencing user behaviour that enables better groundwater management (Desai, 2017). Others are working to protect and rejuvenate old tanks and open wells that held the city's water supply prior to the mid-twentieth Century which can then be used to store water for household consumption or irrigation (Broto et al., 2018), effectively acknowledging the traditional water practices in region.

In both cities, lake rejuvenation is increasingly being prioritized on the municipal agenda, demonstrated by the efforts made by citizens to ensure lakes are brimming with water throughout the year (Desai, 2017). Lakes are also an integral component of proposed solutions to industrial effluent and untreated wastewater in water bodies. The issue is being approached through micro level bioremediation efforts to treat wastewater for reuse through an integrated wetlands system, including an algal pond integrated with a lake (Ramachandra et al., 2019). The treatment of polluted waters in natural systems such as constructed wetlands is being practised across developing countries, as it is a simple and economically viable method of managing wastewater (Ramachandra et al., 2019). As such, community initiatives are an integral part of addressing the water crisis in Bangalore and Chennai by ensuring that local concerns are voiced on a macro scale to governments through large organizations like Isha Foundation and community-level, context-appropriate practices are adopted through small-scale citizens' groups.

Discussion

As a rapidly urbanizing country experiencing a population explosion, water is high on the national political agenda in India due to its essentiality to life and economic and social development. The population explosion especially in the urban centres has increased the demand for water, which adds to the existing challenges that Bangalore and Chennai are currently facing. As such, water issues mobilize stakeholders at all levels, from the national government to small-scale, community groups. In India, the national government takes on the role of overseeing water at a high level, with its legislation prioritizing the state of India's water through the various iterations of the National Water Policy (2012). State governments then have the choice to either incorporate or reject national legislation into state-level policy, as water is under the legislative competence of states (Cullet, 2012) and, in the case of Karnataka and Tamil Nadu, both have accepted the responsibility to manage water affairs within their boundaries predominantly through their Water Resources Departments. Municipal governments are accountable for supplying water to households in their jurisdictions through their water authority boards. Notably, the water regimes in Bangalore and Chennai differ significantly in terms of, *inter alia*, infrastructure, policies, as well as the influence and participation of stakeholders. Therefore, the responsibility of carrying out the oversight, management and supply of water cannot be the responsibility of governments alone. Put differently, while the central government can oversee the policies through official regulations, the state and municipal governments would have more significant impacts on implementing and managing the system, while acknowledging the political, regional and social contexts. The Supreme Court ruling on the Cauvery Water dispute has set a precedent for incorporating IWRM thinking into water issues by recognizing the multidimensionality of the basin system and the interdisciplinarity of stakeholders involved therein (Ghosh et al., 2018). This ruling offers an important opportunity to better align IWRM thinking with action.

In essence, the concept of integrated water resources management provides ideas to assist in considering how social choices can be made with water allocation and access in mind, as well as the sustainability of water resources and the infrastructure used to manage them (Giordano & Shah, 2014). However, the traditional IWRM framework that is employed in the 2012 National Water Policy does not adequately address the social dimensions of water. This is demonstrated through the national and state governments' approaches to IWRM as a 'one-size-fits-all' empirical framework that promotes apolitical, nongeographic solutions to water issues (Giordano & Shah, 2014; Shah & von Koppen, 2016). Many think tanks and international organizations, including the Asian Development Bank, embrace the IWRM discourse and recommend actions to be taken in alignment with the framework (Shah & von Koppen, 2016). Consumption-based water pricing, for instance, is a textbook solution to improving water efficiency in the IWRM framework (Giordano & Shah, 2014). However, water pricing is not compatible with the realities on the ground in India, as efforts to rationalize pricing were met with resistance by citizens who were accustomed to paying extremely low tariffs for water and, perhaps more importantly, water meters are faulty and poorly regulated in Bangalore and Chennai which makes consumption-based pricing next to impossible in most households (GCC, 2019; Giordano & Shah, 2014). This exemplifies the futility of implementing a solution that is suboptimal and disjointed with realities on the ground.

Nevertheless, IWRM in Indian cities has the potential to foster a bottom-up governance structure and a participatory democratic approach that reflects the contextual realities (Ghosh et al., 2018; Goyal et al., 2020). Community-level groups and other civil society organizations play a vital role in ensuring proper implementation and adoption of sustainable water practices through an incorporation of the social dimensions of water (Linton & Budds, 2014). Otherwise stated, macro thinking at the government level is important, but it must be linked to local needs and practices. 'Local IWRM' is emerging as a promising alternative to the traditional IWRM framework that emphasizes stakeholder-inclusive, community-level processes (Goyal et al., 2020). This effectively incorporates macro scale thinking through IWRM while tailoring it to a local context. So, rather than aspiring to the full framework of IWRM, localized IWRM offers greater attention to a variety of entry points to enable the participation of local initiatives in promoting coordinated water management while encouraging greater cooperation from local users (Goyal et al., 2020). The mobilization and engagement of community-level actors bolsters context-appropriate responses to water management by incorporating the flows and uses of water into discussions.

Community-level initiatives are diverse in Bangalore and Chennai, with some operating at the micro level as individuals or small groups, and others operating on the macro scale with great potential to lobby governments, like Isha Outreach. Both are useful, albeit in different ways, as they hold potential for harnessing, storing and supplying water in the face of rapidly changing environments (Broto et al., 2018). As part of an effective water management strategy, initiatives operating at both scales require community participation (Gupta & Ahmad, 2019). Strong community participation and engagement build social capital as well as trust with governments by ensuring local voices are reflected in discussions. While water falls under municipal jurisdiction, many citizens feel disconnected from the issue (Gupta & Ahmad, 2019). A strategy that has seen great success in rural India has been to create *paani panchayats*, or local water governance councils, for citizens and officials to discuss water management issues (Gupta & Ahmad, 2019). Such a strategy holds potential for urban India as part of an effective water management strategy for three reasons. First, it fosters social ties between locals within neighbourhoods which is key for building trust within communities. Second, the council acts as a channel of communication between government and communities and, third, it promotes localized responses to urban water security and includes discussions about the social dimensions of the issue.

As such, a community-focused *paani panchayat* fits within the localized IWRM strategy that will more effectively address urban India's water security woes than the dominant top-down framework. Due to the local nature of the water governance council, it holds great potential to implement small-scale initiatives, like rainwater harvesting (RWH), which are increasingly seen as an integral part of an effective water management strategy in India (Gupta & Ahmad, 2019). The practice of holding water in small structures including tanks, wells and ponds to serve a community is a traditional water supply option in south India, thereby aligning with local practices and capabilities, and has been supported by court judgments (Brunner et al., 2014). By storing rainwater from monsoons, households and communities can complement their municipal water supply to ensure a predictable source of water year-round (Metro Water, 2018a; Vivek, 2016).

Governments and civil society recognize the benefits of these local, small-scale structures and both are actively promoting them in Bangalore and Chennai. Both cities have adopted laws mandating RWH infrastructure on buildings since the early 2000s and while the municipal enforcement rate has been low, citizens are aware of the benefits of the practice thanks to civil society's active engagement in promoting RWH (Brunner et al., 2014; Holland-Stergar, 2018). For instance, an educational centre in Chennai, Rain Center, has been offering programming to communities on the benefits of RWH. A study even suggests that these efforts have played a part in increasing well levels by 30% and groundwater levels by an average of four metres across the city (Holland-Stergar, 2018). The key takeaway from this initiative is that a strategy must be tailored to the local context, which fosters community buy-in, and is backed by sufficient political will and commitment to the issue rather than working in opposition to citizens' efforts. The creation of *paani panchayats* across urban India is a promising approach that can facilitate the engagement between citizens and governments, fostering greater collaboration between stakeholders, which is crucial to capture the realities on the ground. While India's approach to IWRM is a good start, there must be greater recognition that a prescriptive approach for governing water resources is not the best system in a country that is as diverse as the world.

Conclusion

Given the current situations in Bangalore and Chennai, neither city is likely to achieve urban water security, assuming business-as-usual trajectory of development. However, there is a possibility to work toward ensuring urban water security and, as a result, avoiding 'Day Zero' scenarios, but this is conditional upon sufficient political will from governments to address water issues. There needs to be increased regulation and enforcement of urbanization and groundwater extraction policies that are relevant to the contexts, in addition to greater community involvement in conservation efforts to reflect the realities on the ground. As India is an incredibly diverse country, national-level efforts to ensure urban water security are futile. A solution that works in a southern Indian context, for instance, might not be appropriate in northern India due to the variability in cultures and infrastructure. For this reason, the federal government must oversee efforts from a high level while state and municipal governments engage in managing and supplying water, respectively, to ensure context-appropriate solutions are adopted. Active community engagement and participation are crucial to pressure governments to act. The efforts made by the stakeholders need to be aligned with each other instead of limiting the effects of community efforts. Political will can be further fostered through the mobilization of influencers who are individuals whose opinions are held in high regard in India and South Asia, more generally, as Indian society is strongly motivated by social ties and human connection (Thussu, 2016). The strong potential of influencers in the environmental sphere, which can be extrapolated into water security, will enable key figures in Indian society to raise awareness of the issues and call for larger, people-centric, future-oriented approaches to water management and governance that embrace the entire city and its citizens (GCC, 2019). The connecting and interdependent nature of water provides us with a window of opportunity that we cannot ignore. Water can be used to both meet basic needs and fuel impactful and catalytic change in the world's megacities.

References

Advisian. (2017). The cost of desalination. *Worley Group*. Available at: https://www.advisian.com/en/global-perspectives/the-cost-of-desalination. Accessed 2 April 2022.

Akshatha, M. (2019). Lake revival: Bengaluru's Sarakki may welcome 'thousand birds' soon. *The Economic Times*. Available at: https://economictimes.indiatimes.com/news/politics-and-nation/lake-revival-bengalurus-sarakki-may-welcome-thousand-birds-soon/articleshow/67652756.cms?from=mdr. Accessed 2 April 2022.

Allan, T. (2003). *IWRM/IWRAM: A new sanctioned discourse?* (SOAS Water Issues Study Group—Occasional Paper 50). London: School of Oriental and African Studies.

Arunprakash, M., Giridharan, L., Krishnamurthy, R. R., & Jayaprakash, M. (2014). Impact of urbanisation in groundwater of South Chennai City, Tamil Nadu, India. *Environmental Earth Sciences, 71*, 947–957.

Asian Development Bank (ADB). (2019). *India: Karnataka integrated and sustainable water resources management investment program*. Available at: https://www.adb.org/projects/43253-026/main. Accessed 2 April 2022.

Bangalore Mirror. (2021, April 7). *Summer soars and so does water tanker price*. Available at: https://bangaloremirror.indiatimes.com/bangalore/civic/summer-soars-and-so-does-water-tanker-price/articleshow/81937589.cms. Accessed 2 April 2022.

Bangalore Water Supply and Sewerage Board (BWSSB). (2017). *About BWSSB*. Available at: https://bwssb.karnataka.gov.in/info-1/About+BWSSB/en. Accessed 2 April 2022.

Bharadwaja, A. S. (2016, January 11). Bengaluru lost its water bodies, and here's what is remaining. *Citizen Matters*. Available at: https://bengaluru.citizenmatters.in/bangalore-water-bodies-ndwi-images-research-7994. Accessed 2 April 2022.

Bharath Joshi, E. T. B., & Sivapriyan, D. H. N. S. (2019). River Cauvery is heading down a deadly spiral. *Deccan Herald*. Available at: https://www.deccanherald.com/exclusives/river-cauvery-is-heading-down-a-deadly-spiral-734640.html. Accessed 2 April 2022.

Biome Environmental. (2016). *Rainwater harvesting regulations in Bangalore*. Available at: https://www.slideshare.net/biomeshubha/biome-rainwater-harvesting-2016. Accessed 2 April 2022.

Broto, V. C., Unnikrishnan, H., & Nagendra, H. (2018, June 30). Colonial infrastructure to blame for Bangalore running out of water. *The Print*. Available at: https://theprint.in/india/governance/colonial-infrastructure-augments-the-threat-on-bangalore-of-running-out-of-water/76840/. Accessed 2 April 2022.

Brunner, N., Starkl, M., Sakthivel, P., Elango, L., Amirthalingam, S., Pratap, C. E., Thirunavukkarasu, M., & Parimalarenganayaki, S. (2014). Policy preferences about managed aquifer recharge for securing sustainable water supply to Chennai City, India, *Water, 6*, 3739–3757.

Bureau of Indian Standards. (1993). Code of basic requirements for water supply, drainage and sanitation, ISN: 1172-1993. Available at: https://law.resource.org/pub/in/bis/S03/is.1172.1993.html. Accessed 2 April 2022.

Cauvery Water Disputes Tribunal. (2007). Volume I: Background of the dispute and framing of issues, the report of the Cauvery Water Disputes Tribunal. Available at: https://www.thehinducentre.com/resources/article9142806.ece. Accessed 2 April 2022.

Census. (2011). *India*. Available at: https://www.census2011.co.in/. Accessed 27 June 2022.

Central Ground Water Board. (2012). *Ground water information booklet: Bangalore urban district, Karnataka*. Government of India, Ministry of Water Resources.

Central Pollution Control Board. (n.d.). *Water pollution*. Available at: https://cpcb.nic.in/water-pollution/#:~:text=The%20Water%20(Prevention%20and%20Control,Act%20was%20amended%20in%201988. Accessed 2 April 2022.

Chaitanya, S. V. K. (2020, February 5). Action plan on climate change released. *The New Indian Express*. Available at: https://www.newindianexpress.com/cities/chennai/2020/feb/05/action-plan-on-climate-change-released-2099193.html. Accessed 2 April 2022.

Chennai Metropolitan Water Supply and Sewerage Board (CMWSSB). (2022). *Water supply system*. Available at: https://chennaimetrowater.tn.gov.in/watersupplysystem.html. Accessed 2 April 2022.

Cullet, P. (2012). The groundwater model bill: Rethinking regulation for the primary source of water. *Economic and Political Weekly, 47*(45), 40–47.

Deepika, K. C. (2017). Where do tankers source water from? *The Hindu*. Available at: https://www.thehindu.com/news/cities/bangalore/where-do-tankers-source-water-from/article18311097.ece. Accessed 2 April 2022.

Desai, P. (2017, September 14). Citizens participate in mapping Bengaluru's groundwater. *India Water Portal*. Available at: https://www.indiawaterportal.org/articles/citizens-participate-mapping-bengalurus-groundwater. Accessed 2 April 2022.

Dhillon, A. (2019, June 19). Chennai in crisis as authorities blamed for dire water shortage. *The Guardian*. Available at: https://www.theguardian.com/world/2019/jun/19/chennai-in-crisis-water-shortage-with-authorities-blamed-india. Accessed 2 April 2022.

Dutta, P. K. (2019). How Chennai lost its water, a story that should worry you. *India Today*. Available at: https://www.indiatoday.in/india/story/how-chennai-lost-its-water-a-story-that-should-worry-you-1555096-2019-06-24. Accessed 2 April 2022.

Earth Observatory. (2019). Unusual monsoon season causes flooding in India. *NASA*. Available at: https://earthobservatory.nasa.gov/images/145703/unusual-monsoon-season-causes-flooding-in-india. Accessed 2 April 2022.

Ghosh, N., Bandyopadhyay, J., & Thakur, J. (2018). *Conflict over Cauvery waters: Imperatives for innovative policy options*. Observer Research Foundation.

Giordano, M., & Shah, T. (2014). From IWRM back to integrated water resources management. *International Journal of Water Resources Development, 30*(3), 346–376.

Gopakumar, G. (2009). Investigating degenerated peripheralization in urban India: The case of water supply infrastructure and urban governance in Chennai. *Public Works Management and Policy, 14*(2), 109–129.

Government of Karnataka. (2011). *The Karnataka Ground Water (Regulation and Control of Development and Management) Act, 2011*. Government of Karnataka.

Government of Tamil Nadu. (1987). *The Chennai Metropolitan Area Groundwater (Regulation) Act, 1987*. Government of Tamil Nadu.

Government of Tamil Nadu. (2003). *The Tamil Nadu Groundwater (Development and Management) Act, 2003*. Government of Tamil Nadu.

Goyal, V. C., Garg, A., Patil, J. P., & Thomas, T. (2020). Formulation of integrated water resources management (IWRM) plan at district level: A case study from Bundelkhand region of India. *Water Policy, 22*, 52–69.

Greater Chennai Corporation (GCC). (2019). *Resilient Chennai strategy*. Available at: https://resilientchennai.com/wp-content/uploads/2019/07/Resilience-Strategy_20190703.pdf. Accessed 2 April 2022.

Gronwell, J.T. (2008). *Access to water: Rights, obligations and the Bangalore situation*. Linköping Studies in Arts and Science 439. Linköping: Linköping University, Department of Water and Environmental Studies.

Gupta, J., & Ahmad, O. (2019, July 31). India: Community participation is a must for water management. *Prevention Web*. Available at: https://www.preventionweb.net/news/india-community-participation-must-water-management. Accessed 2 April 2022.

Hegde, S. (2019). Climate change is not the only reason to blame for India's Chennai water crisis. *The Water Center Blog, University of Pennsylvania*. Available at: https://watercenter.sas.upenn.edu/climate-change-is-not-the-only-reason-to-blame-for-indias-chennai-watercrisis/. Accessed 27 June 2022.

Holland-Stergar, B. (2018). The law and policy of rainwater harvesting: A comparative analysis of Australia, India, and the United States. *UCLA Journal of Environmental Law and Policy, 36*(1), 127–165.

Hoornweg, D., & Pope, K. (2014, January). *Socio-economic pathways and regional distribution of the world's 101 largest cities* (Global Cities Institute Working Paper No. 04). Toronto: Global Cities Institute.

Isha Foundation. (2017). *Revitalization of rivers in India: Draft policy recommendation*. Available at: https://isha.sadhguru.org/ca/en/blog/article/revitalization-rivers-india-draft-policy-recommendation-fundamentals. Accessed 2 April 2022.

Kumar-Rao, A. (2019, July 15). India's water crisis could be helped by better building, planning. *National Geographic*. Available at: https://www.nationalgeographic.com/environment/2019/07/india-water-crisis-drought-could-be-helped-better-building-planning/. Accessed 2 April 2022.

Lakshmi, K., & Radhakrishnan, V. (2019). Mismanaged urbanisation and encroachments: Chennai continues to lose out on its water resources. *The Hindu*. Available at: https://www.thehindu.com/news/cities/chennai/the-shrinking-shape-of-chennais-water/article28426933.ece. Accessed 2 April 2022.

Linton, J., & Budds, J. (2014). The hydrosocial cycle: Defining and mobilizing a relational-dialectical approach to water. *Geoforum, 57*, 170–180.

Manasi, S., & Umamani, K. S. (2013). Water conservation in urban areas: A case study of rainwater harvesting Initiative in Bangalore city. In S. Nautiyal, K. S. Rao, H. Kaechele, K. V. Raju, & R. Schaldach (Eds.), *Knowledge systems of societies for adaptation and mitigation of impacts of climate change* (pp. 303–328). Springer.

Menezes, N., (2018). Bengaluru water supply and Sewerage Board Lax in enforcing rules, says CAG report. *The Economic Times*. Available at: https://economictimes.indiatimes.com/news/politics-and-nation/bengaluru-water-supply-and-sewerage-board-lax-in-enforcing-rules-says-cag-report/articleshow/65333219.cms. Accessed 2 April 2022.

Metro Water. (2018a). *CMWSSB initiatives in RWH*. Available at: https://chennaimetrowater.tn.gov.in/initiatives.html. Accessed 2 April 2022.

Metro Water. (2018b). *FAQ*. Available at: https://chennaimetrowater.tn.gov.in/publicinfo_faq.html. Accessed 2 April 2022.

Ministry of Water Resources. (2002). *National water policy*. Government of India.

Ministry of Water Resources. (2005). *Model bill to regulate and control the development and management of ground water*. Government of India.

Ministry of Water Resources. (2012). *Draft national water policy*. Government of India.

Natarajan, P. M., & Kalloikar, S. (2017). Urban resilient integrated water management pathways to achieve sustainable water resources development in Chennai metropolitan city, Tamil Nadu, India. *Water Practice and Technology, 12*(3), 564–575.

Raj, K. (2013). *Where has all the water gone? An analysis of unreliable water supply in Bangalore city* (Working Paper 307). Bangalore: Institute for Social and Economic Change.

Ramachandra, T. V., Sincy, V., Asulabha, K. S., Mahapatra, D. M., Bhat, S. P., & Aithal, B. H. (2019). Optimal treatment of domestic wastewater through constructed wetlands. *Journal of Biodiversity, 9*(1–2), 81–102.

Ramachandra, T. V., & Bharath, H. A. (2017, January 31). Bangalore's tragedy: A dead city with unabated, unplanned and untenable urbanisation. *eSS Current Affairs: Urbanscapes*, 1–4.

Ramakrishnan, T. (2016). Adieu to Tamil Nadu groundwater law. *The Hindu*. Available at: https://www.thehindu.com/news/national/tamil-nadu/adieu-to-tamil-nadu-groundwater-law/article5147072.ece. Accessed 2 April 2022.

Ramesh, N. (2015). Local waterscapes and global technologies: Micro-politics of desalination in Chennai. *SOAS South Asia Institute Working Papers, 1*, 32–47.

Roul, A. (2019). Who will provide water security to Chennai? *Down to Earth*. Available at: https://www.downtoearth.org.in/blog/water/who-will-provide-water-security-to-chennai--64855. Accessed 2 April 2022.

Sahu, S. (2016). Sustainable urban water supply in India: Some issues of governance. *Journal of Governance and Public Policy, 6*(2), 105–111.

Shah, K. (2018). Garden city is warming up: Why climate change must be an election issue for Bengaluru. *The News Minute*. Available at: https://www.thenewsminute.com/article/garden-city-warming-why-climate-change-must-be-election-issue-bengaluru-80176. Accessed 2 April 2022.

Shah, T., & Van Koppen, B. (2016). The precept and practice of integrated water resources management (IWRM) in India. In V. Narain & A. Narayanamoorthy (Eds.), *Indian water policy at the crossroads: Resources* (pp. 15–33). Springer International Publishing.

Shankar, P. S. V. (2011). India's groundwater challenge and the way forward. *Economic and Political Weekly, 44*(2), 37–45.

Sudhira, H. S., & Nagendra, H. (2013). Local assessment of Bangalore: Graying and greening in Bangalore—Impacts of urbanisation on ecosystems, ecosystem services and biodiversity. In T. Elmqvist, M. Fragkias, J. Goodness, B. Guneralp, P. J. Marsotullio, R. I. McDonald, S. Parnell, M. Schewenius, M. Sendstad, K. C. Seto, & C. Wilkinson (Eds.), *Urbanisation, biodiversity and ecosystem services: Challenges and opportunities* (pp. 75–91). Springer.

Supreme Court of India. (2018). *Civil Appeal No. 2453, 2454, 2456 of 2007*. Available at: https://web.archive.org/web/20180417132747/http://sci.gov.in/supremecourt/2007/11993/11993_2007_Judgement_16-Feb-2018.pdf. Accessed 2 April 2022.

The Economist. (2019, July 6). *Thirsty Indian cities have a management problem, not a water problem*. Available at: https://www.economist.com/asia/2019/07/06/thirsty-indian-cities-have-a-management-problem-not-a-water-problem. Accessed 2 April 2022.

The Hindu. (2019a). Private water tankers shelve indefinite strike plan. Available at: https://www.thehindu.com/news/cities/chennai/private-water-tankers-shelve-indefinite-strike-plan/article28314306.ece. Accessed 2 April 2022.

The Hindu. (2019b). The shrinking shape of Chennai's water. Available at: https://www.thehindu.com/news/cities/chennai/the-shrinking-shape-of-chennais-water/article28426934.ece. Accessed 2 April 2022.

Thussu, D. K. (2016). The soft power of popular cinema: The case of India. *Journal of Political Power, 9*(3), 415–429.

Times of India. (2019). Chennai: 30 percent of water samples fail quality test. Available at: https://timesofindia.indiatimes.com/city/chennai/30-water-samples-fail-quality-test/articleshow/72132907.cms. Accessed 2 April 2022.

Times of India. (2020, November 6). Bengaluru: After electricity, brace for 12% water tariff hike. Available at: https://timesofindia.indiatimes.com/city/bengaluru/bengaluru-after-electricity-brace-for-12-water-tariff-hike/articleshow/79072338.cms. Accessed 2 April 2022.

UNDESA (United Nations, Department of Economic and Social Affairs, Population Division). (2019). *World urbanization prospects: The 2018 revision*. United Nations.

United Nations (UN). (2019, June 17). *9.7 billion on earth by 2050, but growth rate slowing, says new UN population report*. Available at: https://news.un.org/en/story/2019/06/1040621. Accessed 2 April 2022.

Visakha, S. (2019, October 23). Averting Day Zero: How Bengaluru should manage its water. *Citizen Matters*. Available at: https://bengaluru.citizenmatters.in/bengaluru-water-resource-management-scarcity-price-day-zero-bwssb-supply-38373. Accessed 2 April 2022.

Vivek, V. (2016). Rainwater harvesting in Chennai: What made it work? *IIM Kozhikode Society and Management Review, 5*(1), 91106.

Water Resources Department. (2020). *Advanced centre for integrated water resources management*. Government of Karnataka.

World Bank. (2020). *World Bank signs agreement to improve groundwater management in select states of India*. Available at: https://www.worldbank.org/en/news/press-release/2020/02/17/improving-groundwater-management-india. Accessed 2 April 2022.

World Bank. (2021, April). *India: Chennai city partnership: Sustainable Urban Services Program (P175221)—Environmental and Social Systems Assessment Report*. Available at: https://chennaimetrowater.tn.gov.in/pdf/ESSA13April2021.pdf. Accessed 2 April 2022.

CHAPTER 6

A Pathway for Beijing: Avoiding 'Day Zero'

Cassandra Hayward, Mohamed Mohamud, and Larry Swatuk

Introduction

Beijing bears most of the problems that are faced by megacities (Wei, 2005). Its rivers are polluted, its groundwater overexploited, and its air quality badly deteriorated. The change in its physical environment has reduced the city's overall capacity to cope with extreme events. Since 1949, Beijing's population has increased from 4.2 million people to more than 21 million today. 'In parallel with that, the built-up area of the city expanded and increased its size by more than 12 times ... from 109 to 1401 km^2 (Sun et al., 2021)'. These problems have been further exacerbated by Beijing's rapidly growing economy. The booming economy brings many benefits for its citizens and, therefore, entices more people to

C. Hayward
University of Cambridge, Cambridge, UK

M. Mohamud · L. Swatuk (✉)
University of Waterloo, Waterloo, ON, Canada
e-mail: lswatuk@uwaterloo.ca

L. Swatuk and C. Cash (eds.), *The Political Economy of Urban Water Security under Climate Change*, International Political Economy Series,
https://doi.org/10.1007/978-3-031-08108-8_6

move into the city. Thus, rapid economic growth, increased urban population and a relatively higher standard of living have increased Beijing's annual water consumption. Simultaneously, the climate has been changing since the late 2000s to be warmer with decreased precipitation. Beijing is facing a great challenge as water resources begin to constrain the nation's economic and social development.

Beijing has made intensive efforts during the past decades to promote responsible and sustainable use of water resources. In addition, the Chinese Central government invested heavily into the South-North Water Diversion Project (SNWDP), which is the largest water diversion project in the world (Asian Development Bank, 2016). Whether these efforts will be sufficient to ensure water security in a climate changing world is yet to be demonstrated.

This chapter critically reflects on Beijing's actions in support of water security in light of existing and future challenges. It argues that a more holistic water management approach needs to be taken to avoid 'day zero'. Various measures need to occur including, the transition to integrated urban water management, reformed water pricing and laws, increased public awareness and improved governance structures including coordination and collaboration among all relevant stakeholders.

Background

Water resource development and management is as old as China itself (Ball, 2016). Since the mid-1950s, a number of national and global factors combined to increase pressure on China's water resources, augmenting governing elites' abiding tendency for centralized command and control of large-scale projects in support of the 'national interest'. Annual freshwater availability in Beijing is approximately 123.8 m^3/per capita or 339.17 litres per capita per day as of 2016 (Xiaoqin et al., 2017). As of 2018, water supply was meeting demand, as the residential daily water consumption averaged 198.7 litres per person (Ministry of Housing and Urban Development, 2018). Although demand was being met in 2018, much of the water was being provided by unsustainable measures. This becomes a greater concern when looking at how demand has grown, as Beijing's annual water consumption went from one billion m^3 in 2000 to 3.6 billion m^3 in 2011, an annual increase of nearly 230 Mm^3 (Wang et al., 2015).

Beijing has four main water resources: surface water, groundwater, diverted water and reclaimed water. As of 2016, the available surface water was comprised of 88 reservoirs, 30 major lakes and around 400 rivers running through Beijing (Yang et al., 2016). Of the 400 rivers, there are five main ones, the Yongding River, North Canal, Chaobai River, Daqing River and the Jiyun River to which all other rivers and creeks are connected (Fu et al., 2018). The amount of water available for use from these river systems and reservoirs is 1.67 billion m^3 during a regular year (Fu et al., 2018), accounting for 13% of Beijing's water use in 2016 (Xiaoqin et al., 2017). The second source is from groundwater, which in 2010 Beijing had developed 2.2 billion m^3 but the annual sustainable yield was 1.8 billion m^3 (Shen, 2015). By 2011, Beijing had over 84,748 groundwater extraction wells (Yang et al., 2016). Of groundwater use, 62, 31%, and seven percent were for agricultural, domestic and industrial uses, respectively (Yang et al., 2016). Prior to the water diversion project, groundwater was responsible for 70% of water use in Beijing; however, since around 2016 it has decreased to 55% (Xiaoqin et al., 2017).

Post-2014, diverted water from the Yangtse River was pumped to Beijing through the SNWDP, supplying 1.4 billion m^3 of water per year by the end of 2020 (Gao & Yu, 2018). The SNWDP represented 10% of water use in 2016 and is expected to stay at that amount due to the finite amount of water able to be diverted (Xiaoqin et al., 2017). The final source of Beijing's water is reclaimed wastewater, which was 22% of Beijing's water resources in 2016, with roughly 860 million m^3 (Xiaoqin et al., 2017).

Governance Structure

Water Laws

In China, the national constitution has legal authority over all other decision-making bodies (Jiang, 2018). Although the constitution does not specifically mention water, it does state in Article 26 that the national government must protect and improve the ecological and living environment of citizens and must prevent and remedy pollution issues (Jiang, 2018). This Article was drafted into the 1989 Environmental Law, which was amended in 2014, and still stands (Jiang, 2018).

Although not directly linked to the constitution, the Water Law was developed in 1988 and was significantly revised in 2002 and renamed the New Water Law (Jiang, 2018). The law relies on the Competent Department of Water Administration, which deals with all of China's water resource administration, such as utilization and development (Jiang, 2018). Other water laws include the 1984 Water Pollution Prevention and Control Law, 1991 Water and Soil Conservation Law and the 1997 Flood Control Law. Despite these other laws, the New Water Law is most influential (Jiang, 2018). Regulations and rules are set by the central government and local governments are responsible for implementation. Although there appears to be a substantial legal framework for water resources, there is considerable critique (World Bank, 2018). For Jiang (2018), it is vague, fails to recognize integrated water resources management and is silent on market-based water allocation mechanisms (which Beijing uses).

Beijing Water Governance

The Beijing Water Authority is primarily responsible for distributing water throughout the municipality; however, in the case of wastewater, the decentralized system allows for the private sector to distribute wastewater (Hou, 2000). The Beijing Water Authority falls under the Beijing municipal government and interacts with various State Council (central government) institutions to manage water use in the city.

The Beijing Water Authority is responsible for coordinating with many different bodies, including 26 subordinate organizations, 14 water authorities, 18 district governments and various central government ministries (Hou, 2000). Although it might read as extensive cooperation, it is a deeply fragmented system. Under the New Water Law, a mechanism was supposed to be built to help integrate water management; however, each administrative body has its own respective jurisdiction of water resources (Fan et al., 2015). This is a major challenge within the system, as there is no single document or policy to guide these different bodies on best or standardized resource management practice (Fan et al., 2015).

Despite this challenge, the Beijing municipal government committed to a sustainable development strategy in 2008, which emphasized limiting pollution, improving urban ecology and increasing the protection and uses of resources. Various successful policies have emerged from this strategy, including the Three-year Project of Rainwater Pumping Stations

Upgrading and Rainwater Harvesting in Beijing Urban Districts and the West Suburb Sandpit Construction (Fu et al., 2018).

Key Challenges

Water Pollution

The success of Sustainable Development Goal 6 (SDG 6), clean water and sanitation for all, is directly linked to decreasing water pollution. China has prioritized ensuring clean water for all citizens; however, this goal is far from achieved. In 2011, it was reported that 634 Chinese water sources, including rivers and reservoirs, failed to meet safe drinking standards year-round (Tao & Xin, 2014). The cost of combating pollution was estimated at 4.5% of China's GDP (Chunyan et al., 2013). This provides a clear sense of the scale of the issue. More concerningly, water pollution has resulted in a national health crisis. In 2014, 'approximately 190 million people in China fall ill and 60,000 people die from diseases caused by water pollution per year' (Tao & Xin, 2014).

Large-scale pollution began in the 1950s due to industrial development, which has not slowed over the past seventy years (Jusi, 1989). Pollutant discharge from sectors such as industry and agriculture has caused eutrophication, ecological damage and organic and toxic pollution across the country's water systems. The Chinese Ministry of Land and Resources found that between 2011 and 2015, there was an increase in low or poor quality groundwater across the country (Asian Development Bank, 2016). It is estimated that currently 'four fifths of shallow groundwater are heavily polluted' (Asian Development Bank, 2016).

In comparison, an estimated one-third of all surface water in China is polluted (Asian Development Bank, 2016). In the early 1980s, it was found that out of 878 Chinese rivers, 82% of them were polluted to some degree (Jusi, 1989). This issue has not lessened over time as the Asian Development Bank reports that the Chinese river health index, 'continues to register very low values, especially in the lower Yangtze River Basin' (Asian Development Bank, 2016). The Yangtze River basin is a key source of water for many citizens, including a large portion of the city of Beijing through the SNWDP. The city of Beijing is also impacted by its own polluted river system, as it is estimated that 85% of the water in the city's major rivers was undrinkable in 2015, according to official standards, and 56.4% was unfit for any purpose (Tingting, 2017).

Climate Change

In Beijing, the average annual precipitation rate from 1950 to 2012 ranged from a low of 383.9 mm in 1965 to a high of 1005.6 mm in 1954 (Song et al., 2014). The overall precipitation average between 1950 and 2012 was 584.7 mm (Song et al., 2014). It is clear from this evidence that annual precipitation varies immensely between years (Li et al., 2019). This variability is caused by climatic wet and dry periods over time, such as El Niño weather patterns (Asian Development Bank, 2016; Song et al., 2014). Throughout this wet and dry period variability, the average rainfall in Beijing has been consistently decreasing since the 1960s, with an overall decrease of 32% by 2012 (Song et al., 2014). This decrease has been consistent throughout the Haihe River basin as well, one of Beijing's largest sources of water.

The decrease in precipitation over the past thirty years has impacted Beijing's water reservoirs. The city has 88 reservoirs, with eighteen of them considered to be large, each having the capacity to store 10 million m^3 of water. The largest reservoir for Beijing, the Miyun Reservoir, has been incrementally declining over the past twenty years (Song et al., 2014). The second largest reservoir, the Guanting, received 99% less water in 2012 than it did in the 1950s, with the adjoining rivers now being dry for much of the year (Song et al., 2014).

Although the water amounts are impacted by yearly fluctuation, it has also been found that there are significant monthly variations in precipitation amounts. One study has found that seasonally, while precipitation in the spring and autumn has marginally increased at a rate of 0.7 mm/decade and 0.9 mm/decade respectively, there has been a significant decline of 32.8 mm/decade in the summer season when Beijing traditionally receives most of its precipitation (Song et al., 2014).

The concentration in precipitation between the summer months creates a major problem for water security. This uneven precipitation amount makes annual inflows to Beijing reservoirs highly unreliable, especially considering the variability of precipitation from year to year (Li et al., 2019). This unreliability is an impact of climate change.

The exact formula causing Beijing's precipitation variation is not fully understood (Song et al., 2014). However, one major factor which impacts the variation is increasing temperature. Between 1978 and 2009, the average annual temperature in Beijing increased by 1.7 °C (Zhang, 2011). This temperature increase is a result of high energy consumption which releases carbon dioxide into the atmosphere (Song et al., 2014). In cities like Beijing, these temperatures are further exacerbated by the heat island effect, as megacities create large amounts of anthropogenic heat. These changes produce atmospheric conditions that impact local patterns of precipitation and air circulation. The resulting impact across Beijing and much of Northern China has been the weakening of the onshore monsoon winds and diminished water vapour transfers (Song et al., 2014).

As temperatures rise, more extreme precipitation events including flooding and droughts will become more common. Beijing has already experienced some of these climate events, as rainstorms and floods have become more common (Song et al., 2014). In July of 2012, Beijing experienced one of its worst floods to date. A severe rainstorm produced a total rainfall amount of over 460 mm of precipitation in eighteen hours, which is just under the average precipitation amount the city typically receives per year (Song et al., 2014). The flood resulted in 79 casualties, impacted 1.9 million people and caused 1.6 billion dollars in economic losses (Asian Development Bank, 2016). Events such as these, and droughts experienced in Southern China, will worsen in future (Hong et al., 2019). It is estimated that by 2050, Beijing's average annual temperature will be 2.33 °C above 2000s average, suggesting that extreme climatic conditions are only just beginning (Zhang, 2011).

Groundwater Withdrawals

Closely linked to the decreasing amount of precipitation is the increasing and unsustainable reliance on groundwater. Beijing currently relies on groundwater to meet 55% of the city's water demand (Li et al., 2019). In 2010, 2.2 billion m^3 was abstracted in comparison to an estimated annual sustainable yield of 1.8 billion m^3 (Shen, 2015). This kind of overdraft has resulted in Beijing's monthly groundwater levels to decrease by more than 20 metres between 1980 and 2010 (Shen, 2015).

Tied to groundwater exploitation is the lack of adequate groundwater governance. Shen highlights several problems and states, 'Although China has set up some management systems and promoted self-regulation in groundwater development ... the government has had little success in controlling extraction or protecting quality within the existing formal laws and regulations' (Shen, 2015: 76).

Population and Growing Demand

China's population is estimated to peak at 1.4 billion people in 2029 and drop to 1.36 billion people by 2050 (Fensom, 2019). Beijing, China's capital city, currently has a population of roughly 21 million people and is one of the largest cities in the world (You, 2018). The municipal government has released a development plan outlining that the population of Beijing will be limited to a 23-million-person population by 2035 (You, 2018). However, this has raised major human rights concerns, as districts in Beijing have been cracking down on migrant worker residences and relocating educational, medical and training facilities to outside of the cities limit to achieve this goal (Pinghul, 2017).

The issue of population becomes further complicated when evaluating how increasing population, and other factors including the growing middle class, impact demand for water. A study conducted by the Beijing Water Science and Technology Institute found that in 2010, the water footprint from direct and indirect water consumption in Beijing was ten times more than the available local water supplies per capita (Ma et al., 2015).

When it comes to groundwater, it is well-known that Beijing has been suffering from water overdraft. The demand will continue, as a simulation conducted by the World Bank estimated that water demand in China will likely double by 2030 (Asian Development Bank, 2016).

Urban Flooding

According to Fu et al. (2018: 3), over a ten-year period (2003–2012), 'short-duration extreme storms that poured over 70mm rainfall in 1 hour happened 82 times ... The figure tended to climb after 2000, as well as the intensity of these storms'. Beijing has struggled to deal with such high concentrations of precipitation and as climate change worsens, extreme storms will become more frequent. Flooding is further exacerbated by Beijing's urban setting, which has altered the natural ability of the land to slow-down and absorb rainfall. As with all megacities, this is caused by the high number of impervious surfaces—roads, buildings, high and low-density housing—and the decline of green space as cities expand into the countryside.

Beijing's stormwater system is designed to deal with surface runoff through a particular management protocol: storage takes place in the west (into the Yongding River system), drainage occurs in the east (flood water in the upper/middle region of the city is directed into the North Canal) and diversion in the north and south (through rubber dams, flood gates, barrages and creeks) (Fu et al., 2018). This system works relatively well for regular rain events; however, it is often overwhelmed during extreme events. Moreover, once the system in Beijing reaches its coping capacity, this impacts everyone living downstream (Fu et al., 2018).

Unequal Access

The largest social concern regarding water resources in Beijing in unequal access. The UN's SDG 6 data tracker shows that approximately 95% of China's urban population has access to safely managed drinking water, while an estimated 86% has access to safely managed sanitation (see https://sdg6data.org/country-or-area/china). According to World Bank data, the percentage of China's urban population living in slums decreased from 43.6% in 1990 to 24.6% in 2018 (see https://data.worldbank.org/indicator/EN.POP.SLUM.UR.ZS?locations=CN). Given China's population increase over the same time period (from 1.135 to 1.403 billion), this suggests an absolute decline of approximately 15 million living in slums—a direct reflection of China's remarkable economic growth over the last three decades. However, those living in 'urban villages'—the Chinese term for slums—lie at the lower end of the data. It was found in 2016 that 40% of inhabitants in Beijing urban villagers had access to internet in their homes and all villages studied had access to some sort of water source (Wu, 2016). However, these villages often lacked sanitation and kitchens within units, as they had to be shared (Wu, 2016). This means that although these citizens have access to water, it should be considered below the bare minimum.

One Beijing municipal government study estimated that 800,000 individuals were living in urban villages in 2002, represented predominantly by working migrants (Foggin, 2008). In 2002, this population would have made up 12.8% of Beijing's population (Texter, 2019). If we are to assume this population has remained a consistent percentage, the population of today's urban villages could be upwards of 2,520,000 people. However, this is an extremely broad assumption given that there are no statistics post-2002 and the Beijing municipal government has been targeting these communities for gentrification and meeting population reduction goals (Liu & Wong, 2018).

Government Efforts and Strategies

Urban Flood Mitigation

The municipal government has made significant investments in flood mitigation. One of the largest initiatives was the 'three-year Project of Rainwater Pumping Stations Upgrading and Rainwater Harvesting in Beijing Urban Districts' which began in 2013 (Fu et al., 2018). The project successfully upgraded 77 pumping stations across the city resulting in a dramatically increased city pumping capacity from 374,000 m^3/h to 718,000 m^3/s. Improvements were also made to rainwater harvesting system whereby 60 storage tanks were installed with a total volume of 210,000 m^3 (Fu et al., 2018: 4).

Also in 2013, the municipal government invested in the 'Beijing Implementation and Construction Plan for Hydraulic Engineering' which successfully improved and dredged 1460 km of river channels that presented high flood risks or had large populations (Fu et al., 2018). Many riverways were also connected to underground drainage pipelines, which is essential to move water out of urban areas quickly (Fu et al., 2018). The government has also taken significant steps to 'soften' the city by increasing green areas. Called the 'Sponge City Initiative', this began in 2015 in 16 Chinese cities, to reduce rainwater runoff and increase infiltration (Biswas & Hartley, 2017). The goal of the project is to ensure that '80 percent of urban areas should absorb and reuse at least 70 percent of rainwater' (Biswas & Hartley, 2017). It has been financed through a three-way partnership between the private sector and the central and local governments (Biswas & Hartley, 2017). This was and continues to be an extremely impressive goal. Although a part of the programme, Beijing is not on track to meet this goal, as in 2018, 85% of surfaces remained impervious (Biswas & Hartley, 2017).

Wastewater Management

In Beijing, there has been an emphasis on wastewater reuse since the 1980s through decentralized wastewater sites (Liang & van Dijk, 2016). In 1987, the government passed legislation that requires all institutes larger than 30,000 m^2 to have their own decentralized wastewater reuse plants (Liang & van Dijk, 2016). In the early 2000s, centralized wastewater reuse plants began to be built, designed to treat wastewater in one place and then distribute the water back to users (Liang & van Dijk,

2016). As of 2016, Beijing had thousands of decentralized plants but only five large, centralized plants (Liang & van Dijk, 2016).

Wastewater reuse in Beijing is not perfect; however, the municipal government has done an exceptional job at increasing its capacity. In 2003, reclaimed water only accounted for 5.73% of all water use in Beijing, mainly due to the decentralized system (Chang & Ma, 2012). In ten years, reclaimed water has increased to 22% of Beijing's water supply, which was roughly 860 million m^3 of water in 2013 (Xiaoqin et al., 2017).

In 2010, the division of wastewater reuse was 47% to agriculture, 30% to the environment, 20% to industry and 3% urban miscellaneous within Beijing (Lili et al., 2011). This incredible progress has been partly attributed to central government overarching policies but mainly due to the rigorous efforts of Beijing's municipal government (Chang & Ma, 2012). This trend is likely to continue, 'as reclaimed wastewater exploitation in Beijing is now [only] at the beginning stage' (Chang & Ma, 2012).

There is still significant room for reclaimed wastewater to infiltrate the water market. In 2010, only 59.3% of wastewater in Beijing was successfully reused (Chang & Ma, 2012). It could be possible that some of this lost water was not a high enough quality to be reused, however, the decentralized system is mainly responsible. Aside from decentralized plants for industrial use, many plants have extensive issues, including not operating regularly due to financial cost and non-functioning systems (Liang & van Dijk, 2016). This wastewater reuse loss has major potential to be reclaimed, as the Beijing municipal government continues to centralize the majority system. In 2011, Beijing's two largest centralized plants, Fang Zhuang Wastewater Reclamation Plant and Jiu Xian Qiao Reclamation Plant, were only producing at 50% of overall capacity (Lili et al., 2011). These plants are not reaching their full capacity as there is a lack of city infrastructure, including pipelines, to divert wastewater from decentralized plants or residential homes (Lili et al., 2011).

The Beijing government is aware of these issues. In 2013, the Beijing municipal government launched a three-year plan to create more wastewater treatment and recycling plants (Waterworld, 2016). The goal of the programme is to increase the capacity of reclaimed water to 4.13 million m^3 per day, equaling 1.3 billion cubic metres of water per year by the end of 2020 (Xiaoqin et al., 2017). The municipal government has been encouraging this development through water pricing. For example, in

2010, wastewater prices for household, industrial and carwash use were 25, 16.1 and 1.6% of conventional water prices (Chang & Ma, 2012). It is evident that the Beijing municipal government has created powerful financial incentive to use reclaimed water.

The private sector has also played a considerable role in advancing wastewater use, as 67% of wastewater produced was being used by agriculture or industry in 2010 (Chang & Ma, 2012). Without the private sector, wastewater capacity would not have grown so dramatically, as there are significant issues in mainstreaming wastewater use in the residential sector. In 2010, only 0.03% of recycled water was being used by the residential sector, due to the lack of infrastructure (such as pipes) and consumer reluctance (Chang & Ma, 2012). Partnership between the local government and private sector stakeholders appears to be the best solution to increase wastewater reuse capacity, as the municipal government is made responsible by the central government to provide loans to decrease production costs (Chang & Ma, 2012).

South-North Water Diversion Project

The SNWDP is predominately a central government initiative, however, local governments were also involved. The estimated total cost of the project is more than USD 70 billion. The purpose of the project is to bring water from the water rich southern areas of China, which hold 82% of the country's water, into the arid northern region (Yang et al., 2018). The project diverts water in three routes—Eastern, Middle, Western—linking China's four main rivers, the Yangtze, Huaihe, Yellow and Haihe (Yang et al., 2018). According to Wilson et al. (2017: 8), 'with two of the three routes operational, the SNWDP can move up to 18.5 km^3 of water/year. Even without the [Western Route] this figure is expected to rise to 27.8 km^3/year in the near future, making the SNWDP one of the grandest attempts by humans to alter their environment at regional and super-regional scales'. Upon completion in 2050, the project will deliver 44.8 km^3 of water to the growing population in the north. In addition, it is intended to bring significant relief to over-exploited groundwater aquifers. Yao et al. (2019) show that the baseline measure of Beijing's overdraft approximately 600 Mm^3, so highlighting the scale of the problem.

Beijing has been receiving drinking water via the Middle Route since 2014. 'The gravity-fed Middle Route ... moves water from the heightened dam at the Danjiangkou Reservoir through a main canal and a tunnel under the Yellow river at Zhengzhou, with local infrastructure enabling withdrawals from the main canal' (Rogers et al., 2020: 51). The total length of the Middle Route is 1432 km, delivering an estimated 13 billion m^3 of water to 119 cities along the route. In its first year completed, it was estimated that Beijing received 23 million m^3 of water that year (Gao & Yu, 2018). By the end of 2020, Beijing is estimated to receive 1.4 billion m^3 of water per year (Gao & Yu, 2018). As of 2019, the project represented 10% of Beijing's overall water use, with 70% used for residential uses (Xinhua, 2019).

The SNWDP was built in the full knowledge that it would not end water scarcity. The purpose of the project is to create immediate relief for groundwater resources and act as a supplementary water source to help meet demand (Yang et al., 2018). By the end of 2019, the project had helped increase Beijing's groundwater reserves by 2.88 metres, making it the first year in sixteen that groundwater levels increased (Xinhua, 2019). According to Yao et al. (2019: 552, 553), the 'roadmap' for China's groundwater pumping control policy (issued in 2013) intends to displace 4 billion m^3 of over-exploited groundwater with 'transferred water, local surface and recycled water'. The roadmap projects overall groundwater use to decrease to 31% of total water use, with Beijing groundwater use declining by 78% by 2025 (see also Zhang et al., 2021). Despite reaching many of its water goals, there is significant critique around the project.

Two important criticisms about the project are social displacement and ongoing environmental risk. The eastern and central routes required the acquisition of 63,000 hm^2 of land, which required over 340,000 residents to be involuntarily resettled (Rogers et al., 2020: 55). The central government had promised fair compensation; however, the rates of compensation varied drastically by geographical region and were considered very low by residents who relied on the land for livelihoods (Zhao et al., 2017). Undeterred by this opposition, the central government resettled residents without changing the compensation policies (Zhao et al., 2017). An increasing number of studies focused on the environmental impact of the SNWDP are emerging (Rogers et al., 2020; Wilson et al., 2017). In an extensive review of the literature, Wilson et al. (2017) suggest that while there will be significant negative environmental impacts in water-providing areas the environmental benefits thought to accrue to water-receiving areas are not well established. Among other things, there is concern that the project will cause significant impacts on the Han River and Yangtze Delta, where it is diverting 35% of the available water (Wilson et al., 2017). Additionally, there is concern that there is a possibility of secondary salinization in moving water through the SNWTP, contributing to decreasing water quality (Wilson et al., 2017).

Water Pricing

The central government has encouraged the implementation of increasing block tariffs (IBT) for water use (Ma et al., 2018). IBTs raise the price of water per unit as the rate of consumption increases. In China, the goal of block tariffs 'is to improve water use efficiency as well as to provide efficient incentives for water saving' (Ma et al., 2018). However, Beijing struggles with these goals due to the 'oversized initial block' (Ma et al., 2018). In 2018, the initial block included consumers who ranged in use from 3.8 to 15 m^3/month (Ma et al., 2018). In this block, consumers pay $0.63 US per m^3 of water (Ma et al., 2018).

The initial block is intended to help low-income consumers; however, it also includes households that are considered to have 'luxurious' water consumption (Ma et al., 2018). This is demonstrated in how in 2019 the average amount of residential water used that year was 31.1 m^3 per capita (Li et al., 2019). It is important to note that this only represents residential water use, not the entirety of water use per capita. However, this still means that consumers hitting the higher end of the block are using almost 80% more water than the average person in Beijing per year. Academics in the Xunzhou Ma study argue that for the IBT system to work, the initial block should only be for consumers who use between 2.0 and 2.5 m^3 per month at the current rate that is being charged (Ma et al., 2018). Past this amount, they argue that consumers must pay much higher prices (Ma et al., 2018).

Discussion

Throughout this chapter, it has become evident that although Beijing struggles with many challenges related to water scarcity, the Central and local Beijing governments are putting in significant efforts to improve Beijing's situation. This is best demonstrated by the partnership between the public and private sectors to accelerate the growth of reclaimed wastewater as a foundational source of city water. These efforts should not be taken lightly, as water scarcity presents the complex challenge of balancing ecological, social and economic well-being. However, if Beijing is to avoid day zero and reach the sustainable development goals, a concentrated effort needs to be made in creating an integrated water resources management system (IWRM).

In Northern China, the Haihe River basin serves as an example of how integrated water resource management can be successful within the local context. The Haihe basin is connected to six provinces, including the Beijing and Tianjin municipalities (World Bank, 2012). The World Bank partnered with the Central and local governments of the Haihe basin to create the Haihe basin Integrated Water and Environment Management Project (World Bank, 2012). The project ran from 2003 to 2011 with the aim to address water quality, pollution and relieve exploited groundwater and surface water (World Bank, 2012). The project achieved substantial success due to establishing, 'a mechanism for cooperation between water and environment departments and the central, provincial and local levels' (World Bank, 2012).

Thinking back to Beijing's complex water governance system, the establishment of a cooperation mechanism to incorporate all levels of governance across six provinces is impressive. The project also relied heavily on stakeholder participation, by creating 400 water user associations to allow communities to decide how best to manage their local water resources (World Bank, 2012). Due to the project, the Haihe basin area's level of shallow groundwater over-exploitation decreased by 63% and deep groundwater by 46% between 2004 and 2010 (World Bank, 2012). Discharged wastewater decreased by 129.34 million tonnes by 2010 due to coordinated efforts in Tianjin and the Dagu Canal (World Bank, 2012).

The Haihe basin example demonstrates a basin-level integrated water resource management system. Given China's long history of 'pushing rivers around' in support of creating what Worster (1985) called a 'hydraulic society', one doubts the likelihood of its achieving SDG 60.5.1 on IWRM implementation. Indeed, China continues to display characteristics of classically high-modern 'distintegrated' water resources management where (i) decisions are taken by the state in support of a narrowly defined 'national interest'; (ii) experts are enlisted to determine the technical and financial possibilities for achieving state-defined goals; and (iii) water is treated as an input into socio-economic development resulting in nature being 'adapted' to human needs and not the other way around. According to UN SDG data, China reports that it is 80% of the way toward achieving SDG 6.5.1 (see https://sdg6data.org/country-or-area/china#anchor_6.5.1). Least progress has been made in relation to appropriate institutional forms including stakeholder participation. This, however, does not rule out IWRM-oriented decision-making. In the absence of appropriate basin-level institutions, progress toward sustainable IWRM can be achieved through the deliberate application of a 'basin sensibility', even at city level.

Beijing can use systems like these within their municipal boundaries. City level management is defined by, 'holistic governance of finite and fragile water, with coordinated and flexible strategic planning, decision-making processes involving stakeholder participation and optimizing the interface between urban water and activities beyond urban boundaries, down-stream use and agriculture' (Van den Brandeler et al., 2019). This is a more possibility than it is current reality. Using this understanding of IWRM, Beijing has considerable gaps within water governance and programmes.

Recommendations

- The Beijing Water Authority should adopt an integrated urban water management system within city governance, to reflect the successful Haihe Basin structure. This system can help coordination and cooperation, through mechanisms such as improving data collection and information sharing. Additionally, this system could encourage more cohesive policies and incentives to encourage wastewater and rainwater reuse, more stringent environmental policies and community participation.
- Citizens have a key role to play in the future of Beijing's water resource management. A study conducted in 2014 found that most Beijing citizens cared and were aware of the water scarcity problem but did not know which measures they needed to take to help (Fan et al., 2015). Education regarding wastewater reuse offers one possibility. Among wealthier citizens, water efficiency must be encouraged within their homes, such as using high-efficiency water taps or washing machines.
- The Beijing Water Authority should do more outreach with the local community and help provide education on what citizens can help

achieve. Citizen participation and mobilization could centre around local, small-scale 'sponge city' initiatives, such as park development. Working with government officials in practical and beneficial ways may provide a pathway for enhanced state-citizen trust-building.

- The Beijing municipal government and Beijing Water Authority need to stabilize water use from the SNWDP, as it is unsustainable to keep relying on enhancing supply to meet ever-increasing demand. Although it does serve as an important substitute for now, Beijing needs to develop more sustainable water resources, such as wastewater, and increase water efficiency. As the capital city of China, Beijing has an essential role to play in setting the precedent for sustainable resource management.
- The New Water Law needs to be updated to better reflect the current water situation and market across China. It has been two decades since the legislation was updated, meaning that there are significant gaps, such as zero national legislation on water trading and pricing systems. Additionally, the New Water Law needs to include integrated water resource management and detail the legal practices and expectations for Chinese cities.
- Beijing's water pricing system needs to accurately reflect citizens' ability to pay. Block tariffs must not negatively impact low-income communities while encouraging more well-off households, companies and enterprises to be more water wise in their consumption patterns.
- The government of Beijing needs to strive to establish institutional systems that clearly define and regulate water withdrawal and use. Also, the government must build basin-level decision-support systems that are designed to integrate urban hydrological processes and the socio-economic dynamics of the water demand issue.
- Institutionally, water conservation crosses several themes and sectors and, thus, many government agencies, civil society and the private sector are involved. Institutional arrangements and stakeholders' engagement are key success factors for any water conservancy programme. Water production, treatment, distribution; then wastewater collection, treatment and disposal usually are a city's largest energy consumers. Educating residents as water consumers and stakeholders on the implications from the water and sanitation sector can draw strong public support for water conservation,

in addition to health and environmental co-benefits. Having all government agencies on board will help ensure implementation.

Conclusion

Supporting human life and socio-economic activities in urban regions requires continuous water supply as well as high resilience against adverse effects of floods, pollution, groundwater depletion and wastewater management. Growing population, rapid urbanization and socio-economic activities on one hand, and emerging effects of climate change on the other hand seriously threaten water security in Beijing.

Efforts have been made by different levels of government to promote a reasonable utilization of existing water supplies through, inter alia, conservation measures, wastewater reclamation, mitigation of urban flooding through 'sponge city' interventions and enhanced supply through water transfer schemes. Despite these massive measures and efforts, there is not enough water to meet Beijing's future needs.

In terms of management issues, many agencies are involved in water governance but lack coordination. Coordination must cross organizational levels and sectors. Many water-related laws and policies are not implemented because central and local governments' efforts are not coordinated. The institutional systems necessary for integrated urban water security must be strengthened in support of more effective water resource management strategies, plans, programmes and practices, including water pricing systems, water use efficiency and water-saving practices, public awareness and participation, flood mitigation, non-point source pollution abatement, wastewater reuse and rainwater harvesting.

References

Asian Development Bank. (2016). *Addressing water security in the People's Republic of China the 13th five-year plan (2016–2020) and beyond*. Asian Development Bank.

Ball, P. (2016). *The Water Kingdom: A secret history of China*. Bodley Head.

Biswas, A. K., & Hartley, K. (2017, September 26). Tackling the challenges of sponge cities. *China Daily*.

Chang, D., & Ma, Z. (2012). Wastewater reclamation and reuse in Beijing: Influence factors and policy implications. *Desalination*, *297*, 72–78.

Chunyan, L., Chen, L., Zhao, H., Guo, S., & Wang, G. (2013). Challenges facing socioeconomic development as a result of China's environmental problems and future prospects. *Ecological Engineering, 60*, 199–203.

Fan, L., Wang, H., Lai, W., Wang, C., & Fan, L. (2015). Administration of water resources in Beijing: Problems and countermeasures. *Water Policy, 17*(4), 563–580.

Fensom, A. (2019, September 16). Dangerous demographics: China's population problem will eclipse its ambitions. *The National Interest*. Available at: https://nationalinterest.org/feature/dangerous-demographics-chinas-population-problem-will-eclipse-its-ambitions-80961. Accessed 4 April 2022.

Foggin, P. (2008). Urban poverty and urban slums in China. *Lausanne World Pulse Archives*. Available at: https://lausanneworldpulse.com/urban-php/977/07-2008. Accessed 4 April 2022.

Fu, C., Liu, J., Wang, H., Xiang., C., Fu, X., & Luan, Q. (2018). Urban storm flooding: Characteristics and management in Beijing. *MATEC Web of Conferences, 246*, 01042.

Gao, Y., & Yu, M. (2018). Assessment of the economic impact of South-to-North Water Diversion Project on industrial sectors in Beijing. *Journal of Economic Structures, 7*(1), 1–17.

Hong, C., Zhang, Q., Zhang, Y., Davis, S. J., Tong, D., Zheng, Y., Liu, Z., Guan, D., He, K., & Schellnhuber, H. J. (2019). Impacts of climate change on future air quality and human health in China. *PNAS, 116*(35), 17193–17200.

Hou, E. (2000, April 20). *Briefing paper on water governance structure in Beijing, PRC*. Available at: https://citeseerx.ist.psu.edu/viewdoc/download?doi=10.1.1.453.9299&rep=rep1&type=pdf. Accessed 4 April 2022.

Jiang, M. (2018). *Towards tradable water rights: Water law and policy reform in China*. Springer.

Jusi, W. (1989). Water pollution and water shortage problems in China. *Journal of Applied Ecology, 26*(3), 851–857.

Li, Y., Zhang, Z., & Shi, M. (2019). Restrictive effects of water scarcity on urban economic development in the Beijing-Tianjin-Hebei city region. *Sustainability, 11*(8), 2452.

Liang, X., & Van Dijk, M. P. (2016). Evaluating the interests of different stakeholders in Beijing wastewater reuse systems for sustainable urban water management. *Sustainability, 8*(11), 1098.

Lili, Y., Jiao, W., Chen, X., & Chen, W. (2011). An overview of reclaimed water reuse in China. *Journal of Environmental Sciences, 23*(10), 1585–1593.

Liu, R., & Wong, T. (2018). Urban village redevelopment in Beijing: The state-dominated formalization of informal housing. *Cities, 72*, 160–172.

Ma, D., Xian, C., & Zhang, J. (2015). The evaluation of water footprints and sustainable water utilization in Beijing. *Sustainability, 7*(10), 13206–13221.

Ma, X., Wu, D., & Zhang, S. (2018). Multiple goals dilemma of residential water pricing policy reform: Increasing block tariffs or a uniform tariff with rebate? *Sustainability, 10*(10), 3526.

McDonald, R., Weber, K., Padowski, J., Flörke, M., Schneider, C., Green, P., & Montgomery, M. (2014). Water on an urban planet: Urbanization and the reach of urban water infrastructure. *Global Environmental Change, 27*(1), 96–105. https://doi.org/10.1016/j.gloenvcha.2014.04.022

Ministry of Housing and Urban-Rural Development. (2018). *China CN: Water consumption: City: Daily per capita: Residential: Beijing. CEIC.* Available at: https://www.ceicdata.com/en/china/water-consumption-daily-per-capita-residential/cn-water-consumption-city-daily-per-capita-residential-beijing. Accessed 4 April 2022.

Pinghul, Z. (2017, October 3). Beijing's population set to fall as government's efforts to trim migrant numbers pay dividends. *South China Morning Post.*

Rogers, S., Chen, D., Jiang, H., Rutherfurd, I., Wang, M., Webber, M., Crow-Miller, B., Barnett, J., Finlayson, B., Jiang, M., Shi, C., & Zhang, W. (2020). An integrated assessment of China's South-North Water Transfer Project. *Geographical Research, 58*(1), 49–63.

Shen, D. (2015). Groundwater management in China. *Water Policy, 17*(1), 61–82.

Song, X., AghaKouchak, A., He, R., Liu, C., Sen Roy, S., Xuan, W, Wang, G., Wang, X., & Zhang, J. (2014). Rapid urbanization and changes in spatiotemporal characteristics of precipitation in Beijing metropolitan area. *Advanced Earth and Space Sciences, 119*(19), 11250–11271.

Sun, L., Fertner, C., & Jørgensen, G. (2021). Beijing's First Green Belt—A 50-year long Chinese planning story. *Land, 10*, 969.

Tao, T., & Xin, K. (2014). Public health: A sustainable plan for China's drinking water. *Nature, 511*, 527–528.

Texter, C. (2019). China: population of Beijing from 1980 to 2035. *Statista.* Available at: https://www.statista.com/statistics/466949/china-population-of-beijing/. Accessed 4 April 2022.

Tingting, D. (2017, June 2). In China, the water you drink is as dangerous as the air you breathe. *The Guardian.* Available at: https://www.theguardian.com/global-development-professionals-network/2017/jun/02/china-water-dangerouspollution-greenpeace. Accessed 27 June 2022.

Udimal, T. B., Jincai, Z., Ayamba, E. C., & Mensah Owusu, S. (2017). China's water situation; the supply of water and the pattern of its usage. *International Journal of Sustainable Built Environment, 6*(2), 491–500.

UNDESA (United Nations, Department of Economic and Social Affairs) (2014). *World urbanization prospects: The 2014 revision.* United Nations.

United Nations. (2020). Water scarcity. Available at: https://www.unwater.org/water-facts/scarcity/. Accessed 4 April 2022.

Van Den Brandeler, F., Gupta, J., & Hordijk, M. (2019). Megacities and rivers: Scalar mismatches between urban water management and river basin management. *Journal of Hydrology, 573*, 1067–1074.

Wang, J., Shang, Y., Wang, H., Zhao, Y., & Yin, Y. (2015). Beijing's water resources: Challenges and solutions. *JAWRA Journal of the American Water Resources Association, 51*(3), 614–623.

Waterworld. (2016). *China's largest underground wastewater recycling plant moves ahead*. Available at: https://www.waterworld.com/international/wastewater/article/16202882/chinas-largest-underground-wastewater-recycling-plant-moves-ahead. Accessed 4 April 2022.

Wei, D. (2005). Beijing water resources and the south to north water diversion project. *Canadian Journal of Civil Engineering, 32*(1), 159–163.

Wilson, M., Xiao-Yan, L., Yu-Jun, M., Smith, A., & Wu, J. (2017). A review of the economic, social, and environmental impacts of China's South-North Water Transfer Project: A sustainability perspective. *Sustainability, 9*(8), 1489.

World Bank. (2012). *China: Improving water resource management and pollution control in the Hai Basin*. Available at: https://www.worldbank.org/en/news/feature/2012/09/03/china-improving-water-resource-management-pollution-control-in-hai-basin. Accessed 4 April 2022.

World Bank. (2018). *Watershed: A new era of water governance in China*. Policy Brief. Washington, DC: The World Bank.

Worster, D. (1985). *Rivers of empire: Water, aridity, and the growth of the American West*. Oxford University Press.

Wu, F. (2016). Housing in Chinese urban villages: The Dwellers, conditions and tenancy informality. *Housing Studies, 31*(7), 852–870.

Xiaoqin, Z., Zifu, L., Chad, S., Xuejun, W., & Han, S. (2017). Issues and challenges of reclaimed water usage: A case study of the dragon-shaped river in the Beijing Olympic Park. *Water International, 42*(4), 486–494.

Xinhua. (2019). China's South-to-North water diversion. *China Daily*. Available at: https://www.chinadaily.com.cn/a/201912/11/WS5df0a307a310cf3e3557d7f2.html. Accessed 4 April 2022.

Yang, W., Hyndman, D., Winkler, J., Viña, A., Deines, J., Lupi, F., & Liu, J. (2016). Urban water sustainability framework and application. *Ecology and Society, 21*(4), 4.

Yang, J., Zhao, H., Yang, Z., Huang, Z., Bai, G., & Liu, C. (2018). The strategy of reducing groundwater exploitation and the south-to-north water diversion project. *The International Journal of Environmental Studies, 75*(1), 59–67.

Yao, Y., Zheng, C., Andrews, C., He, X., Zhang, A., & Liu, J. (2019). Integration of groundwater into China's south-north water transfer strategy. *Science of the Total Environment, 658*, 550–557.

You, L. (2018). Beijing's future mapped out for two decades. *China Daily*. Available at: https://www.chinadaily.com.cn/cndy/2017-10/18/content_33395011.htm. Accessed 4 April 2022.
Zhang, B. (2011). The climate change, water crisis and forest ecosystem services in Beijing, China. In H. Kheradmand (Ed.), *Climate change—Socioeconomic effects* (pp. 115–130). InTech.
Zhang, C., Duan, Q., Yeh, P.J.-F., Pan, Y., Gong, H., Moradkhani, H., Gong, W., Lei, X., Liao, W., Xu, L., Huang, Z., Zheng, L., & Geo, X. (2021). Sub-regional groundwater storage recovery in North China Plain after the South-to-North water diversion project. *Journal of Hydrology, 597*, 126156.
Zhao, Z., Zuo, J., & Zillante, G. (2017). Transformation of water resource management: A case study of the South-to-North Water Diversion project. *Journal of Cleaner Production, 163*, 136–145.

CHAPTER 7

Confronting the System: An Exploration of the Water Security Crisis in Melbourne

Christine Kitoko, Margot Whittington, and Larry Swatuk

Introduction

Melbourne is the capital of the Australian state of Victoria and serves as the home of approximately 75% of Victoria's population (World Population Review, 2020). Water security is at the forefront of Melburnians' minds due to a multiplicity of factors, including the impacts of climate change and population growth (Ives et al., 2013; Moran, 2006; Sousa Júnior et al., 2016; Werbeloff & Brown, 2011a). In the aftermath of the Millennium Drought, which lasted from 1997 to 2009, citizens of Melbourne have become highly aware of the city's declining water storage levels and of their personal water consumption (Low et al., 2015; Rowley, 2016). In the past five years, the city's water storage has decreased by an average of 61 billion litres due to successive droughts, leading the Victoria State Government to adopt a 'security through diversity'

C. Kitoko · M. Whittington · L. Swatuk (✉)
University of Waterloo, Waterloo, ON, Canada
e-mail: lswatuk@uwaterloo.ca

L. Swatuk and C. Cash (eds.), *The Political Economy of Urban Water Security under Climate Change*, International Political Economy Series,
https://doi.org/10.1007/978-3-031-08108-8_7

approach (Heggie, 2019; Werbeloff & Brown, 2011a). This approach includes initiatives to increase storage levels such as building the Victoria Desalination plant, and to decrease demand through initiatives such as permanent water-saving rules restricting outdoor water consumption, and the voluntary 'Target 155' campaign (Victoria State Government, 2015, 2020). While the Victoria State Government and the Melbourne Municipal Government have embraced the philosophy of the security through diversity approach, in practice they appear to have placed an over-reliance on the desalination plant to increase storage levels (Werbeloff & Brown, 2011a). Hence, these governments need to consider alternative solutions to improve water security for the long term, particularly as Melbourne faces the threats of climate change and population growth. Further, although Melbourne's current strategy is considered an improvement on the city's previous methods of conducting urban water management, the city remains dependent on the same system that made way for present vulnerabilities to emerge in the first place (Werbeloff & Brown, 2011b); Therefore, the city's water security strategy needs to be transformed, if it is to be able to adapt and respond to these urgent challenges.

The urban water management system presently in place in Melbourne is not entirely suited to tackle the impacts of climate change and population growth, as it dates from the colonial era. Thus, it is predicated on historical processes which have altered and significantly degraded the natural environment, water resources included (Brown et al., 2009; Werbeloff & Brown, 2011b). This includes the centralized nature of the strategy, which has meant that certain stakeholders have been excluded from its development and operation, and its reliance on methods transplanted from the United Kingdom (UK), meaning that it has not been tailored exclusively to meet local needs (Brown et al., 2009; Werbeloff & Brown, 2011b). In the face of current challenges, therefore, reliance on such a system is not sustainable. The population is booming, the city is expanding, and climate change is continuing to evolve (Ives et al., 2013; Moran, 2006; Sousa Júnior et al., 2016; Werbeloff & Brown, 2011b). It is hence important for Melbourne to alter its approach to water security, according to the changing nature of these challenges.

This could be achieved by implementing a truer embodiment of the principle of diversification, as outlined in the security through diversity model promoted by state and federal governments (Werbeloff & Brown, 2011a, 2011b). Melbourne should include a broader range of relevant stakeholders in the city's urban water management scheme to not only confront, but also address, its centralized nature and inherent colonial methods which are unsuited to meet evolving local needs. Such stakeholders should be local and derive from civil society, as many of them have demonstrated a commitment to fighting for the adoption of more sustainable methods of managing water resources in the area. They include Traditional Owner Groups[1] (e.g. the Wurundjeri Woi Wurrung Cultural Heritage Aboriginal Corporation and the Bunurong Land Council Aboriginal Corporation), as seen through their activities centred on the recalling and application of traditional Aboriginal[2] ways of perceiving and engaging with nature within the context of modern-day Melbourne (e.g. the Wurundjeri Cultural Values Project in partnership with Melbourne Water and the Victorian Environmental Water Holder) (BLCAC, n.d.; State Government of Victoria, 2019a; Wurundjeri Woi Wurrung Cultural Heritage Aboriginal Corporation), along with other community and environmental actors such as Friends of the Earth Melbourne and Environment Victoria whose activities have included opposing municipal plans for desalination.

Community and environmental actors are important collaborators, as they defend the preservation of natural resources and advocate for what is in the common interest of their communities (see, e.g. Brown et al., 2009: 853). Thus, their inclusion in decision-making processes related to water resources could arguably serve to hold Melbourne's current public and private water managers accountable and lead to the management of water resources in ways that demonstrate consideration for the well-being of people and the environment. Furthermore, Aboriginal organizations are highly relevant to this discussion because, in addition to their activism, they comprise and represent segments of the population publicly recognized as the rightful owners of the land in Melbourne. Considering, therefore, the historical and present-day implications of their dispossession of land and water (see, e.g. Hall, 2019), particularly in light of the cultural significance of these resources to them, involving local Aboriginal groups in the region's urban water management could constitute an important step in the process of 'reconciliation'. More specifically, it would demonstrate willingness on the part of authorities to work toward

[1] The term refers to Aboriginal groups formally recognized as Traditional Owners of Country, as outlined by the State Government of Victoria (2019b).

[2] The terms Aboriginal and Indigenous are used interchangeably in this chapter.

redefining and improving their relationship with Indigenous people, by partnering with them to establish mechanisms through which together they can effect change more concretely. Nonetheless, as actors such as O'Bryan (2017) contend, partnerships of the like must move beyond the symbolical. These partnerships must enable Indigenous people to partake in meaningful decision-making over the management of water resources. This could lead to a diversion from the current situation, both in terms of the reconfiguration of Melbourne's urban water management system to render it more sustainable, and through the inclusion of Indigenous groups among the more diversified ensemble of stakeholders, as a step toward reconciliation.

A deeper exploration of the water security issue in Melbourne through historical and modern-day facets will provide greater understanding of the aforementioned challenges. In this chapter, we argue that Melbourne's approach to water security fails to address the following two important elements: broader stakeholder inclusion in water resource management, and environmental protection. Melbourne's water security measures neglect to meaningfully include important stakeholders such as Indigenous, community and environmental actors in decision-making processes; lack adequate consideration of the impacts of desalination on marine life and the ocean; and fail to acknowledge the limits of the natural world.

Historical Overview: Differing Perceptions of Water and Land

Water security is indeed under threat in Melbourne, due to several climate and population-related factors as described. However, these components do not paint a full picture of the issue. Before European settlement in the area, and its gradual development into a metropolis, present-day Melbourne served as a ceremonial meeting ground for Aboriginal clans, who sustained themselves on surrounding ecosystem goods and services (Ives et al., 2013; Oakley & Johnson, 2013; Presland, 2014). Their cultural gatherings were regular and involved hundreds of people for up to 3–4 consecutive weeks (Ives et al., 2013; Oakley & Johnson, 2013). They benefited from clean drinking water provided by the Yarra River, and food from abounding vegetation and wildlife (Ives et al., 2013; Oakley & Johnson, 2013; Presland, 2014). Much of their environment is comprised of low-lying wetlands and alluvial plains; the former resulting from beach ridges that inhibited drainage. They included swamps and lagoons and varied in size depending on seasons and rainfall. Water and land, including the swamps, were indivisible from one another, as they were together considered by Aboriginal people to be one and indispensable to their spiritual and physical survival. Accordingly, natural resources were managed in such a way as to enable them to last and continue to be relied upon for tens of thousands of years (Ives et al., 2013; Oakley & Johnson, 2013; Presland, 2014).

This manner of engaging with nature, however, belonging to the Woi wurrung and Boon wurrung clans of the Eastern Kulin nation, did not correspond to that of the subsequent British colonizers who seized control of their territory (Ives et al., 2013; Oakley & Johnson, 2013; Presland, 2014). On the contrary, the latter perceived nature as needing to be subdued and put to meaningful use by Man, based on their understanding of Genesis 1:28 in the Bible (Presland, 2014). 'Man' in this case meant European men of a certain standing and did not include Indigenous people or women, both of which had no rights under the British Crown (Moses, 2000). Undertaking this task, therefore, required appropriating the new environment that was to become Melbourne, and dramatically altering it in accordance with European wants, needs and desires. As such, settlement was initiated in 1835 (Ives et al., 2013; Oakley & Johnson, 2013; Presland, 2014).

This occurred upon European people's encounter with the chosen site's natural wealth. It comprised of arable land on the alluvial plains, and timber that could be sourced from forests, in addition to the available potable water. It was situated along the northern banks of the Yarra River, at the top of Port Philip Bay, and was protected against flooding (Ives et al., 2013; Oakley & Johnson, 2013; Presland, 2014). The latter was due to the area's rocky and elevated nature, which formed the limits beyond which tides could not attain (Presland, 2014). Hence, once agreed upon as the ideal place, development began.

Initial activities involved converting waterways into ports and building industry zones to export goods such as gold and wool to the metropole (Ives et al., 2013; Oakley & Johnson, 2013; Presland, 2014). These led to population and economic growth during the 1850s, and necessitated town expansion beyond the initial site's confines. Surrounding ecosystems, therefore, had to be either cleared to create space or converted according to other needs (Ives et al., 2013). The process began with the tackling of swamps, which covered much of the area and were viewed unfavourably by the Europeans.

The wetlands had been valued by Indigenous Australians, as they perceived water and land to be undifferentiated from one another. However, for the Europeans it was not so. In their culture, swamps were considered futile and detrimental to health. They could not be cultivated or built upon like dry land, nor be put to use in the same manners as rivers, lakes and oceans (Ponting, 1991).

Beyond the direct physical transformation of the land, these practices contained ideological meaning. They not only reinforced the establishment and dominance of British culture in the environment, but further signified local Indigenous people's dispossession of and exclusion from it (Moses, 2000). Many among them succumbed to the onslaught of diseases, while others found themselves relegated to precariousness within the town, and then entirely moved to grounds that would later become reserves, a process that some have labelled 'cultural genocide' (Moses, 2000). The new powers thereby consolidated British settlers' vision for Melbourne, proceeding with its execution in a manner that could be understood to have constituted a transplantation of Europe to the colony. Further, encompassed within it was the establishment of a water system modelled after that of the UK.

The need for a water supply system surfaced alongside other developments in the town, as it would enable the processing of industrial goods and improve on waste management, among other things (Oakley & Johnson, 2013). Therefore, plans were launched to extend the centralized system that had been established in other parts of colonial Australia in the early 1800s to Melbourne (Brown et al., 2009). The country's urban water management system occurred in three stages, categorized by Brown et al. (2009) as the 'historical transition'.

The first stage unfolded in the early Nineteenth Century, resting on the knowledge of hydraulic engineers brought in from the metropole. The foreign experts sought to provide clean and safe water to a growing urban population, using an effective centralized scheme. Their focus was particularly on supplying the elite, due to the social movement of cleanliness at the time that was tied to social status. They therefore orchestrated the planning, construction and management of the system; relying on dams, pipes and the extraction of large volumes of water from a source considered benign (Brown et al., 2009). Once operational and secure, prevailing thoughts then shifted. They turned to the idea of 'limitless fresh water' being a public right, that should be provided by governments at an affordable cost, to all people equally—as in the UK (Brown et al., 2009).

As such, a centralized system of taxation emerged (i.e. the hydro-social contract) to enable water infrastructure and delivery to be funded and achieve this new vision. It came to be enforced by regional and subsequently metropolitan governments, and symbolized the provision of safe, affordable and 'limitless' water, from a benign environment to booming cities (Brown et al., 2009).

The second stage focused on the development of a sewerage system. It occurred between the mid to late 1800s, when public health concerns were prevalent across the UK and Europe due to outbreaks of cholera and typhoid. Researchers in London discovered that pathogen infections from effluents, not bad air, caused people to be ill (Johnson, 2007). In accordance, a combined and networked sewerage system was developed to dispose of industrial and wastewaters in waterways outside of cities. The method was thought to be environmentally sound and was subsequently adopted in Australia (Brown et al., 2009). Sydney led the way in realizing these developments, investing in a combined sewerage and stormwater drainage system in 1850. Other cities followed suit, starting from the late 1800s (Brown et al., 2009).

The third stage focused on drainage. The practice had already been occurring at a micro level, however, it came to be incorporated into the centralized system post-World War II (Brown et al., 2009). Government public spending at the time had risen substantially, allowing the new discipline of urban hydrology to establish itself firmly in Australia. Professionals in the field consequently innovated techniques to efficiently transport stormwater out of urban centres, into external waterways, through pipes underground (Brown et al., 2009). This transformed the public perception of stormwater, and by extension, dramatically impacted urban development. On one hand, stormwater turned into a nuisance; on the other hand, waterways came to be viewed as dumping grounds and hence were also undesired (Brown et al., 2009). Meanwhile, rivers in floodplain areas became channelized to make room for continuing expansion, altogether further modifying the hydro-social contract. The latter became such that cost-effective flood protection services were expected to be provided by a centralized authority structure, which was to convey the water to an external environment and facilitate urbanization (Brown et al., 2009). Such is how the initial development states of the urban water management system in Australia—and Melbourne—were established. An important point to be made here is how ill-suited European stormwater management systems were to Australian rainfall regimes. As shown in

Table 7.1, whereas London and Melbourne receive approximately equal amounts of precipitation per annum, Melbourne receives the bulk of its rainfall over a six-month period. Being 'locked-in' to European models of urban planning as they have evolved over centuries lie at the heart of Melbourne's 'water woes'.

Following the historical transition, the arrival of environmentalism in the late 1960s and early 1970s brought even greater changes and complexities to the hydro-social contract. A greater number of stakeholders began demanding improvements in the urban water management scheme, to have the extensive pollution it was causing in waterways redressed (Brown et al., 2009). Yet, even in some of the changes that resulted, the system did not wholly adapt to evolving times or needs (Brown et al., 2009; Werbeloff & Brown, 2011b). This is presently evidenced in the fact that Melbourne's urban water management scheme has maintained centralized operating structures and procedures, which have ultimately proved to be ineffective in protecting the city against the mounting threats to water security (Brown et al., 2009; Werbeloff & Brown, 2011b). Hence, the vulnerabilities currently observed are due to a combination of present socio-ecological dynamics and past practices and philosophies.

Not only have the traditional ways of engaging with nature and stewarding its resources, as done by the Woi wurrung and Boon wurrung peoples been done away with, but these have been replaced with practices

Table 7.1 Melbourne[a] water use by sector (billion litres)

Year	*Residential*	*Non-residential*	*System losses (e.g. leakages; fire fighting)*	*Western water*[b]	*Total*
2000–2001	303	138	60	14	515
2004–2005	265	118	48	12	433
2008–2009	223	97	41	11	372
2012–2013	252	100	42	13	407
2018–2019	287	108	47	16	458
2020–2021	298	88	38	16	440

[a]Melbourne Water is owned by the state of Victoria and sells bulk water to 4 corporations: City West, Western Water, South East Water and Yarra Valley Water. In July 2021 City West and Western Water merged to create Greater Western Water

[b]Western Water delivers water and sewerage services to Melbourne's Western Suburbs

Source Melbourne Water (2021)

that have consisted of encroaching on nature, permanently transforming it, and doing so through a consolidated power structure that implements processes predicated on institutions established elsewhere, and therefore unsuited for local circumstances and needs (Crosby, 1986; cf. Swatuk, 2001 for the case of Africa). Melbourne's evolution should be understood as a direct reflection of the interests and philosophical positions of the powerful. With the emergence of democratic forces over time, these approaches have been modified to accommodate the interests of others, with the environmental movement noted above being one example. The point to be made here is that achieving water security in Melbourne—as everywhere in the world—is a combination of questioning past practices and engaging in social struggle for more just and sustainable outcomes. Given the socio-economic and socio-political challenges likely to arise from such an approach, policymakers have tended to lean toward technological 'fixes' in the belief that achieving water security is not a political issue. This is the case with Melbourne as is demonstrated below.

Water Profile

Melbourne is primarily reliant on 'freshwater dominated surface water systems', thus, the city is especially vulnerable to the increasingly apparent impacts of climate change such as drought and reduced rainfall (Werbeloff & Brown, 2011a: 3). A majority of Melbourne's water comes from 'remote, forested mountain streams', which are collected in protected catchments (Melbourne Water, 2020a). Melbourne is one of very few cities in the world with catchments that are protected from bushfire pollution and human use and recreation, resulting in high quality drinking water (Melbourne Water, 2020a). The catchments are carefully protected from bushfires, which contaminate the water with ash and sediment, through 'strategic planned burns that reduce the risk of intense bushfires', monitoring technology and periodic patrols for rapid fire identification, and frequent grass-cutting in the summer (Melbourne Water, 2020a). Patrol teams keep the catchment areas safe from human contamination through activities such as recreational boating, fishing and camping, which are treated as serious offences and can result in expensive fines for violators (Melbourne Water, 2020a). Additionally, Parks Victoria leads an annual trapping and baiting programme to clear the areas of animals and pests that could potentially contaminate the catchment areas (Melbourne Water, 2020a).

Melbourne's catchments are connected by streams to some of the city's ten major reservoirs (Melbourne Water, 2020b). On-stream reservoirs collect water from the catchments, while off-stream reservoirs collect water from other sources, such as the recently built Victoria Desalination plant (Melbourne Water, 2020b). The city's reservoirs have a combined storage capacity of 1,810 billion litres of water (Melbourne Water, 2020b). The reservoirs are connected through pipelines so that water can be transferred, as needed, according to rainfall levels and demand variation (Melbourne Water, 2020b). Most of Melbourne's urban water supply derives from the Silvan reservoir, which was built in 1932 (Melbourne Water, 2020e).

Notably, only 30–50% of rainfall in catchment areas reach Melbourne's reservoirs (Melbourne Water, 2020a). A large portion of rainfall in the catchments is either consumed by vegetation, stored in the soil as groundwater, or evaporated into the atmosphere (Melbourne Water, 2020a). In the summer, only about ten percent of rainfall becomes runoff because the soil soaks up most of the rain before it can 'flow into streams' (Melbourne Water, 2020a).

Since the late 1990s, Melbourne's precipitation has been highly uneven. The Millennium drought which lasted more than a decade (circa 1997–2010) created massive challenges for water management in all of Australia's southern cities. As shown in Table 7.1, Melbourne's water consumption fell dramatically over this time period but has increased steadily since the drought ended. As of March 2022, Melbourne Water's reservoirs were 86% full. However, the downward trend in rainfall is predicted to continue punctuated by more extreme events (drought/flood). Additionally, experts predict that Melbourne will face substantial increases in temperatures, and longer warm spells with more days reaching temperatures above 35 °C in the future (Victoria State Government, 2015). As Melbourne becomes hotter and drier, there is an increased risk of bushfires, which can further reduce water supplies (Melbourne Water, 2020d). The devastating outcomes of these temperature increases became apparent in January 2020, as deadly wildfires in New South Wales and Victoria, caused by record high temperatures and prolonged drought, destroyed thousands of homes and impacted millions of hectares of land (BBC, 2020). Further, as a result of lower rainfall levels and higher temperatures, the protected catchment areas become drier and provide less water to the reservoirs (Melbourne Water, 2020a). Thus, Melbourne's reliance on rainfall and surface water systems, where a large portion of water is lost to soil and the atmosphere, is unsustainable and unreliable in the face of increased drought and decreased rainfall resulting from the impacts of climate change.

Population growth further challenges Melbourne's water security. Melbourne is currently Australia's fastest growing city, with a population of about five million residents (ABS, 2020). The capital city of Victoria continues to grow rapidly, with experts estimating Melbourne's population will reach eight million by 2051 (Barry & Coombes, 2018). In 2020–2021, the average water consumption across Melbourne's City, South East and Yarra Valley districts was 159 litres per capita per day (l/c/d). This contrasts markedly with consumption in the Western suburbs which stood at 178 l/c/d (Melbourne Water, 2021). This is an increase from the 2010/2011 fiscal year, when, for 49 out of 52 weeks people in Melbourne used less than 155 litres of water per day following the introduction of the state-wide 'Target 155 program', which will be discussed later in this chapter (Low et al., 2015). In 2020–2021, residential consumption accounted for 69% of Melbourne's water usage across City West, South East and Yarra Valley water supply areas. Twenty-one percent of the water in these areas was used for industry and commercial purposes, and 10% resulted from system losses (Melbourne Water, 2021). Western Water consumption was slightly different: 80% residential; 13% non-residential and only 7% system losses. In 2018–2019, 31% of water consumed by residents was used for taking showers (Melbourne Water, 2019). Additional research shows that roughly half of per person water consumption in Melbourne is related to outdoor consumption such as car washing, sprinklers, and hosing driveways (Heggie, 2019). Despite these somewhat shocking statistics, as shown in Table 7.1, consumption has fallen dramatically since the beginning of the Twenty-first Century. Upon closer scrutiny, one sees three trends: commercial/industrial water usage has decreased significantly; unaccounted for water due to system loss has dramatically decreased; and total residential consumption in 2020–2021 is about equal to that of two decades earlier despite significant population increase.

Customers of Melbourne's South East water utility company in 2019–2020 pay AUD 2.63 per kilolitre for the first 440 kilolitres of water used per day, and AUD 3.35 per kilolitre if they use more than 440 kilolitres in a day (South East Water, 2020b). Therefore, as Melbourne's population continues to grow, so will its water security challenges, particularly in the face of increased demand.

Governance and Management

Melbourne Water Corporation

Melbourne Water Corporation, which is owned entirely by the Victoria State Government, manages the city's catchments and rivers, as well as the city's water supply and sewage services (IbisWorld). Aside from its role as the wholesaler of Melbourne's drinking water, the not-for-profit corporation's operations include managing Melbourne's ten water storage reservoirs, treating most of Melbourne's sewage, producing and supplying recycled water, protecting local creeks and rivers, flood management, implementing projects to improve livability and reduce environmental impacts, and mitigating climate change (IbisWorld).

City of Melbourne

In response to the Millennium Drought, the Melbourne City Government created the 2002 Total Watermark Strategy, which was updated in 2009 and again in 2014 (City of Melbourne, 2014; Low et al., 2015). A key target set for 2018 and 2030 involves increasing the amount of water sourced from 'alternative sources' for city council and the municipal government to improve water quality (City of Melbourne, 2014). Notably, Melbourne became carbon neutral certified in 2013 (CNCA, n.d.). The city aims to be one of the most sustainable cities in the world and works with various stakeholders to attempt to improve the city's integrated water resource management (IWRM) strategies (see Table 7.2) (City of Melbourne, 2014, 2017).

Following extensive community-engagement, the city released its Integrated Water Management (IWM) Plan in 2017, which includes a ten-year stormwater harvesting plan and reviews whether the city has met the 2014 Total Watermark goals (City of Melbourne, 2017). The 2017 report reviews the goals laid out in the 2014 Total Watermark strategy, and claims the city reached most of the 2014 goals, including 'modelling effects of green infrastructure on reducing flooding' and improving flood mitigation measures (City of Melbourne, 2017: 32). However, the 2017 report also acknowledges a failure to sufficiently research areas such as the city's heat island effect and the 'linkages between human health and access to waterways and public open spaces' (City of Melbourne, 2017: 32).

Additionally, although the report includes a diagram mentioning the United Nations Sustainable Development Goals (SDGs), it provides no

Table 7.2 City of Melbourne stakeholder engagement for IWM

Stakeholder group	*Interest/method of engagement*	*Example of proposed/on-going collaboration*
Melbourne Water	– Flood Strategy – Healthy Waterways Strategy – Moonee Ponds Creek Collaboration	Continue to partner with Melbourne Water and other councils to deliver on the relevant actions from the Port Phillip Bay and Westernport Flood Management Strategy
Department of Environment, Land, Water and Planning (DELWP)	– Water for Victoria/IWM forums – Yarra River Action Plan – Climate Change Adaptation Plan – Fishermans Bend Taskforce	Partner with DELWP and others to consider the benefits of an impermeability charge to incentivise the private realm to provide green space, retain rainwater and provide urban cooling and improved amenity
Victorian Planning Authority	– Precinct planning for Arden-Macaulay	Partner with Victorian Planning Authority and Melbourne Water to develop an Integrated Open Space and Drainage Strategy for Arden-Macaulay that builds on international best practice and opportunities to capture water upstream in the Moonee Ponds catchment and implement agreed actions
Environmental Protection Authority Victoria	– State environmental protection policy (Waters of Victoria)	Advocate for a consistent Planning Scheme approach across Victoria for climate change and extreme weather event mitigation including provision for onsite/on-lot flood retention in flood prone catchments

(continued)

Table 7.2 (continued)

Stakeholder group	*Interest/method of engagement*	*Example of proposed/on-going collaboration*
Greater West/South East Water	– Water retailers – IWM plans – Precinct based projects	Continue to partner with Greater West Water, South East Water, Melbourne Water and/or others to further investigate the feasibility of an Alternative Water ring main around the inner city, connecting the many alternative water supplies for optimal use
Resilient Melbourne	– Part of Global Resilient Cities Network funded by Rockefeller Foundation – Network of state, civil society and private sector actors – Project led by Chief Resilience Officer financed by 100 Resilient Cities Initiative	Partner with Resilient Melbourne to develop decision-support tools that encourage water-sensitive urban design and IWM
Cooperative Research Centre for Water-Sensitive Cities	– Academic research entity – Research/action-based research	Partner with academic institutions, such as the CRC for Water-Sensitive Cities to learn from and further best practice
C-40 Cities, ICLEI	– Sharing best practice for water-sensitive urban design	Partner with international associations of cities such as C40 and ICLEI to share and learn from international best practice

details regarding the city's efforts to meet these goals, particularly SDG 6, which pertains to water and sanitation and includes a target to reduce water scarcity (City of Melbourne, 2017; United Nations). The 2017 plan contains three new targets, in addition to the existing targets from the 2014 Total Watermark Report, including ensuring a 'minimum 20 percent of each catchment's surface is considered permeable by 2030' (City of Melbourne, 2017: 13).

Moreover, in 2015, the City of Melbourne engaged the public through roundtables, events, public forums, and online participation to create a document called Future Melbourne 2026 outlining priorities for the city's future (City of Melbourne, 2016). The document includes two sentences describing the goal to 'conserve water and improve the health of... waterways by capturing stormwater' (City of Melbourne, 2016: 11). The document also outlines the goal of including Aboriginal experts in future land management planning. However, it fails to mention Aboriginal people's role in water management and fails to mention any efforts to include Aboriginal participation during the public engagement phases of the report itself (City of Melbourne, 2016).

State of Victoria

As previously mentioned, the State of Victoria owns and operates the municipal water wholesaler known as Melbourne Water (IbisWorld). The state's Ministry for Water sets water targets and restrictions for the state, including Target 155, which was initially implemented in 2008 and aims to encourage residents to limit water usage to 155 litres per day (Low et al., 2015; Victoria State Government, 2020). The initiative was cancelled in 2011, despite evident success in reducing per person water consumption (Ker, 2011). Recently, the programme has been re-instated, and is promoted by both the provincial government and Melbourne's municipal government; however, it is too early to tell if the newly reinstated programme will help reduce per person water usage in Melbourne (Victoria State Government, 2020). Further, the state has implemented five permanent water-saving rules that regulate outdoor water use by limiting what time of day citizens can water lawns and public gardens and prohibiting residents from washing driveways (Victoria State Government, 2019).

Security Through Diversity Approach

Traditionally, water needs of growing populations in Australian urban centres have been met with large-scale infrastructure solutions, delivered through centralized mechanisms to cheaply deliver water to a broad number of people (Werbeloff and Brown, 2011a). However, there has recently been a push to move away from this linear approach to water delivery, in favour of a security through diversity approach (Werbeloff & Brown, 2011a). All three levels of government—federal, state, and municipal water utilities—have promoted the security through diversity approach to water management, 'as a means of maximizing resilience to a range of possible water futures' (Werbeloff & Brown, 2011a: 782). This approach aims to reconfigure the traditional linear approach by harnessing numerous demand and supply initiatives, and recycling previously used water, promoting making use of 'diverse water sources, demand management and multiple scales of water service delivery' (Werbeloff & Brown, 2011a). The approach includes three pillars: diversifying water sources, implementing various initiatives to reduce consumption and manage demand and diversifying at both centralized and decentralized scales (Werbeloff & Brown, 2011a). In one study, researchers found that among senior water officials in Melbourne 'desalination was widely perceived to be the silver bullet solution to the water scarce conditions faced by [the city]' (Werbeloff & Brown, 2011a: 784). Interestingly, this perception directly contrasts the philosophy of the security through diversity approach, which advocates for avoiding over-reliance on a singular mode of infrastructure to deliver municipal water (Werbeloff & Brown, 2011a).

Melbourne Water follows a strategy of maintaining a high reserve in support of water security. At the end of 2021, water storages were at 89.6% of total capacity. Approximately 20% of this stored capacity comes from desalinated water. According to Melbourne Water (2021: 3), 'It's been more than 20 years since we've had water storage supplies at the current level and the Desalination Plant played a major role in this ... Since 2017, around 394 billion litres of desalinated water have contributed to our supply ... For the 2021–2022 year, the Desalination Plant is delivering 125 billion litres of desalinated water'.

The City of Melbourne defines its IWRM approach as 'the coordinated management of all components of the water cycle including water consumption, rainwater, stormwater, wastewater and groundwater, to secure a range of benefits for the wider catchment' (City of Melbourne,

2017). While this definition is promising, Melbourne's approach to water security lacks two important elements that could improve the city's water management approach and allow for greater security diversity and inclusion. Firstly, the city's current approach fails to achieve meaningful inclusion of Indigenous Peoples and environmental stakeholders in decision-making processes. Principle Two of the Dublin-Rio Principles states that 'water development and management should be based on a participatory approach, involving users, planners and policymakers at all levels' (GWP, n.d.: 1). Our vision of this participatory approach involves the direct inclusion of Indigenous peoples at all levels of decision-making in relation to water security.

Secondly, Melbourne's approach to water security neglects some important environmental considerations. While Melbourne's desalination plant was built to include some sustainable measures, such as the green roof and surrounding green area (Water Technology, 2020), the plant still has the potential to cause environmental damage. Recent studies have found that the brine produced by desalination processes, which is returned to the ocean, has the potential to disrupt marine ecosystems, including the potential to harm marine species due to high concentrations of salination, and could also potentially introduce toxic chemicals into the ocean (Gies, 2019). Many scholars have noted the importance of protecting the environment when building water security capacity. Cook and Bakker (2011: 97) note, 'the anthropocentrism ... framing of water security risks neglecting the importance of the ecosystem as an integral component of both human and water security'. Melbourne's approach does consider the environment in many ways, including the conversion of pavement into green spaces to improve permeability (City of Melbourne, 2017). Unfortunately, the city's over-reliance on costly technology, such as desalination, may lead to a persistent ignorance of the limits of the ecosystem. Further, over-reliance on the desalination plant as 'diversity', ignores what Werbeloff and Brown (2011b: 2368) refer to as a 'more integrated blend of supply and demand initiatives'.

Reducing Consumption Through the 'Target 155' Campaign

During the Millennium Drought, policymakers realized the need to reduce residential consumption in Melbourne (Rowley, 2016). In 2008, the state of Victoria implemented various water consumption reduction strategies, including the voluntary 'Target 155' programme, encouraging voluntary water consumption reduction through advertisements on television, billboards, radio and newspapers (Low et al., 2015; Rowley, 2016). In creating the Target 155 programme, the Yarra Valley water utility was charged with consulting a team of experts and behavioural psychologists to find ways to make reducing water consumption a social norm (Rowley, 2016). They began with easy targets, such as giving away free water-reducing showerheads and hose nozzles, and eventually moved toward other steps such as training staff at 80 garden centres in Melbourne to encourage customers to plant drought-resistance native plants (Rowley, 2016).

The Target 155 initiative helped the city reduce per person water usage from 247 litres per day in 2000–2001, to 147 in 2010–2011 (Rowley, 2016). Additionally, a study commissioned by Melbourne's water retailers found 'the T155 Campaign netted 53 GL in water savings from December 2008 to August 2010, based on comparing observed water use to a model-predicted water use without this campaign, after correcting for climate variability' (Low et al., 2015). The campaign also successfully strengthened social norms around reducing water consumption (Rowley, 2016). Despite these successes in reducing Melbourne's water consumption, the Victorian government's Water Minister ended the Target 155 campaign in 2011, claiming the programme had minimal significant outcomes in reducing water consumption in Melbourne, in contrast to reports that found evidence proving otherwise (Ker, 2011). However, the programme has recently been re-instated and is promoted by both the provincial government and Melbourne's municipal government (Victoria State Government, 2020).

Today, the city of Melbourne encourages residents to 'take the Target 155 pledge' to reduce water consumption to 155 litres per person per day, thereby reducing the city's overall water consumption. Melbourne's South East Water company claims that 'right now, all it takes to help reach Target 155 is to each save less than a bucket of water a day' (South East Water, 2020a). Suggestions provided by the city's website to reduce water consumption include taking showers that are one minute shorter than usual, getting leaks fixed, and scraping plates before placing them in the dishwasher, as opposed to rinsing them (Victoria State Government, 2019). The programme also encourages water users to read their water utility bill, which informs customers whether they are meeting Target 155 or not and compares their water consumption to that of their neighbours (Rowley, 2016; Victoria State Government, 2020).

Management Profile

Melbourne Water, the water wholesaler owned by the State of Victoria, provides water to the city through the following three retail distributors: Greater Western Water, Yarra Valley Water and South East Water (Melbourne Water, 2021). Each retailer provides water to citizens in different areas of the metropolitan area (Melbourne Water, 2021). Melbourne Water also supplies water to the rural areas outside of Melbourne, and to water suppliers in Melbourne's outer regions: Barwon Water, Gippsland Water, South Gippsland Water, Western Water and Westernport Water (Melbourne Water, 2021).

The ownership and management of Melbourne's water catchments and their locations can be broken into the following four categories: 90,800 hectares are located in national parks, protected by Melbourne Water and Victoria Parks (both are state-owned entities); 56,300 are located in state forests, managed by Victoria State's Department of Environment, Land, Water, and Planning; 7,500 hectares are owned and managed by Melbourne Water Corporation; and 2,100 hectares are on private land (Melbourne Water, 2020a).

During the Millennium Drought, the state government decided to build a new desalination plant to create a buffer for water storage levels and reduce reliance on Melbourne's reservoirs (Melbourne Water, 2020c). The plant removes 'dissolved salts from seawater' using reverse osmosis technologies (Melbourne Water, 2020c). The water from the plant is distributed through an 84-km-long pipeline (Melbourne Water, 2020c). Notably, the plant runs on 100% renewable energy and has a green roof consisting of native plant species (Water Technology, 2020). Victoria's desalination plant is responsible for keeping Melbourne's water storage levels about eight percent higher than they would be otherwise (Melbourne Water, 2019, 2020c).

However, there is some controversy around the privatization of Victoria's desalination plant. The plant's contract was written as a public–private partnership between the state's Department of Environment, Land, Water, and Planning and the operator of the plant, a consortium called Aquasure (Water Technology, 2020). The consortium comprises three companies: a German mining company called Theiss; an Australian financial services and investment company called Macquarie Capital; and a French water treatment company called Degrémont (Water Technology, 2020). The plant cost AUD 4.5 billion to build and costs over half a million Australian dollars per year to maintain and operate (Poposki, 2020; Rowley, 2016).

Discussion

The threats to water security in Melbourne emanate from both present-day and historical factors. These factors include the dispossession of the environment from the Aboriginal people who initially presided and maintained the land through a distinct cultural lens; followed by the destruction, conversion and minimisation of water in its natural forms and ecosystems overall to make way for population and urban expansion; and the execution of these processes based on frameworks developed in and for external places (Brown et al., 2009; Ives et al., 2013; Oakley & Johnson, 2013; Presland, 2014). Centuries later, authorities have not diverted from or rectified many of these practices in the strategy they have adopted to tackle mounting water security concerns. Instead, government approaches have constituted the perpetuation of the status quo. While Melbourne's strategy has included some demand-side interventions, such as permanent water-saving rules and campaigns such as Target 155, one study found that the city's senior water managers viewed these measures as secondary to supply-side interventions, such as the Victoria desalination plant, which increase access to supply without requiring a departure from the urban water management system currently in place (Werbeloff & Brown, 2011a, 2011b). At the same time, supply-side approaches ask little of consumers regarding behavioural change, and encourage urban sprawl: the more water saved, the more to be supplied to new developments. Desalination-dependent approaches fail to adequately consider potential negative consequences to the environment such as ocean pollution and degradation of marine life habitats, as well as significantly increased energy consumption (Gies, 2019).

Whereas desalination may appear to government as 'diversity of sources', it replicates the high-modern obsession with increased supply. Put differently, is 'enhanced supply' diversity or old wine in new bottles? The Victoria Government's website claims that 'with rainfall and streamflow trends suggesting less water will be available from surface water sources in the future, we will increasingly use desalinated water to maintain water supply resilience' (Victoria State Government, 2019). Further, although initiatives such as the Target 155 programme and permanent water-saving rules have reduced individual, household and industrial water consumption in Melbourne, total use today is about the same as it was at the turn of the Twenty-first Century. Thus, although residential water usage is responsible for over half of Melbourne's water consumption, relying on voluntary residential demand-side reductions in consumption is potentially not a strong enough solution to Melbourne's water concerns, particularly as the population continues to grow.

Notably, the state owns Melbourne's water wholesaler and seems to control a great deal of the efforts to reduce water in Melbourne rather than the City itself. This approach is effective because it ensures regulations apply to a broader range of people whose water resources are connected. However, given that 75% of the state's citizens reside in Greater Melbourne, it seems like the city should play a stronger role in water resources management (World Population Review, 2020). Clearly, the City's 2017 Integrated Urban Water Management Plan is an important step in this direction.

However, it is clear that water security in Melbourne and across Australia is heavily oriented toward high technology and expensive built infrastructure. Is there no room for reimagining less expensive, more inclusive and locally embedded ways and means of building water security? Put slightly differently, there are more ways of 'knowing' than through the narrow lens of Western science. While the city's 2016 Future Melbourne 2026 report does give consideration to including Aboriginal peoples in land management, it fails to include any mention of Aboriginal authority over water management and failed to seek Indigenous inclusion during its public engagement phase. Further, questions arise around desalination, and whose interests the Wonthaggi plant serves, given that it is partly owned by three foreign multinational companies (Water Technology, 2020). It is worth considering whether these companies have the best interests of the public, the environment and Indigenous groups in mind. Without a direct line of communication to the citizen of Melbourne, it seems likely these companies are largely not engaged with the concerns of the public around water security. Thus, the city should consider creating a direct channel for which Indigenous and environmental stakeholders, as well as the public, can communicate concerns to not only the municipal and state governments regarding water management measures as a whole, but also to the companies that own and operate the Wonthaggi desalination plant. This approach would ensure greater accountability and would amplify local voices, allowing them to be heard by those in control of the plant. Therefore, to reflect more accurately the principle of diversification, the city should address the centralized nature of the urban water management system on which it depends to tackle the threats posed to water security, by including a broader range of stakeholders in the process, particularly, Indigenous people, and creating means for direct communications between them and decision-makers, such as the consortium of foreign companies that own a major share of the Wonthaggi desalination plant.

This inclusion is extremely important, as Indigenous people constituted the first people to preside over the area, and held a particular cultural lens through which they perceived water and land which allowed them to rely upon these resources for tens of thousands of years (Ives et al., 2013; Oakley & Johnson, 2013; Presland, 2014). This Indigenous cultural lens persists in Melbourne today among Traditional Owner Groups, for example, who preserve it through activities and initiatives centred on promoting Indigenous cultural heritage within the present-day context. Such groups could be very helpful in transforming Melbourne's approach to urban water management, by providing valuable insight to decision-making processes. Additionally, and more importantly, doing so would arguably be an important step toward reconciliation, especially considering the reality of certain Aboriginal people in remote localities today, who lack access to water (Hall, 2019). Granting these groups management rights over water resources could help make way for this unequal distribution of water resources to be addressed more concretely and urgently.

In addition, the inclusion of other community and environmental stakeholders in the urban water management system could also help the city better embody diversification in its strategy, and thus allow the city to better mitigate the urgent threats to water security that it is facing. The contribution of such actors is highly important, as they advocate for doing things differently, according to what is in the best interest of their communities and nature (see, e.g. Brown et al., 2009: 853). Their inclusion in stakeholder forums and decision-making processes relating to water resources, therefore, could arguably help hold Melbourne's current water managers accountable and lead to the management of water resources in ways that demonstrate consideration for the well-being of all people and the environment.

Conclusion and Recommendations

To manage growing water security pressures, all three levels of government have promoted a security through diversity approach in Melbourne (Werbeloff & Brown, 2011a). However, the city's approach reveals significant limitations when juxtaposed with the idea of attaining security (Werbeloff & Brown, 2011a). This is due to the methods inherent to the approach, constituting a perpetuation of the status quo, and as such, of insecurity. These methods include the enactment of guidelines and restrictions to reduce residential and industrial consumption; the sensitization of residents to foster compliance; and the implementation of sea water desalination to broaden sourcing (Melbourne Water, 2020d; Sousa Júnior et al., 2016; Werbeloff & Brown, 2011a). Desalination is considered of central importance by city water managers, as it vastly expands stock availability without requiring a shift away from the system already in place. That is, a shift away from the vested interests the system incorporates (Werbeloff & Brown, 2011a).

However, questions regarding the potential adverse effects of desalination aside, Melbourne's strategy is not a sustainable approach to urban water management due to existing limitations within the system it relies on. These comprise the following: the centralized nature of the system, which means it is untailored to local needs; its datedness, which means it precedes the emergence of present social and environmental challenges; its restricted adaptive capacity, which enabled the emergence of the present water-related vulnerabilities; and its lack of inclusivity, which left arguably important stakeholders, such as Indigenous, community and environmental actors unable to contribute to management processes (Presland, 2014; Sousa Júnior et al., 2016; Werbeloff & Brown, 2011b). If Melbourne is to be able to respond more effectively to the rapidly increasing pressures of a drying climate and an expanding population, the city's urban water management scheme will need to be reconfigured. Authorities will need to take proactive steps toward creating more inclusive decision-making mechanisms, where voices from organized civil society bodies can be heard and have direct influence in the stewardship of local water resources. Specifically, this process can be launched by creating spaces that facilitate and encourage discussion and collaboration such as town halls, public events and online forums regarding not only the development of strategies for water security but also broader discussions about the value of water and the appropriate content of 'water sensitive urban design'. Ultimately, creating spaces and means for meaningful inclusion of community, environmental and Indigenous groups in decision-making processes would facilitate an important conversation regarding sustainable solutions for urban water security. Enhanced supply may buy time—at a very high financial and environmental cost—but it won't buy long-term urban resilience.

References

Australian Bureau of Statistics (ABS). (2020, March 25). *Regional population growth, Australia, 2018–19*. Available at: https://www.abs.gov.au/ausstats/abs@.nsf/mf/3218.0. Accessed 5 April 2022.

Barry, M. E., & Coombes, P. J. (2018). Planning resilient water resources and communities: The need for a bottom-up systems approach. *Australasian Journal of Water Resources, 22*(2), 113–136.

BBC. (2020, January 31). *Australia fires: A visual guide to the bushfire crisis*. Available at: https://www.bbc.com/news/world-australia-50951043. Accessed 27 June 2022.

BLCAC (Bunurong Land Council Aboriginal Corporation). (n.d.). Available at: https://www.bunuronglc.org/. Accessed 5 April 2022.

Brown, R. R., Keath, N., & Wong, T. H. F. (2009). Urban water management in cities: Historical, current and future regimes. *Water Science and Technology: A Journal of the International Association on Water Pollution Research, 59*(5), 847–855.

City of Melbourne. (2014). *Total watermark—City as a catchment*. City of Melbourne.

City of Melbourne. (2016). *Future Melbourne 2026*. City of Melbourne.

City of Melbourne. (2017). *Municipal integrated water management plan*. City of Melbourne.

CNCA (Carbon Neutral Cities Alliance). (n.d.). *Melbourne, Victoria, Australia*. Available at: https://carbonneutralcities.org/cities/melbourne/. Accessed 5 April 2022.

Cook, C., & Bakker, K. (2011). Water security: Debating an emerging paradigm. *Global Environmental Change, 22*(1), 94–102.

Crosby, A. W. (1986). *Ecological imperialism: The biological expansion of Europe 900–1900*. Cambridge University Press.

Gies, E. (2019, February 7). Slaking the world's thirst with seawater dumps toxic brine in Oceans. *Scientific American*. Available at: https://www.scientificamerican.com/article/slaking-the-worlds-thirst-with-seawater-dumps-toxic-brine-in-oceans/. Accessed 5 April 2022.

Global Water Partnership (GWP). (n.d.). *Dublin-Rio principles*. Available at: https://www.gwp.org/contentassets/05190d0c938f47d1b254d6606ec6bb04/dublin-rio-principles.pdf. Accessed 5 April 2022.

Hall, N. L. (2019). Challenges of WASH in remote Australian Indigenous communities. *Journal of Water, Sanitation and Hygiene for Development, 9*(3), 429–437.

Heggie, J. (2019). Failing rains and thirsty cities: Australia's growing water problem. *National Geographic*. Available at: https://www.nationalgeographic.com/environment/2019/08/partner-content-australia-water-problem/. Accessed 5 April 2022.

IbisWorld. (n.d.). *Melbourne Water Corporation—Premium Company Report Australia*. Available at: https://www.ibisworld.com.au/australian-company-research-reports/electricity-gas-water-waste-services/melbourne-water-corporation-company.html accessed 5 April 2022.

Ives, C. D., Beilin, R., Gordon, A., Kendal, D., Hahs, A. K., & Mcdonnell, M. J. (2013). Local assessment of Melbourne: The biodiversity and social-ecological dynamics of Melbourne, Australia. In T. Elmqvist, M. Fragkias, J. Goodness, B. Güneralp, P. J. Marcotullio, R. I. McDonald, S. Parnell, M. Schewenius, M. Sendstad, K. C. Seto, & C. Wilkinson (Eds.), *Urbanization, biodiversity and ecosystem services: Challenges 385 and opportunities: A global assessment* (pp. 385–407). Springer.

Johnson, S. (2007). *The Ghost Map*. Penguin Random House.

Ker, P. (2011, March 3). Dumped Target 155 water scheme 'was working'. *The Sydney Morning Herald*.

Low, K., Grant, S., Hamilton, A., Gan, K., Saphores, J., Arora, M., & Feldman, D. (2015). Fighting drought with innovation: Melbourne's response to the Millennium Drought in Southeast Australia. *Wires Water, 2*(4), 315–328.

Melbourne Water. (2019). *Melbourne's Water Outlook 2020*. Available at: https://media-2.yvw.com.au/inline-files/ANNUAL%20WATER%20OUTLOOK%202020_long%20version_Final.pdf. Accessed 23 March 2022.

Melbourne Water. (2020a, March 31). *Water catchments*. Available at: https://www.melbournewater.com.au/community-and-education/about-our-water/why-melbournes-water-tastes-great-tap/water-catchments. Accessed 5 April 2022.

Melbourne Water. (2020b, March 31). *Water storage reservoir*. Available at: https://www.melbournewater.com.au/community-and-education/about-our-water/why-melbournes-water-tastes-great-tap/water-storage. Accessed 5 April 2022.

Melbourne Water. (2020c, April 16). *Desalination*. Available at: https://www.melbournewater.com.au/water/securing-our-water-supply/how-water-sector-taking-action/desalination. Accessed 5 April 2022.

Melbourne Water. (2020d, February 15). *Our water supply challenges*. Available at: https://www.melbournewater.com.au/water/securing-our-water-supply/our-water-supply-challenges. Accessed 5 April 2022.

Melbourne Water. (2020e). *Silvan Reservoir* (28 March). Available at: https://www.melbournewater.com.au/community-and-education/about-our-water/why-melbournes-water-tastes-great-tap/water-storage/silvan accessed 5 April 2022.

Melbourne Water. (2021). *Melbourne's Water Outlook 2022*. Available at: https://welcome.gww.com.au/sites/default/files/2021-12/Melbourne%27s-Water-Outlook-2022.PDF. Accessed 23 March 2022.

Moran, A. (2006). *Water supply options for Melbourne: An examination of costs and availabilities of new water supply sources for Melbourne and other urban areas in Victoria* (Occasional Paper). Melbourne: Institute of Public Affairs.

Moses, D. (2000). An antipodean genocide? The origins of the genocidal moment in the colonization of Australia. *Journal of Genocide Research, 2*(1), 89–106.

Oakley, S., & Johnson, L. (2013). Place-taking and place-making in waterfront renewal, Australia. *Urban Studies, 50*(2), 341–355.

O'Bryan, K. (2017). More aqua nullius? The Traditional Owner Settlement Act 2010 and the neglect of indigenous rights to manage inland water resources. *Melbourne University Law Review, 40*(2), 547–593.

Ponting, C. (1991). *A green history of the world*. Penguin Books.

Poposki, C. (2020, May 20). Melbourne desalination plant costs tax-payers an eye-watering $649 million in annual operating charges. *Daily Mail Australia*.

Presland, G. (2014). A boggy question: Differing views of wetlands in 19th century Melbourne. In M. Gjerde & E. Petrovic (Eds.), *UHPH_14: Landscapes and ecologies of urban and planning history. Proceedings of the 12th conference of the Australasian Urban History/Planning History Group* (pp 617–630). Australasian Urban History/Planning History Group and Victoria University of Wellington.

Rowley, S. (2016, November 1). Australia's lesson for a thirsty California. *The New York Times*.

Sousa Júnior, W., Baldwin, C., Camkin, J., Fidelman, P., Silva, O., Neto, S., & Smith, T. (2016). Water: Drought, crisis and governance in Australia and Brazil. *Water, 8*(11), 493.

South East Water. (2020a). *Target 155 to make every drop count*. Available at: https://southeastwater.com.au/CurrentProjects/Programs/Pages/Target155.aspx. Accessed 5 April 2022.

South East Water. (2020b). *Prices and charges*. Available at: https://southeastwater.com.au/Residential/Pages/WaterPricesCharges.aspx. Accessed 5 April 2022.

State Government of Victoria. (2019a). *The aboriginal water program*. Available at: https://www.water.vic.gov.au/aboriginal-values/the-aboriginal-water-program. Accessed 5 April 2022.

State Government of Victoria. (2019b). *Formal recognition processes in Victoria*. Available at: https://www.aboriginalvictoria.vic.gov.au/traditional-owner-formal-recognition-victoria/formal-recognition-processes-victoria. Accessed 5 April 2022.

Swatuk, L. A. (2001). The brothers Grim: Modernity and 'international' relations in Southern Africa. In K. C. Dunn & T. M. Shaw (Eds.), *Africa's challenge to international relations theory* (pp. 163–184). Palgrave.

United Nations. (n.d.). *Sustainable development goals—Goal 6: Ensure access to water and sanitation for all*. Available at: https://www.un.org/sustainabledevelopment/water-and-sanitation/. Accessed 5 April 2022.

Victoria State Government. (2015). *Climate-ready Victoria—Greater Melbourne*. Available at: https://www.climatechange.vic.gov.au/__data/assets/pdf_file/0019/60742/Greater-Melbourne.pdf. Accessed 5 April 2022.

Victoria State Government. (2019). *Permanent water saving rules*. Available at: https://www.water.vic.gov.au/liveable/using-water-wisely/advice-and-rules/permanent-water-saving-rules. Accessed 5 April 2022.

Victoria State Government. (2020, January 16). *Target 155*. Available at: https://www.water.vic.gov.au/liveable/using-water-wisely/target-155-target-your-water-use. Accessed 5 April 2022.

Water Technology. (2020). *Wonthaggi desalination plant*. Available at: https://www.water-technology.net/projects/wonthaggidesalinatio/. Accessed 5 April 2022.

Werbeloff, L., & Brown, R. (2011a). Security through diversity: Moving from rhetoric to practice. *Water Science and Technology, 64*(4), 781–788.

Werbeloff, L., & Brown, R. (2011b). Working towards sustainable urban water management: The vulnerability blind spot. *Water Science and Technology, 64*(12), 2362–2369.

World Population Review. (2020). *Victoria population 2020*. Available at: https://worldpopulationreview.com/territories/victoria-population/. Accessed 5 April 2022.

Wurundjeri Woi Wurrung Cultural Heritage Aboriginal Corporation. (n.d.). Available at: https://www.wurundjeri.com.au/. Accessed 5 April 2022.

CHAPTER 8

MENA Megacities Approaching Day Zero: A Comparative Study Between Cairo and Istanbul

Elena Edo, Goncha Sadayeva, Nesma Hassan, and Larry Swatuk

Introduction

Urban water scarcity is a growing global dilemma faced by numerous megacities. Water security could be defined as 'sustainable access, on a watershed basis, to adequate quantities of water, of acceptable quality, to ensure human and ecosystem health' (Bakker et al., 2010). To tackle the water security challenge in general, states have committed to developing functioning integrated water resources management (IWRM) systems at the Basin level by 2030 as part of the Sustainable Development Goals (SDGs). IWRM is a holistic approach of water management based on

E. Edo · G. Sadayeva · N. Hassan · L. Swatuk (✉)
University of Waterloo, Waterloo, ON, Canada
e-mail: lswatuk@uwaterloo.ca

E. Edo
e-mail: eedo@uwaterloo.ca

L. Swatuk and C. Cash (eds.), *The Political Economy of Urban Water Security under Climate Change*, International Political Economy Series,
https://doi.org/10.1007/978-3-031-08108-8_8

the four key principles of the 1992 Dublin Statement on Water and Sustainable Development: '(1) fresh water is a finite and vulnerable resource essential to sustain life, development and the environment; (2) water development and management should be based on a participatory approach, involving users, planners and policy-makers at all levels; (3) women play a central part in the provision, management and safeguarding of water; and (4) water has an economic value in all its competing uses and should be recognized as an economic good' (ICWE, 1992).

In assessing the likelihood of achieving urban water security, five factors should be considered in relation to IWRM: socio-demographic, economic, technological, environmental and governance (SETEG) (Romero-Lankao & Gnatz, 2016). Socio-demographic factors refer to satisfactory access to water and sanitation; economic factors refer to water demand and the allocation of budgets; technological factors refer to the adequacy of the water supply and sanitation (WSS) infrastructure; environmental factors refer to climate change, watershed uses and water pollution and contamination; and, finally, governance factors refer to institutional frameworks, plans or strategies and performance (Romero-Lankano & Gnatz, 2016).

Two megacities in the Middle East and North Africa region with different geographical characteristics—Cairo, Egypt and Istanbul and Turkey—are experiencing day zero type scenarios that pose a serious threat to the sustainable management of water resources. Water scarcity is a rapidly growing problem in both cities where the infrastructure and wastewater treatment facilities seem to be insufficient in the long-term perspective. Both cities continue to mobilize their resources within different organizational frameworks to address water scarcity, mainly caused by supply shortages, population growth and climate change impacts. This chapter provides an in-depth analysis of the cities while critically reflecting on the adequacy of the different approaches they adopt toward achieving water security.

G. Sadayeva
e-mail: gsadayev@uwaterloo.ca

N. Hassan
e-mail: n25hassa@uwaterloo.ca

The chapter is organized as follows. The Background section provides a review of the general situation in Cairo and Istanbul. It assesses their water resources, needs, infrastructure, governance and actors and overall performance. This is followed by two sections which describe Cairo's and Istanbul's key challenges for achieving water security, current efforts toward sustainability and opportunities for moving away from 'day zero'. The penultimate section, labelled 'Discussion', analyses the research by comparing both cities within the context of the SETEG framework described above. The final section presents our conclusions and recommendations.

Background

Cairo

Cairo, Egypt's sprawling capital, is situated in northern Egypt and has an arid, dry climate. It receives 24.7 mm of rainfall annually, which is a 25–50% decrease caused by climate change (ECC, 2014). Cairo has a yearly average evaporation rate of 10.1 mm/year (Abd Ellah, 2020; El-Sayed, 2018). Cairo's main water resource is the Nile River and is situated downstream of more than 40 Egyptian and African cities and towns. Under the 1959 agreement, Egypt receives 55.5 billion cubic metres annually from the Nile (El-Sayed, 2018), part of which supplies 90% of Cairo's water (Myllylä, 1995). This is expected to decrease by 25% in the years of filling the Grand Ethiopian Renaissance Dam (GERD) (Schlanger, 2019). Cairo is also surrounded by groundwater aquifers which supply 4.6 billion cubic metres of water annually (Abd Ellah, 2020; El-Sayed, 2018). However, they are becoming increasingly contaminated from industry discharge.

Cairo has 20.5 million inhabitants (Macrotrends, 2020a) who consume an average of 330 litres/capita/day (lcd) (MHUUC, 2012). Much of the unaccounted-for water is attributed to the informal settlements in the city as they install self-made pipe extensions to the formal water supply infrastructure (Khalil, 2019). The informal settlements account for approximately 60% of Cairo (Khalil, 2019). Currently, Cairo is working toward extending its WSS infrastructure—part of which is over a century old (Sada Elbalad, 2017)—to incorporate the expected population of 38 million by 2050 (GOPP, 2008).

Egypt's WSS institutional framework is centralized and operates at the national level (World Bank, 2014). The Ministry of Housing, Utilities and Urban Communities (MHUUC) is the main actor responsible for decision-making and supervision. The Cairo and Alexandria Potable Water Organization (CAPWO) is responsible for the planning and implementing infrastructure investments in Cairo and Alexandria and reports to the MHUUC. The Holding Company for Water and Wastewater (HCWW) performs the operation and management of assets through its subsidiaries—the Water and Sanitation Companies (WSCs). The HCWW is responsible for developing master plans that are then implemented by the WSCs and monitors their performance. The Egyptian Water Regulatory Agency (EWRA) regulates the quality of WSS service delivery, monitors WSS tariffs and undertakes consumer protection responsibilities. It operates under the MHUUC. Table 8.1 provides a summary of the different actors and their roles.

Cairo is constantly expanding its water and wastewater infrastructure to accommodate its growing population. The current potable water capacity is 7,233,000 m^3/day and is expected to double by 2027 (MHUUC, 2012). Regarding its reuse of wastewater, Cairo has six wastewater treatment plants with a collective capacity of 4,290,000 m^3/day, which is also expected to double by 2027 (MHUUC, 2012). Cairo adopts a tiered pricing system (see Table 8.2). The cost of domestic water in Cairo ranges from 0.65 L.E. to 3.15 L.E. (Daif, 2018), and 3.00 L.E. to 10.00 L.E. for industrial use (Egypt Today, 2018).[1]

There have been ongoing efforts to introduce effective water governance and management in Egypt and Cairo that are discussed at length in Sect. 3. Although there have been national efforts such as establishing a specific water sector regulator (the EWRA), establishing water laws and incorporating IWRM into the National Water Resources Plan, there remain institutional challenges in overlapping responsibilities, poor law enforcement and outdated plans. Additionally, while the national and local governments acknowledge the risks of increased droughts due to climate change, there is no climate change mitigation strategy relevant to Cairo in place. Egypt is also a powerful member of the Nile basin Initiative set to achieve sustainable strategies for the transboundary water source.

[1] L.E. stands for livre égyptienne or Egyptian pound. As of April, 2022, 1 LE = 0.05 USD.

Table 8.1 Main institutions in the WSS sector in Egypt

Organization	*Main roles and responsibilities*
Financing	
Ministry of Finance	Allocation of capital for WSS sector
Policy Making	
MHUUC	Established in 1996 Provides leadership for the WSS sector, sets policies and coordinates investment programmes Oversees agencies and companies including EWRA, HCWW, NOPWASD and CAPWO
MWRI	Sets standards for discharges into the Nile basin Development, distribution and management of water resources Development of operations and maintenance Assesses water quality of various water sources
Ministry of Health	Monitors municipal water quality
Ministry of Environmental Affairs	Environmental planning, policy setting and legislation Oversees environmental legislation enforcement
Infrastructure Delivery	
CAPWO	Investment planning, design and supervision of construction of WSS infrastructure in Greater Cairo and Alexandria
Service Delivery	
HCWW	Established in 2004 Public owned company Helps to improve the performance of WSCs and improve their management practices
WSCs	Provides drinking water and wastewater services on the governorate level Maintenance work and repairs
Regulation	
EWRA	Established in 2004 Ensures sustainability and quality of services at reasonable prices

There are three relevant government plans. First, the National Vision 2030 addresses the national economy and sustainable development and encompasses 11 programmes relevant to water, sanitation and sustainability. Second, the National Water Resources Plan 2037 focuses on developing new water supplies, strengthening demand management, enhancing water quality control and ensuring sustainability (World Bank,

Table 8.2 Water systems in Cairo and Istanbul

	Cairo	*Istanbul*
Needs	• The current population of 20.5 million (Macrotrends, 2020a) • Expected to grow to 38 million by 2050 (GOPP, 2008) • Meet the water demand of 330 litres/capita/day • Improve supply to informal settlements. 60% of Cairo's areas are classified as informal (Khalil, 2019) • Reduce heavy wastewater discharges and drainage to River Nile and its aquifers (Abd-Elaty et al., 2019) • The yearly average evaporation rate attains 10.1 mm/year (El-Sayed, 2018)	• The current population is 15 million (World Population Review, n.d.) • Expected to grow to up to 40 million by 2050 (Saatci, 2013) • Average daily water supply to Istanbul: 2,733,288 m^3/day • Improve water supply to informal settlements. Approximately 70% of the housing stock in Istanbul are classified as informal (Uzun et al., 2010) • Annual precipitation is 812.8 mm throughout the year (Weather Atlas) • Gross water demand in the city is estimated to be 175L/capita, and this figure is expected to reach 225L/capita by 2050 including industrial usage (Cuceloglu et al., 2017) • More demand in European side (leading to the transfer of water from Asian to European side)

	Cairo	*Istanbul*
Actors	• International: USAID for funding, EU for technical assistance • Regional: Nile basin countries through the Nile basin Initiative • National: Ministry of Housing, Utilities and Urban Communities; Ministry of Water Resources and Irrigation; Ministry of Agriculture and Land Reclamation; Ministry of Water Supply and Sanitation Facilities; Egyptian Water and Wastewater Regulatory Agency; Holding Company for Water and Wastewater • Municipal: Cairo and Alexandria Potable Water Organization (CAPWO). Water Sanitation Company (WSC) • Local: residents, informal settlers, industry	• International: EU IPA Regional development programmes • National: Ministry of Forestry and Water Affairs (MoFWA); Turkish Water Institute (SUEN) • Municipal: Istanbul Water and Sewerage Administration (ISKI) • Local: residents, informal settlers, industry

(continued)

Table 8.2 (continued)

	Cairo	*Istanbul*
Resources	**The River Nile** • The assigned amount of Nile water to Egypt is about 55.5 billion cubic metres a year **Groundwater Aquifers** • Cairo: the withdrawal quantity of groundwater from the aquifer system is 4.6 BCM a year (El-Sayed, 2018) • 78.9% of the groundwater is safe for human consumption (El-Sayed, 2018) **Rainfall** • There are 14.7 days of rain in Cairo, amounting to 24.7 mm accumulated precipitation (Weather Atlas, n.d.-a)	• Surface water collected in reservoirs of Asian and European side: Bosphorus, Eastern Thrace, Istranca stream, Black Sea basin • 98% of water resources in İstanbul are surface water resources, and 2% from groundwater (ISKI, n.d.-a) • 18 surface water resources in İstanbul: one natural lake, eight dams, eight regulators and embankments (ISKI, n.d.-a) • 18 drinking water reservoirs operate to meet the demand for potable water in Istanbul European side resources: • Terkos, Alibeykoy, Büyükçekmece, Sazlıdere Asian side resources: • Ömerli, Darlık and Elmalı Resources in neighbouring cities (i.e. outside Istanbul's watershed): • Kazandere, Papucdere reservoirs; Istranca River; Melen system (Cuceloglu et al., 2017) • The total annual yield of drinking water resources: 1,660,000 m^3/year (ISKI, n.d.-a)

	Cairo	*Istanbul*
Infrastructure	• Drinking water capacity: 7,233,000 m^3/day (MHUUC, 2012) • Wastewater capacity: 4,290,000 m^3/day (MHUUC, 2012) • 6 wastewater treatment plants • Cost of water for domestic use in Cairo: 0–10 cubic metres: 0.65 L.E 11–20 cubic metres: 1.60 L.E 21–30 cubic metres: 2.25 L.E 0–40 cubic metres: 2.75 L.E >40 cubic metres: 3.15 L.E • Range of cost of water for industrial use: 3.00—10.00 L.E	• Greater Melen project, providing 1.18 billion m^3 water per year (3 million m^3/d) until the year 2040 (Altinbilek, 2006) • Average water delivered to the city: 2,733,388 m^3/day (ISKI, n.d.-a) • 21 Drinking Water Treatment Plants Capacity: 4,428,860 m^3/day (ISKI, n.d.-a) • 88 Wastewater Treatment Plants Capacity: 5,815,910 m^3/day (ISKI, n.d.-a) • 150 Water Storage Tanks Volume: 1 million 727 thousand 080 m^3 (ISKI, n.d.-a)
Outside Issues	• Arid, desert climate with minimal rainfall. Rainfall has further decreased by 25–50% due to climate change • Discharge of waste from the 43 towns between the Aswan Dam and Cairo, as well as other upstream African cities and towns • Contamination from industry • Grand Ethiopian Renaissance Dam: provisioned to decreased Egypt's water supply from the Nile by 25%	• Water availability and annual precipitation is predicted to diminish by 2050 due to climate change • Surface water pollution is mainly caused by factories and plants in Istanbul (ISKI, 2019) • Existing water reservoirs are polluted due to illegal settlements on watershed zones (Van Leeuwen & Sjerps, 2016)

(continued)

Table 8.2 (continued)

	Cairo	*Istanbul*
Effective Water Governance and Management	• Nationally: - IWRM incorporated in the MWRI plan - Establishing a special regulatory agency: EWRA - MWRI agreement with the EU to use modern irrigation and water treatment systems • Regionally: participation in the Nile basin Initiative for peaceful transboundary water agreements	• Nationally - Water Framework Directive (WFD) adopted in 2000 with a new, combined approach into EU water policy - WFD incorporated the whole aspects of IWRM in its Article 3 - SCADA (Supervisory Control and Data Acquisition) technology was provided by ISKI for potable water distribution to reduce water losses and monitor water quality
Relevant Government Plans	• National Vision 2030 • National Water Resource Plan 2037 • Greater Cairo Urban Development Strategy 2050	• Turkey's National Climate Change Adaptation Strategy and Action Plan (2011–2023) • Environmental Law (1983) • Water Pollution Control Regulation (1988) • Environmental Impact Assessment (EIA) in Environmental Law (1993) • Regulation on Water Pollution Control (2004) • Legislation related to Protection of watershed and preparation of watershed management plans (2012) • Legislation related to surface water quality for drinking water and water pollution control (2012) • Legislation related to the protection of groundwater resources (2012) • Melen Project from Melen River basin to Istanbul

	Cairo	*Istanbul*
SDG 6 Country Performance	• Overall Performance: Moderately Improving • Target 6.1: On track for maintaining the target. 98.4% of the population using at least basic drinking water services • Target 6.2: Stagnating efforts. 93.2% of the population using at least basic sanitation services • Target 6.3: (no data on improvement status). 28.4% of anthropogenic wastewater receives treatment • Target 6.4: (no data on improvement status). 159.9% freshwater withdrawal of total renewable water resources, causing water stress. 2.8 m3/year/capita of groundwater depletion • Target 6.5: 40% implementation of IWRM, which is incorporated in national plans. There is no data on its implementation on all levels • Target 6.6: no data	• Overall Performance: Moderately Improving • Target 6.1: On track for maintaining the target. 98.9% of the population using at least basic drinking water services • Target 6.2: On track for maintaining the target. 96.4% of the population using at least basic sanitation services • Target 6.3: Moderately improving. 48.8% of anthropogenic wastewater receives treatment • Target 6.4: (no data on improvement status). 27.5% freshwater withdrawal of total renewable water resources, causing water stress. 6.5 m^3/year/capita of groundwater depletion • Target 6.5: 70% implementation of IWRM, which was ranked as medium-high performance by the UNEP report for SDG 60.5 • Target 6.6: no data

2014). Third, the Greater Cairo Urban Development Strategy 2050 focuses on the economic development of Greater Cairo and expects the economic returns to trickle-down to water and sanitation infrastructure—especially that of slums.

In 2019, Egypt in general, and Cairo by extension, have been 'moderately improving' their actions toward the sixth Sustainable Development Goal (SDG 6): Clean Water and Sanitation (Bertelsmann Stiftung & SDSN, 2019). Particularly, Egypt has been on track for maintaining target 6.1 with 98.4% of the population (on record) using at least basic drinking water services (Bertelsmann Stiftung & SDSN, 2019). 93.8% of Egypt's population has access to basic sanitation services, which has been a stagnating effort. On the other hand, Egypt's performance for SDG target 6.4 is decreasing in the freshwater withdrawal but improving in groundwater depletion. Egypt withdraws 159.9% of freshwater as a percentage of total renewable water resources, but also maintains a small 2.8 m^3/year/capita of groundwater depletion (Bertelsmann Stiftung & SDSN, 2019). Egypt's degree of IWRM implementation is 40% in accordance with the National Water Resources Plan. The challenge with the above data is that they do not accurately reflect informal settlements, and therefore true performance may be poorer than the numbers shown above. Table 8.1 provides a summary of WSS in Cairo in comparison to Istanbul.

Istanbul

Istanbul is a transcontinental city of Turkey situated in Europe and Asia facing the Bosphorus Strait and Golden Horn, between the Black Sea to its North and the Sea of Marmara to its South. Because of its geography, the city has a transitional Mediterranean characteristic resulting in various types of microclimates in its different zones, such as humid subtropical and oceanic. Annual precipitation is 812.8 mm (Weather Atlas, n.d.-b). Istanbul has a population of 15 million as of 2020 (World Population Review, n.d.; Macrotrends, 2020b) and is projected to reach 40 million by 2050 (Saatci, 2013). As one of the 38 megacities in the world, the city has experienced exponential population growth over the last century and sets a clear example of urban water scarcity. Istanbul is characterized by an unproportionate distribution of its water resources and population. Although only 30% of the population lives on the Asian side of Istanbul, it holds 77% of the water resources, creating challenges to maintain an uninterrupted water supply for the whole city (Cuceloglu et al., 2017).

The water systems of this megacity are composed of dams, reservoirs, water treatment plants and pipelines with a total length of 17,000 km. According to the most recent information provided by the Istanbul Water and Sewerage Administration (ISKI), the average water supply to the city was 2,733,388 m^3/day. 98% of the city's water resources is made up of surface water resources. Currently, a total of 18 surface water resources provide water supply to Istanbul in various capacities, including a natural lake, eight dams, eight regulators and embankments. Furthermore, groundwater resources—which amount to 161 water wells and spring water bodies—constitute 2% of the drinking water demand. Some of the drinking water reservoirs, namely the Kazandere reservoir, Papucdere reservoir, Istranca River and the Melen system are in the neighbouring cities outside of Istanbul's watershed (Cuceloglu et al., 2017). However, most of the reservoirs (Terkos, Alibeykoy, Büyükçekmece, Sazlıdere) are situated on the European side and three (Ömerli, Darlık and Elmalı) on the Asian side of Istanbul. Among the mentioned water resources, the Ömerli Watershed is the major contributor, providing approximately 32% of the total freshwater supply. Regarding wastewater management, 88 wastewater treatment plants operate in Istanbul with a capacity of 5,815,910 m^3/day (ISKI, n.d.-a).

Water resources management in Turkey involves many stakeholders at the decision-making and executive levels. The Ministry of Forestry and Water Affairs (MoFWA) holds the key responsibility for water resources management, including surface and groundwater planning. Turkish Water Institute (SUEN, n.d.), under the authority of MoFWA, is involved in developing long-term sustainable strategies and national policies for water management (World Bank, 2016). The water management system of Istanbul Province, including WSS, lies under the responsibility of the Istanbul Water and Sewerage Administration (ISKI), which was established in 1981. Being a public utility of the Istanbul Metropolitan Municipality, ISKI performs its functions with an independent budget where most of its investments are made through the income generated from water sales (ISKI, 2019).

Historically, Istanbul has always faced water scarcity because of being located remotely from potable water resources. To address this persistent problem, big underground reservoirs were constructed to curb water scarcity and meet the water demand of its population. However, considering the unprecedented scale of urbanization at present, managing water is more complex than ever (Easton et al., 2017). Istanbul has made significant efforts to provide sufficient drinking water and sanitation through water and wastewater treatment systems. However, the city's water resources are threatened in the long run by the impacts of climate change, unplanned urbanization and uncontrolled settlements in watershed areas, causing water pollution, groundwater depletion and saltwater intrusion (Van Leeuwen & Sjerps, 2016). In this regard, Turkey has made considerable progress in its water policy framework by formulating various laws and regulations on water management and environmental protection (Demirbilek & Benson, 2019). Moreover, several projects have been initiated toward the long-term solution for water security in Istanbul. The implementation of the Greater Melen project on the Asian side which passes through the Bosphorus Strait via a pipeline of 189 km in length and is targeted to meet the water demands of the European side. This project is set to provide 1.18 billion m^3 year (3 million m^3/day) until the year 2040 (Altinbilek, 2006).

According to recent SDSN data, Turkey in general, and Istanbul by extension, has moderate progress toward SDG 6, although year-on-year trends show no change (Bertelsmann Stiftung & SDSN, 2019). In a recent study, the Economist Impact scores Istanbul's performance toward sustainable water use at 71.8 on a scale of 0—100. This places it 25th out of 51 cities in the study. In comparison, Cairo scored 49.7 and was ranked 45th (see https://impact.economist.com/sustainability/project/water-optimisation/calculator-app/?city=Istanbul).

Key Challenges in Achieving Water Security in Cairo

Cairo's geography, economy and institutional structure create a myriad of challenges in ensuring water security. Cairo is faced with the mismanagement of water resources and an increase in water crowding. Additionally, its trend in water governance raises some issues. These challenges can be broadly divided into demand-side and supply-side challenges.

Demand-Side Challenges

To begin with, Cairo faces an overwhelmingly increasing demand for water. Cairo's population is projected to almost double by 2050, reaching 38 million inhabitants (GOPP, 2008). This is compounded by the fact that Cairenes have one of the highest urban water consumption rates worldwide: 330 l/c/d (MHUUC, 2012). This exacerbates Cairo's vulnerability because 90% of Cairo's drinking water is drawn from the Nile (Myllylä, 1995)—an amount expected to decrease due to GERD and climate change. GERD is expected to reduce Egypt's water intake by 25% (Schlanger, 2019). Therefore, urban growth will further increase water stress. Furthermore, Cairo has excessively exceeded its watershed—a phenomenon common to urban areas (Hoekstra et al., 2018), and its decision-makers fail to adopt a watershed perspective.

The second challenge that Cairo faces is its urban-scape. In an interview on Maspero Memory (2016), vernacular architect Hasan Fathy explains that the modern planning and architecture of Cairo imitate Europe's and are incompatible with Cairo's climate. As opposed to the traditional structures of old Cairo, modern Cairo creates the heat island effect, which increases heat and evaporation and decreases water absorption. Additionally, Cairo's per capita share of green spaces is only three m^2 which may be compared with Paris (15 m^2), Athens (23 m^2) and Vienna (64 m^2) (MHUUC, 2012). These factors ultimately increase the water demand of nature, humans and the built environment. Cairo's modern urban-scape also causes flooding from rainfall every winter, drowning the city and requiring the deployment of hundreds of trucks to drain the rainwater (Almal News, 2020).

Supply-Side Challenges

Fundamentally, the overarching supply-side challenge is that water security is not a priority of Cairo's government, despite it being water resource-poor. The Greater Cairo Urban Development Strategy's primary focus is economic development (MHUUC, 2012). This could be because the National Water Resources Plan mainly addresses large water—i.e. agriculture—and does not prioritize urban water supply and sanitation (WSS). Nonetheless, this lack of prioritization creates challenges in governance and water management.

There is disjointed coordination between governance actors (Myllylä, 1995) that is evident in the lack of alignment across the various national and municipal development plans. This results in competing demands and, at times, unfinished efforts. There is also a gap between policy-making and implementation (Khalil, 2019; Myllylä, 1995), and between government plans and day-to-day affairs (Khalil, 2019). Another common underlying challenge is the inequitable delivery of water supply in informal settlements. As with all other case studies in this collection, a great portion of Cairo's population resides in informal settlements (GOPP, 2008) and rely on illegal, self-installed pipe extensions (Khalil, 2019). Although the national government has been extending the formal water and wastewater infrastructure post-Arab Spring to include informal settlements, the services' inconsistency, poor water quality, unreliable accountability of charged fees and the cost of water still exclude many informal settlers (Khalil, 2019).

In terms of management, although the government is striving to meet the city's rising demands, the fact remains that Cairo relies almost entirely on a transboundary resource: The Nile River. Although Egypt has regional negotiation powers over the Nile and the timeframe of filling the GERD, Egypt (and Cairo by extension) are vulnerable. Another entrenched management challenge is the poor infrastructure system, which has not been upgraded for 100 years (Sada Elbalad, 2017). Although water is purified to global standards in the treatment plants, the neglected pipe system leads to unaccounted-for water and increased health risks (CGTN Africa, 2018). Upgrading the piping system is a challenging and costly undertaking as it lies underneath the subway system (Sada Elbalad, 2017).

Efforts Toward Sustainability

The government has made significant strides in monitoring water pollution on the Nile River. There has been an advancement in the mode of monitoring from the conventional traditional approaches to the new advanced technological solutions. Twenty-one stations were built to track both the quality of the Nile River and the quality of direct industrial wastewater discharged into the river, and by 2030 the number of monitoring stations is projected to be 95. In addition, there has been a substantial decrease in the number of facilities that discharge their waste into the Nile River from twenty-seven to only nine facilities (MPMAR,

2018). Several programmes and projects have been carried out by the MWRI to ensure the optimal use of the water resources and water management for sustainable development that have taken place as per the National Water Policy till the year 2017 (Alnaggar, 2003). Regarding the water quality status, there are preventative measures taken through the regular assessment of the status of water quality and suitability for its various uses as well as regulations set to protect the water resource against pollution. Furthermore, the MWRI has developed and operates a National Water Quality Monitoring System in the Nile, canals and drains and lake Nasser (Alnaggar, 2003). The Regional Center for Training and Water Studies (RCTWS) programme was developed to support capacity building, training, education and public awareness, and applied studies focused on IWRM. The Water Communication Unit was established to strengthen the ministry's capacity for raising public awareness to prompt water-saving and protection measures. The programme was launched to inform citizens of the importance of the role of water resources in development plans and to invite consumers to participate in the decision-making process (Alnaggar, 2003).

The MWRI has signed an agreement with the European Union (EU) for cooperation under the National Plan for Water Irrigation until 2037 as well as projects such as modern irrigation and water treatment in drainage systems (Takouleu, 2018). The government relies on water reuse techniques, particularly for irrigation, to overcome water scarcity. The agricultural drainage water is reclaimed at 10% of irrigation capacity, and the amount of reused wastewater amounted to 2 billion m^3 in 2017 (Alnaggar, 2003). The treated wastewater from Cairo is used to cultivate mainly timber trees and industrial non-food crops (Khalifa, 2017). The government plans to upgrade the existing secondary wastewater treatment plants to save a total of 11.67 billion m^3 water through tertiary wastewater treatment and reuse. The Government has committed to extending the use of natural methods such as wetland and soil aquifer treatment techniques that are known to be highly efficient and cost-effective (Helmecke et al., 2020). Rapid population growth and urban sprawl have created immense pressure on the existing WSS services in cities. The government, therefore, planned to build the New Cairo wastewater treatment plant to meet current and future demand. The Cairo wastewater treatment plant has a capacity of 500,000 m^3/day, providing the city and the surrounding area with a cost-effective and environmentally sound wastewater treatment plant to meet the current water demand and demand of the projected population growth (Water Technology, n.d.). Furthermore, there are ongoing attempts to transform the irrigation system into a drip system. These efforts are matched on the private sector side, where companies like Sekem have pioneered organic farming, sustainable irrigation methods as well as the processing of wastewater. This has ensured the efficient use of water resources due to the lower water requirement for organic cultivation (40% less) and the use of sprinkler and drip irrigation methods. Moreover, all the wastewater produced is reused after treatment (MPMAR, 2018).

Key Opportunities in Achieving Water Security in Cairo

Demand-Side Opportunities

Opportunities for Cairo include maximizing the natural circumstances and enhancing human-made infrastructures. Although Cairo receives less rainfall than Egypt's other urban cities (Gado & El-Agha, 2020), recent studies prove that rainwater harvesting is suitable (Elsaeed, 2019). Since this rainfall is concentrated over few days and results in flooding, the Cairo governorate could adapt the existing flash flood guidelines of other Egyptian governorates such as Sinai, Aswan and Qena (UNECE, n.d.) and effectively plan to reuse this water. In addressing built infrastructure, Cairo should be keen to minimize evaporation demands and maximize infiltration through sponge city initiatives, i.e. softening and greening the urban-scape, looking to nature for solutions as opposed to expensive, energy-intensive technology. Simple solutions such as adding shading to the treatment of plant water pools to decrease evaporation are easily implemented.

Supply-Side Opportunities

Cairo in specific, and Egypt, in general, should work toward collective transboundary efforts to ensure water security for, and responsible use by all Nile basin territories. Another key opportunity is effective coordination among local decision-makers. By coordinating different projects and priorities across ministries, water security could be practically addressed within the urban agenda. With effective laws and policies in place about water use and protection—some of which are aligned with IWRM principles—the government could also mobilize stakeholders from across society to enforce the laws. To bridge the gap between government planning and day-to-day affairs, the government could work toward formalizing the existing extensive expertise of the informal sector. Instead of building the formal infrastructure alongside the informal ones—as is currently occurring—the Cairo and Alexandria Water Organization (CAPWO) could examine the existing informal infrastructure, incorporate needs and challenges faced by inhabitants, and rectify the existing infrastructure, and expand it to meet growing demands.

Key Challenges in Achieving Water Security in Istanbul

Istanbul is threatened by a water crisis due to its distant location to drinking water resources, both geologically and geographically. Many reservoirs operate under an integrated system to meet the water demand of the European and Asian parts of the city. As mentioned in the background, the City Blueprint approach with 24 indicators has been applied to Istanbul to provide a long-term framing of the city's performance in managing its water resources. The indicators are scored on a scale between 0 (very poor performance) to 10 (excellent performance) based on three frameworks, namely: (i) Trends and Pressures Framework (TPF) indicating the city's challenges on main social, environmental and financial aspects; (ii) City Blueprint Performance Framework (CBF) indicating the IWRM performance and its bottlenecks in Istanbul and the city's adequacy to water management; (iii) and Governance Capacity Framework (GCF) indicating the capacity in the improvement of city's water governance. Based on this preliminary assessment, the indicators for drinking water sufficiency, consumption and quality and safe sanitation in Istanbul are scored on a noticeably higher scale due to large-scale engineering projects. However, complex challenges in surface and groundwater quality and climate adaptation commitments have been recognized to avoid the anticipated water shortage in the long-term (Van Leeuwen & Sjerps, 2016).

Demand-Side Challenges

Istanbul has implemented large-scale projects to provide the increasing population with safe drinking water. However, a major challenge jeopardizing the existing water supply infrastructure is the pollution of Ömerli and other reservoirs due to illegal settlements in watershed zones. Population growth in Istanbul is around twice the overall rate for Turkey because of massive in-migration. From the 1950s, rapid and chaotic urbanization has led to an increase in the number of unauthorized and uncontrolled settlements in coastal areas without adequate sanitation. The enforcement of the regulations enacted in 1949 and 1966 to demolish slums and prohibits the construction of new ones closer to the reservoirs in Istanbul has been neglected due to social, economic and political reasons that posed a serious threat to water resources (Van Leeuwen & Sjerps, 2016).

As the economic centre of Turkey, around 40% of Turkish industry is based in Istanbul. Manufacturing plants, industries and widespread use of chemical products contaminate the city's water resources (ISKI, 2019). Surface water pollution is mainly caused by the effluent that is disposed of by factories into the rivers. In response to preventing water quality deterioration by industrial activities, every factory is required by law to have a purification unit to prevent the disposal of contaminated water. However, this is often ignored due to high infrastructure and operational costs (Albut et al., 2007).

Supply-Side Challenges

Climate change and its main impacts are expected to pose severe threats to water security and deteriorate the quality and quantity of surface water. Because of its latitude, Istanbul feels the effects of climate variability more significantly. Despite the high annual precipitation rates in Istanbul, the city experienced a drought from 2006 to 2008, recording the lowest rainfall in 50 years, which has since increased concerns over urban water supply among water management stakeholders (Easton et al., 2017). Water availability (m^3/year/capita) in Turkey is predicted to diminish from 3070 in 1990 to 1910 by 2050 due to droughts, floods and decreases in annual precipitation that may lead to the loss of economic, social and natural resources (Aktash, 2014). This would mean that in the next 50 years, changes in precipitation are likely to diminish the water supply of dams and exacerbate water losses through evaporation (Turoglu, 2013).

Efforts Toward Sustainability in Istanbul

Istanbul poses an asymmetric situation regarding its water supplies and a non-homogeneous distribution of the population between the European and Asian sides. The Asian side accounts for 77% of the water resources, including Greater Melen, while only 35% of the population resides there (Van Leeuwen & Sjerps, 2016). To accommodate for the water deficit of the European side, the Melen system in the Water Supply Master Plan was developed by ISKI. Water resources of Istanbul are mainly surface waters that are beyond the provincial boundaries. Following the 1994 severe drought, the emphasis has been made on the development of water resources and the total capacity has been increased from 590 Mm^3/year in 1994 to 2100 Mm^3/year in 2014 (Öztürk & Altay, 2015). The Istanbul Master Plan Consortium (IMC) was assigned by ISKI to prepare a master plan for water supplies, stormwater and wastewater investments in the Istanbul Metropolitan Area (Altinbilek, 2006). Additional water resources are to be developed for the periods after 2040 to meet the future water demand and their annual water supply, as proposed in the masterplan (Öztürk & Altay, 2015).

The inadequate supply of water resources within the provincial borders prompted the protection of water catchment basins that have been acknowledged to ensure sustainable water supply in future. The national framework legislation of the Water Pollution Control Regulation was implemented to protect the watershed against pollution. The first 300 metres of the boundary line of the reservoir (maximum water level) have been expropriated by the ISKI and designated as an absolute protection zone where settlement within this zone is prohibited. ISKI has expropriated and forested 65% of absolute protected areas in all associated watersheds, except for the Greater Melen (Öztürk & Altay, 2015). While between the border of the protection zone and the dividing line of water, industrial activities where manufacturing is directly involved with water are prohibited, and only low density and regulated settlements are permitted. A 10-m-wide strip has been expropriated on both sides of the river where wastewater and stormwater channels and service roads are being contoured (Altinbilek, 2006; Öztürk & Altay, 2015). Furthermore, in attempts to protect the Melen resource, the ISKI has taken over the construction and operation of wastewater treatment plants in Duzce Province that encompasses most of the watershed (Öztürk & Altay, 2015).

There are currently 12 potable water treatment plants in Istanbul with a total capacity of nearly 4.4 million m^3/day (ISKI, 2020). The treated water quality is monitored regularly by the Istanbul Metropolitan Municipality and Provincial Directorate of the Ministry of Health. The urban drinking water has increased significantly through the improvements in water treatment plants and the renewal of pipes in the water distribution network (Öztürk & Altay, 2015). The ISKI operates the water transmission and distribution system in Istanbul. The length of the water distribution had reached over 18,000 km in 2014, and 98% of the network consisted of ductile iron pipes. As proposed by the ISKI's distribution system rehabilitation programme, the remaining cast-iron pipes will be changed in the short term. Effective water pressure control and renewal of the pipes in the water network have decreased the ratio of unaccounted-for water to 24% in 2014 (Öztürk & Altay, 2015).

Istanbul's Key Opportunities in Achieving Water Security

Supply-Side Solutions

With the ongoing water crisis caused by climate change, rapid industrialization and urban sprawl observed in Istanbul, supply-demand management appears to be an urgent necessity for sustainable water resources management. The potential vulnerability of the city to global climate change requires examining hydrological processes and causes of water deficiency, as well as having long-term planning of water resources. Climate adaptation and mitigation strategies including water management policy were adopted within 'Turkey's National Climate Change Adaptation Strategy and Action Plan' for 2011–2023 that targets developing an urban infrastructure master plan and financing strategy, private sector engagement in water investments with new finance methods and use of the most appropriate technologies for water and wastewater facilities (MoEU, 2011). In this context, the Greater Melen project is expected to significantly increase the total water resources capacity of Istanbul on a long-term basis within the Bosphorus Undersea Water Supply Tunnel (Van Leeuwen & Sjerps, 2016). However, climate risk analysis still needs to be carried out on the supply side by identifying droughts and effectively coordinating the city's water distribution systems as part of drought preparedness.

The ISKI has initiated the purification of wastewater through treatment units that may then be used for agriculture, parks or any other purpose that does not need high-quality water (Albut et al., 2007). The introduction of Supervisory Control and Data Acquisition (SCADA) technology for potable water distribution by ISKI has significantly reduced water losses and monitors water quality in dams and pumping stations. SCADA has also been an effective system to measure the water increase level due to weather conditions (ISKI, n.d.-b). To control the pollution of reservoirs, a new model of upgrading illegal settlements in Istanbul and other urban areas was developed by the Turkish Housing Development Administration (TOKI) in 2003. Since around 70% of the housing stock in Istanbul has been informal settlements since the 1950s, water management stakeholders will have to be highly committed and coordinated including private sector participation to see the considerable progress of this model and its impact on watersheds of reservoirs (Uzun et al., 2010).

Demand-Side Solutions

According to City Blueprint Approach, demand-side solutions for complex water security challenges in Istanbul, including efficient wastewater management, reducing water losses and public awareness campaigns, will only be achieved through strong collaboration among national and local governments, private sector, civil society and other stakeholders (Van Leeuwen & Sjerps, 2016). Under the pressures of urban sprawl and climate change, the effective implementation of water supply, sanitation and wastewater treatment necessitates a major transition to sustainable IWRM through Public-Private-Participation (PPP) initiatives. In this context, the implementation of the build-operate-transfer (BOT) model within urban wastewater treatment plants is promoted to carry out water management plans until 2050 in collaboration with the private sector. In the last few years, public outreach campaigns have been extensively carried out by ISKI in educational institutions and public places, but their scale should be further extended to make the community develop awareness on water and environment (ISKI, 2019).

Lastly, to achieve urban water security in Istanbul through contemporary water use and management, developing and operationalizing an inclusive system of good governance should be the primary goal of government. By coordinating the roles of legislative, financial and political authorities, and establishing appropriate entry points for private sector and civil society, a more inclusive, transparent and sustainable form of resource management may emerge over time. Given the scale of present problems, especially in regard to informal settlement, this will be no easy task.

Discussion

Having analysed the current situation, outstanding challenges and efforts from both cities, it becomes clear that there is no one-size-fits-all solution for Cairo and Istanbul in achieving urban water security considering their differences and very few similarities in many aspects given below. The fundamental challenges facing these cities span socio-demographic, economic, technological, environmental and political/governance factors. The chapter now turns to a discussion of these key elements in relation to urban water security.

Although both megacities are near the Mediterranean Sea, they have various geographical features in terms of landforms and ecosystems. Cairo is downstream of its largest water resource which is a transboundary river that begins in another country. On the other hand, Istanbul sits on, and is close to, water bodies through the Bosphorus strait connecting the Black Sea to the Mediterranean by way of the Sea of Marmara. Istanbul's water resources lie within Turkey. This difference gives rise to different outside issues. Cairo's vulnerability lies in not only climate change, but also in reduced water supply due to its transboundary basin. Turkey's greatest vulnerability lies in climate change, which resulted in water shortage due to extreme weather events (droughts) over the last decades. Moreover, the city's water reservoirs are at high risk of contamination due to unauthorized settlements on watershed zones. All these facts have increased the concerns over urban water supply among water management stakeholders in both cities.

Cairo receives considerably less amount of rainfall and has a high evaporative demand compared to Istanbul due to its arid climate that poses a threat to water security in the context of rapid urbanization demands (see Table 1.1). On the contrary, Istanbul experiences high precipitation annually in the humid subtropical Mediterranean zone. However, due to global warming, the city has experienced below-average rainfall annually over the last decades that has amplified the risk of water shortage. Both cities have undergone climate-related events that resulted in water shortage over the last decades. In this respect, effective water resources management in both cities requires incorporating climate variability factors in the long-term water resources management strategies.

Water resources in Cairo are limited to the Nile River, together with minor amounts of rainfall and flash floods. The Aswan High Dam provides storage and guarantees regulated water supplies for municipal, industrial and agricultural uses. Three water supply projects have also been implemented, namely the Bahr El-Ghazal development, Jongile Canal and River Sobat-Machar Marshes in the upper Nile. Another source of water supply is the groundwater in the Nile valley and delta; however, the groundwater potential greatly depends on subsurface drainage. In Istanbul, the Melen regulators and Sakarya pipeline projects, dams and underground reservoirs are the main water supply sources. In the past, dams were the main source of water supply to the city; however, there has been an increasing share of water obtained from the pipeline projects. Nevertheless, both Cairo and Istanbul rely on waste treatment plants. The treated wastewater is mainly used for agriculture in Cairo, while Istanbul has 21 potable water treatment plants to meet the demands of residential use. Both cities are faced with vulnerability of water resources and water supply systems due to significant changes in rates of flow and reduction of water potential due to climate change. Istanbul has taken the initiative to decrease the impacts and increase resilience against climate change by adopting the Climate Change Adaptation Strategy and Action Plan in 2012. Although aware of the impacts of climate change, Cairo has yet to develop a climate change adaptation and mitigation plan. Furthermore, the inadequate supply of water resources within the borders of Istanbul has prompted regulators such as Sakarya to import water from neighbouring cities. Meanwhile, Cairo's withdrawal rate from the Nile is greater than the rate of return.

Cairo and Istanbul have many similarities in terms of water supply needs. Both cities need to meet the water demands of a large, dense population, a significant portion of which are slum dwellers. Both cities must mitigate the risks of climate change on water resources through making better use of the water to which they have access. Within a comparative perspective, Cairo needs to fill the existing gaps in the implementation of water management policies and plans due to the lack of coordination between different governance actors. Regarding Istanbul, the city administration still makes efforts to collaborate with the industrial sector to reduce surface water contamination from manufacturing.

The closed water system of Cairo makes it more vulnerable to quality deterioration. As the population has been growing, and the expansion of urban areas continues, there has been an increase in water pollution. The pollution of surface and groundwater is due to agricultural, industrial and domestic waste. Although a water quality monitoring system of the Nile is in place, the development of other mechanisms including governance, policies, institutions, infrastructure for monitoring, laboratories and skilled human resources is needed. In comparison, surface water pollution in Istanbul is due to the overflow of the sewer system during intense precipitation. Remediation projects have taken place regarding the streams within residential areas, mainly focused on densely populated areas. Moving forward, the sewer network system will consist of separate stormwater and wastewater channels allowing the city to make better use of both stormwater and wastewater.

In assessing the socio-demographic factor and as illustrated above, both Cairo and Istanbul have successfully provided improved piped WSS. Cairo's government is also working toward improving the water infrastructure in informal settlements, albeit not as a priority. Similarly, a new model for upgrading illegal settlements in Istanbul was developed in 2003 by the Turkish Housing Development Administration which plans to demolish unplanned slums from watershed zones and constructs new residential areas in the long term. Although the implementation of this model might require more time due to rapid urbanization in Istanbul, it is likely to significantly reduce the scale of water pollution in reservoirs if implemented systemically.

Regarding governance, Cairo's institutional framework is centralized, with overlapping responsibilities and weak enforcement. This results in national water strategies, plans and reforms which address agriculture and have minimal focus on urban water security. Istanbul's main water actors are decentralized. Although many institutions are engaged in water resources management at the primary and secondary levels, the functioning of the financially independent and centralized administration in Istanbul makes it more capable of taking effective and tailored action. The consequences are also reflected in data collection and availability. It is tremendously challenging to find specific data on Cairo's water, such as its withdrawal from the Nile and the percentage of improved WSS. Data was relatively easier to collect for Istanbul due to the decentralized decision-making and urban-focused institutions. On the other hand, both cities suffer from weak water pollution law enforcement, resulting in water contamination. The performance of both cities toward SDG 6 is ranked as 'moderately improving'. Both cities have made accomplishments on SDG 6.1 and 6.2 by providing basic drinking water services and sanitation services to more than 90% of the population. However, the actions on other targets are still not satisfactory and need to be improved to sustain high performance.

Both cities allocate budgets for their water infrastructure plans. However, it is noteworthy that for Cairo, the priority is to expand the infrastructure and supply to meet the urban sprawl, whereas meeting current demands of poor pipe quality and lack of infrastructure in informal settlements is a lower priority. In fact, it is planned to be tended to through trickle-down: after urban economic development, it will be possible to allocate considerable budgets for that purpose. The funding for water infrastructure comes from the Ministry of Finance, and decision-making is still very centralized. Compared to Egypt, water management plans in Turkey have been formulated for all urban settlements until 2050, with particular attention to Istanbul. The government encourages the public-private partnership through the build-operate-transfer (BOT) model in many infrastructure projects, including urban water management. Due to the large-scale projects to be finalized for Istanbul water supply and treatment, ISKI and associated government agencies encounter difficulties in handling the financial cost of these projects. Upgrading unplanned settlements to prevent the pollution of the reservoirs in this sprawling city requires huge investment and strong commitment from all stakeholders. Therefore, the cooperation between the private sector and the city administration is essential to facilitate the implementation of present and proposed initiatives.

Conclusions and Recommendations

In this final section, we present our conclusions and recommendations. They are set out and discussed in terms of descending scales or domains of action, i.e. national and municipal. As shown, in Table 8.3, each city faces continuing challenges, but there are also many opportunities for improved urban water security.

Table 8.3 Recommendations to achieve water security in Cairo and Istanbul

	Cairo	*Istanbul*
National	• Allow for a decentralized governance system • Include a budget for sustainable urban water among the national water efficiency and treatment projects • Include Cairo in the climate change action project • Collaborate with Nile basin countries for protection and sustainable consumption of the Nile River	• Facilitate the implementation of the illegal settlements upgrading programme • Provide slum owners with housing units with adequate water supply • Achieve an inclusive system of governance by encouraging private sector participation in the decision-making and water supply projects • Apply a multidisciplinary approach to mitigate the impacts of climate change on Istanbul water resources
Municipal	• Prioritize extending the WSS infrastructure to informal settlements • Apply a more effective water pricing strategy to facilitate equitable access to low-income households and discourage excessive use and water waste • Include a climate change mitigation and adaptation plan in the urban development strategy that is aligned with the general national strategies • Maintain and upgrade the WSS infrastructure • Develop governance, policies, institutions and infrastructure to monitor water quality • Reduce evaporation demand of the water system and urban-scape	• Apply a more effective water pricing strategy to stimulate the efficient use of water and discourage its waste • Expand the scope of water use awareness measures to reach to more target audience • Incorporate environmental impacts of water scarcity in the public outreach campaign programmes • Achieve better payment of water tariffs through enforcing municipal laws to increase financial resources of ISKI • Extend the use of up to date technologies for better operation and protection of water systems

Cairo

Cairo's socio-demographic performance is improving, its governance is adequate, but its economic, technological and environmental performances are weak. Therefore, Cairo is less likely to sustainably achieve urban water security if 'business-as-usual' practices persist. There are several steps that may be taken.

On a national level, the centralized institutional framework in Cairo presents considerable challenges. In contrast, Istanbul has instituted a decentralized governance system which, as shown throughout this chapter, provides better outcomes in terms of city-specific sustainable water supply plans, water protection laws, climate change adaptation efforts and data collection and compilation. Therefore, a decentralized governance framework, with a water authority of Cairo with the power of decision- and policymaking, would allow for not only more efficient performance but, in fact, more tailored solutions and projects, as well as better allocation of resources. It would also facilitate better water accountability, which would, in turn, allow for more effective plans and efforts. Also, Cairo could improve its water law enforcement by increasing the authority of the EWRA. Additionally, Egypt's national budget for water efficiency and treatment projects is sizeable; however, it is mostly directed toward agriculture in rural Egypt. The Ministry of Finance can increase the municipal water budget to help mitigate water scarcity.

As the Nile River is Egypt's main water resource, it is imperative that efforts should be made toward ensuring sustainable use of the source. Therefore, it is recommended that Egypt continues to collaborate and also share its existing efforts of sustainable consumption and protection of the Nile River with the other Nile basin countries. Furthermore, the Nile is vulnerable to the impacts of climate change. Since the national government signed a climate change adaptation plan with UNDP that focuses on coastal cities (Maged, 2019), it should also incorporate Cairo. The municipal government should further detail and execute the plan within the urban development efforts.

On a municipal level, ensuring equitable access to water, as a basic human right, is a significant step toward achieving urban water security. Egypt has done well in increasing water supply in urban areas. However, the lack of prioritization for extending infrastructure to informal settlements and unaffordable domestic rates for the poor has led to inequitable access to water. Therefore, increased efforts and resources should be directed toward increasing access to water in informal settlements and incorporating them into the formal water system. Additionally, the government should ensure fair pricing so that the system is maintained and extended. The current system is divided into four tiers reaching to 40 litres. Since average consumption in Cairo is 330 l/c/d, the tariffs could be tiered to allow for more equitability at low consumption rates, and to discourage higher consumption rates. Moving the tiers apart would ensure that a fair price is paid for water and discourage wasting water, as the MHUUC (2012) predicts that affordability for those with access to formal, in-house water supply is the main driver of the high urban water consumption rates in Cairo.

Another challenge faced is the poor quality of the WSS infrastructure in Cairo, which is causing pipe leakage and the flow of impurities into the water supply, posing health risks. Therefore, it is important for Cairo to not only upgrade, but also ensure the regular maintenance of the infrastructure to eliminate pipe leakage and water contamination. Even though a water quality monitoring system of the Nile is in place, the development of other mechanisms, including governance, policies, institutions, infrastructure for monitoring, laboratories and skilled human resources, are needed. Development in these areas can also improve the quality of treated wastewater, increasing the resource supply for food crops and potable water. Moreover, reducing evaporative demand of water treatment plants, water infrastructure and general urban design would effectively reduce water demand.

Istanbul

In comparison with Cairo, Istanbul has made more significant efforts toward achieving water security. Several initiatives have been introduced by the city's policymakers for the protection of water resources and adaptation to climate change. Nevertheless, there are several opportunities for improved performance.

Since the proportion of the informal residential settlements is increasing in Istanbul in the context of urban sprawl, the implementation of the illegal settlements upgrading programme within the new model by TOKI should be facilitated. Within this programme, it is planned to provide the slum owners with compensation for their slums that will allow them to live in new housing units with adequate water supply (Uzun et al., 2010). However, this complex task requires a high level of commitment and strong collaboration among government agencies as well as a high degree of trust between the state and the citizenry in the long term. Significant investment to ameliorate the contamination of water bodies must be a part of the slum upgrading effort.

On a national level, where water is formally provided, underpricing results in the underestimation of real value of water by the industrial sector and households. Therefore, a water pricing strategy that can stimulate the efficient use of water and discourage its waste must be put in place. This can also allow ISKI to get involved in future investments with a sufficient budget. Since 2017, within the framework of social responsibility, ISKI has promoted water use awareness by organizing seminars, training programmes for young generations at approximately 400 educational institutions, and setting up booths in public spaces (ISKI, 2019). However, the scope of these measures must be expanded to incorporate environmental impacts of water scarcity by various means, particularly mass media and the internet to reach a greater target audience, including households and private businesses.

According to UNEP, the implementation of IWRM in Turkey is moderately improving with medium-high performance as of 2018. This was achieved due to progress in laws and policies and long-term management instruments in place for sustainable water use. At the national level, the country reports the existence of the coordination in water resources management between inter-ministerial committees and institutions supporting the sustainable strategy to overcome water shortage. However, Turkey has failed to achieve an inclusive system of governance since the role of the private sector as a stakeholder in the decision structures and as a contractor in water supply projects is at the basic level (UNEP, 2018). Therefore, in order to reach a 'very high' classification of IWRM performance during the next phase, the private sector participation should not be limited to the operation of water and wastewater treatment plants. They should also be actively involved and make a financial contribution to water management (Istanbul International Water Forum, 2011).

Regarding the financial aspects for IWRM implementation, Turkey is ranked by the UNEP among the small percentage of countries that have sufficient funds disbursed for all work. As a growing megacity, Istanbul has been defined among the priority areas for the planning of water supply infrastructure projects, such as the Melen project, which is the largest drinking water project investment in the country's history. Furthermore, Turkey has received financial support from the international development programmes, such as the EU Regional Development Programme in the area of water management cycle (EC, n.d.; EIP, n.d). On a local level, domestic, commercial and industrial water consumption is regulated by different tariff rates in Istanbul. However, industries and public institutions show poor payment records in terms of water and sewerage tariffs.

So, ISKI should enforce municipal laws to achieve the better payment of water tariffs to cover its operation and maintenance expenses and create financial resources for future investments (Altinbilek, 2006).

Water security has also been included in the Climate Change Action Plan of Istanbul. The Golden Horn Environment Protection Project is a great example of environmental rehabilitation efforts initiated by the city (Altinbilek, 2006). In addition to that, the scale of environmental awareness measures should be increased for the conservation of the watersheds of water reservoirs with the support of the Ministry of Environment and Forestry. Additionally, to mitigate the impacts of climate change on water resources, a multidisciplinary approach should be applied, including technical and administrative precautionary measures to prevent the pollution of watersheds in water supply reservoirs.

On a municipal level, Istanbul has made substantial progress toward the technological advancement in water resources management. The introduction of SCADA—the central command system for Istanbul—is one of the biggest achievements by ISKI that transfers all data on water resources, rainfall and water lines to a centralized data system (ISKI, n.d.-b). Another important initiative is ISKABIS (İSKİ Infrastructure Data System), a GIS project enabling spatial inquiries on potable water supply and wastewater infrastructure plants. This technology has been an efficient response to climate variability with its application in Disaster Management Data System in Istanbul (ISKI, n.d.-c). Thus, the use of up to date technologies such as remote sensing and GIS should be further extended for the better operation and protection of water systems in Istanbul.

All in all, urban water scarcity is a challenge faced by several megacities, and there is no single blueprint for achieving water security. Cities vary in climate, resources, governance and challenges as witnessed by the case studies of Cairo and Istanbul. In our view, operating within a general framework provides direction for tailored efforts in achieving urban water security.

References

Abd-Elaty, I., Zelenakova, M., Straface, S., Vranayová, Z., & Abu-hashim, M. (2019). Integrated modelling for groundwater contamination from polluted streams using new protection process techniques. *Water, 11*, 2321.

Abd Ellah, R. G. (2020). Water resources in Egypt and their challenges, Lake Nasser case study. *Egyptian Journal of Aquatic Research, 46*, 1–12.

Aktash, O. (2014). Impacts of climate change on water resources in Turkey. *Environmental Engineering and Management Journal, 13*(4), 881–889.

Albut, S., Istanbulluoglu, A., Konukcu, F., & Kocaman, I. (2007). Probable water crisis in Thrace and Istanbul in the near future and a sustainable strategy to overcome it. *Water International, 32*(4), 590–603.

Almal News. (2020, February 25). *Alqabida limiyah alshorb tadfa' be 725 mo'eda lesahb miyah alamtar fi almohafazat* [The holding company for water and wastewater deploys 725 trucks to drain rainwater across governates]. *Almal News.* https://almalnews.com/ل سحب-معدة-725-ب --ت دف ع-ال شرب-لـم ياه-ال قاب ضة/. Accessed 5 April 2022.

Alnaggar, D. (2003). Water resource management and policies for Egypt. In *Proceedings of the Symposium organized by the Regional Centre on Urban Water Management (RCUWM-Tehran): No. 73. policies and strategic options for water management in the Islamic countries* (pp. 55–69). Paris, UNESCO.

Altinbilek, D. (2006). Water management in Istanbul. *Water Resources Development, 22*(2), 241–253.

Bakker, K., Cook, C., Dunn, G., Allen, D., & Norman, E. (2010). Water security: A primer. In *Developing a Canadian water security framework as a tool for improved water governance for watersheds.* Program on Water Governance.

Bertelsmann Stiftung, Sustainable Development Solutions Network (SDSN). (2019). *Sustainable development report 2019: Transformations to achieve the sustainable development goals*. Bertelsmann Stiftung and Sustainable Development Solutions Network.

CGTN Africa. (2018, January 31). *Cairo among African cities battling water shortage* [Video File]. YouTube. https://www.youtube.com/watch?v=hpHiNwzOPy0. Accessed 5 April 2022.

Cuceloglu, G., Abbaspour, K. C., & Ozturk, I. (2017). Assessing the water-resources potential of Istanbul by using a Soil and Water Assessment Tool (SWAT) hydrological model. *Water, 9*(814), 1–18.

Daif, I. (2018, June 3). *Taaraf 'ala asaar miyah alshorb baad alziyadah alaakhirah: Infograph* (Introducing water prices after the latest increase: Infographic). Masrawy. https://www.masrawy.com/news/news_egypt/details/2018/6/3/1369052/-أسعار-مياه-الشرب-بعد-الزيادة-الأخيرة-إنفوجرافتعرف-على-. Accessed 5 April 2022.

Demirbilek, B., & Benson, D. (2019). Between emulation and assemblage: Analysing WFD policy transfer outcomes in Turkey. *Water, 11*(2), 324.

Easton, P., Sjerps, R., & Van Leeuwen, K. (2017). *Istanbul: City of water.* EIP Water Action Group.

Egypt and Climate Change (ECC). (2014). *Climate change*. https://gcc14egypt.wordpress.com/climate/. Accessed 5 April 2022.

Egypt Today. (2018, June 3). Egypt's government raises drinking water and sewage fees. *Egypt Today*.

EIP Water Action Group of the European Commission. (n.d.). *The city blueprint approach: Improving implementation capacities of cities and regions by sharing best practices on urban water cycle services*. EIP Water Action Group of the European Commission.

Elsaeed, M. (2019, December 3). Jadwa hasad miyah alamtar 'ala almodon almisriya (Feasibility of rainwater harvesting on Egyptian cities). *Scientific American*. https://www.scientificamerican.com/arabic/articles/news/feasibility-of-rainwater-harvesting-on-egyptian-cities/. Accessed 5 April 2022.

El-Sayed, S. A. (2018). Study of groundwater in Northeast Cairo Area, Egypt. *Journal of Geoscience and Environment Protection, 6*, 229–251.

European Commission (EC). (n.d). *IPA regional development programmes in Turkey*. https://ec.europa.eu/regional_policy/en/funding/ipa/turkey/. Accessed 5 April 2022.

Gado, T. A., & El-Agha, D. E. (2020). Feasibility of rainwater harvesting for sustainable water management in urban areas of Egypt. *Environmental Science and Pollution Research, 27*, 32304–32317.

General Organization for Physical Planning (GOPP). (2008). *Vision of Cairo 2050 within a national vision of Egypt*. https://cairofrombelow.files.wordpress.com/2011/08/cairo-2050-vision-v-2009-gopp-12-mb.pdf. Accessed 5 April 2022.

Helmecke, M., Fries, E., & Schulte, C. (2020). Regulating water reuse for agricultural irrigation: Risks related to organic micro-contaminants. *Environmental Sciences Europe, 32*(1), Article 4.

Hoekstra, A. Y., Buurman, J., & van Ginkel, K. C. H. (2018). Urban water security: A review. *Environmental Research Letters, 13*(5), 053002.

ICWE (International Conference on Water and the Environment). (1992). *The Dublin statement on water and sustainable development*. https://wedocs.unep.org/handle/20.500.11822/30961. Accessed 5 April 2022.

Istanbul International Water Forum. (2011). An Istanbul perspective on regional water problems and search for solutions. *Outcomes of the 2nd Istanbul International water forum secretariat*. Mavi Ofset.

Istanbul Water and Sewerage Administration (ISKI). (2019). *2018 annual report*. ISKI.

Istanbul Water and Sewerage Administration (ISKI). (2020). *İSKİ—Potable water treatment plants*. ISKI.

Istanbul Water and Sewerage Administration (ISKI). (n.d.-a). *About ISKI*. https://www.iski.istanbul/web/en-US/kurumsal/iski-hakkinda. Accessed 5 April 2022.

Istanbul Water and Sewerage Administration (ISKI). (n.d.-b). *Scada technology*. https://www.iski.istanbul/web/en-US/kurumsal/iski-hakkinda/scada-technology. Accessed 5 April 2022.

Istanbul Water and Sewerage Administration (ISKI). (n.d.-c). *İSKABİS technology*. http://www.iski.istanbul/web/en-US/kurumsal/iski-hakkinda/iskabis-technology. Accessed 5 April 2022.

Khalifa, E. (2017). *Safe wastewater use in agriculture in Egypt: Case study*. https://www.ais.unwater.org/ais/pluginfile.php/356/mod_page/content/106/Egyptpercent20FAO-Essam_3.pdf. Accessed 5 April 2022.

Khalil, D. (2019). The flexible governance of water in Cairo's informal areas. *Water, 11*, 1644.

Macrotrends. (2020a). *Cairo, Egypt population 1950–2020*. https://www.macrotrends.net/cities/22812/cairo/population. Accessed 5 April 2022.

Macrotrends. (2020b). *Istanbul, Turkey population 1950–2020*. https://www.macrotrends.net/cities/22691/istanbul/population. Accessed 5 April 2022.

Maged, M. (2019, March 15). Egypt to implement €32 mn climate change plan. *Egypt Independent*.

Maspero Memory. (2016). *Autograph: Tariq Habib yastadeef alostaz aldoctor Hasan Fathy ostaz al'Imara fi Misr* (Autograph: Tariq Habib interviews Professor Hasan Fathy, a professor of architecture in Egypt) [Video File]. YouTube. https://www.youtube.com/watch?v=DFvq5J0Lay4andt=1100s. Accessed 5 April 2022.

Ministry of Environment and Urbanization (MoEU). (2011). *Turkey's national climate change adaptation strategy and action plan*. MoEU.

Ministry of Housing, Utilities and Urban Communities (MHUUC). (2012). *Greater Cairo urban development strategy*. MHUUC.

Ministry of Planning, Monitoring and Administrative Reform (MPMAR). (2018). *Egypt's voluntary national review 2018*. MPMAR.

Myllylä, S. (1995, June 19–22). Cairo—A mega-city and its water resources. In *The Third Nordic Conference on Middle Eastern Studies: Ethnic Encounter and Culture Change*. Nordic Society for Middle Eastern Studies.

Öztürk, D. İ., & Altay, D. D. A. (2015, December). Water and wastewater management in Istanbul. In *UNESCO HQ International Conference on Water, Megacities and Global Change*. UNESCO.

Romero-Lankao, P., & Gnatz, D. M. (2016). Conceptualizing urban water security in an urbanizing world. *Environmental Sustainability, 21*, 45–51.

Saatci, A. M. (2013). Solving water problems of a metropolis. *Journal of Water Resource and Protection, 5*, 7–10.

Sada Elbalad. (2017, January 30). *Salat altahrir – Ra'ees sharikat miyah alshorb alqahira: shabakat miyah alshorb lam togadad month 100 'aam* (Liberty room—President of Cairo's potable water company: Potable water pipes have not been upgraded since 100 years) [Video File]. YouTube. https://www.youtube.com/watch?v=hq0wIveHYAk. Accessed 5 April 2022.

Schlanger, Z. (2019, September 17). 250 million people rely on the Nile for water that may not exist by 2080. *Quartz*. https://qz.com/1709757/climate-change-threatens-the-niles-critical-water-supply/. Accessed 5 April 2022.

Takouleu, J. M. (2018, September 10). EGYPT: Cairo signs agreement with EU on better water management. *Afrik 21*. https://www.afrik21.africa/en/egypt-cairo-signs-agreement-with-eu-on-better-water-management/. Accessed 5 April 2022.

Turkish Water Institute (SUEN). (n.d.). *About us*. https://www.suen.gov.tr/Suen/en/page.aspx?pg=about_us. Accessed 5 April 2022.

Turoglu, H. (2013, November 6–7). Possible effects of climate change on water management in Istanbul. In *The Conference on Global Climate Change*. Yildiz Technical University Library and Documentation Center.

United Nations Economic Commission for Europe (UNECE). (n.d.). *The ministry has developed the 2050 Strategy and updated its national water resources plan till 2037 on the governorates level*. UNECE.

United Nations Environment Programme (UNEP). (2018). *Progress on integrated water resources management*. UNEP.

Uzun, B., Çete, M., & Palancıoglu, H. M. (2010). Legalizing and upgrading illegal settlements in Turkey. *Habitat International, 34*, 204–209.

Van Leeuwen, K., & Sjerps, R. (2016). Istanbul: The challenges of integrated water resources management in Europa's megacity. *Environment, Development and Sustainability, 18*, 1–17.

Weather Atlas. (n.d.-a). *Monthly weather forecast and climate: Cairo, Egypt*. https://www.weather-atlas.com/en/egypt/cairo-climate. Accessed 5 April 2022.

Weather Atlas. (n.d.-b). *Weather forecast Istanbul*. https://www.weather-atlas.com/en/turkey/istanbul. Accessed 5 April 2022.

World Bank. (2014). *Status of water sector regulation in the Middle East and North Africa*. World Bank.

World Bank. (2016). *Valuing water resources in Turkey: A methodological overview and case study*. World Bank

World Population Review. (n.d). *World cities: Istanbul*. https://worldpopulationreview.com/world-cities/istanbul-population/. Accessed 5 April 2022.

CHAPTER 9

Achieving Urban Water Security in Tokyo

Mukhnaam Kaur Chattha, Zhen Wei, and Larry Swatuk

Introduction

Water security refers to providing water in the right quantity and quality at the right time for a dependent system. This is a prerequisite for environmental security, human security and economic growth (Petersen-Perlman et al., 2012). Global water resources are not only crucial for personal consumption and the natural environment, but also the agricultural, energy, industrial andtransportation sectors (UN FAO, 2017). As a limited resource, water is affected and restricted by a series of factors such as geophysical conditions, social and cultural dynamics. Changes

Z. Wei · L. Swatuk (✉)
University of Waterloo, Waterloo, ON, Canada
e-mail: lswatuk@uwaterloo.ca

Z. Wei
e-mail: z85wei@uwaterloo.ca

M. K. Chattha
Office of Sustainability, Sheridan College, Toronto, ON, Canada
e-mail: mkchatth@uwaterloo.ca

L. Swatuk and C. Cash (eds.), *The Political Economy of Urban Water Security under Climate Change*, International Political Economy Series,
https://doi.org/10.1007/978-3-031-08108-8_9

in water resources change relative wealth of the country, and in many ways, water is one of the most important components that unites society (Petersen-Perlman et al., 2012). The United Nations defines water security as 'The capacity of a population to safeguard sustainable access to adequate quantities of acceptable quality water for sustaining livelihoods, human well-being, and socio-economic development, for ensuring protection against water-borne pollution and water-related disasters, and for preserving ecosystems in a climate of peace and political stability' (UN-Water, 2013). At the same time, the United Nations listed ensuring the availability and sustainable management of water and sanitation for everyone as the sixth Sustainable Development Goal (UN, 2015).

In 2014, Tokyo was listed as the largest water stressed city by a research paper that evaluated the world's largest cities based on their water infrastructure using WaterGAP model, where Tokyo's water cycle and consumptive water use of different sectors was modelled (McDonald et al., 2014). Some of the key challenges that Tokyo faces are dry spells which occur once in every decade, climate change causing changes in precipitation, and natural disasters that disrupt water provision. Tokyo has made a range of efforts to secure water supply, which include establishment of: (i) IWRM guidelines at the river basin level, (ii) earthquake resistant water infrastructure, (iii) measures against reducing drought and flooding risks, (iv) water tariff structure that promotes efficient water use, (v) reclaimed wastewater use and (vi) water conservation measures, ranging from rainwater harvesting to preserving a 23,000 hectare forest for over a century. In this chapter, we investigate how urban water security is achieved in Tokyo. Despite being water stressed, the government and relevant actors have implemented a creative variety of hard and soft measures to secure water supply.

Background

Study Area

Tokyo is the capital and the largest city in Japan; it is situated in the southern part of the Kanto plain, which lies close to the centre of the Japanese archipelago. The total population of Tokyo is 13.63 million people (as of January 1, 2018) which is nearly 10% of the total population of Japan. Tokyo accounts for 0.6% of the total area of Japan and covers a total area of 2,190 km^2 (as of October 1, 2016) (TMG, 2018).

Water Resources

In terms of water resources, Tokyo accesses its entire water supply from surface water sources: 78% from the Tone and Arakawa Rivers, 19% from the Tamagawa River and the remaining 3% from other water resources (TMG, 2018). The region has abundant ground-water resources because of the topsoil in the region being highly permeable. However, this resource is no longer tapped into because of land subsidence issues as a result of excessive pumping of ground-water for industrial use (Sato et al., 2006).

Tokyo's Water Supply System and Water Needs

Tokyo's water supply system depends 70% on above-ground-water sources such as melted snow, lakes, rivers and four months of concentrated rainfall (TMG, 2018). A majority of urban water needs for domestic and industrial use are met by drawing water from rivers, dams and other water resource development facilities in the Kanto region (Priscoli & Hiroki, 2016). According to population movement, lifestyle, weather conditions and social economic conditions, the water demand in the region fluctuates. In Tokyo, per day, the maximum water delivery at its peak is approximately 6 million m^3 (TMG, 2018).

The Bureau of Waterworks supplies water to Tokyo city and as of March, 2017, Tokyo's network of distribution pipes was a total length of 27,038 kilometres. To prevent leakages during delivery, the water supply equipment uses stainless steel pipes which supply water from branch points to distribution pipes to meters; this was done because it was found that over 90% of water leakages during delivery were related to the type of water supply equipment used (TMG, 2018). With the prevention of water leakages from pipelines, the water distribution rate in terms of drinking water that reached customers was 92.8% in 2012, from 81.1% in 1975 (Priscoli & Hiroki, 2016). The Tokyo Waterworks Bureau decreased leakage rates by repairs to three percent, which is the lowest in the world (TSS Tokyo Water, n.d.) and remarkable for a city of its size.

Water Tariff Structure in Tokyo

The Tokyo water utility is operated by the Bureau of Waterworks, Tokyo Metropolitan Government (TMG). Water tariffs have been established not only to cover administration costs but also promote efficient water use in Tokyo (World Bank, 2006). As an effort to control user demand, a majority of water agencies adopt tiered water rates or increasing block rates (Priscoli & Hiroki, 2016). Domestic and sewerage water tariffs with increasing-block charges encourage efficient water use. Based on the user's request, the industrial water tariffs are set to an upper limit for the volume of water that can be used. In addition to this, industrial and domestic water pricing systems include differential charges for the type of water pipe sizes installed. For example, where supply pipes are smaller than 25 mm in diameter, the first five m^3 of water is provided for free (though there is a service charge), after which charges increase in stepwise fashion. Where pipe diameters are 30 mm or 40 mm, the charge is 213 Yen/m^3 up to 100 m^3. For pipes, with the largest diameters (i.e. 100 mm to over 300 mm), the fee is 404 Yen/m^3; however, service charges vary dramatically (Bureau of Waterworks, n.d.-a). The aim of the Bureau of Waterworks is to provide customers with the necessary water required for daily use at affordable rates and discourage wastage through block tariffs (Bureau of Waterworks, n.d.-a). Over a twenty year period (1998–2018), the cost and unit selling price of water has come down from a high of about 220 Yen/m^3 to slightly less than 210 Yen/m^3 (TMG, 2018).

Water Governance and Management

In Japan, water is the responsibility of the national government. There are numerous laws and policies that impact on water governance and management (see Tables 9.1 and 9.2). Notable among these, the Ministry of Land, Transport and Infrastructure developed the Comprehensive National Water Resources Plan in line 'with the Comprehensive National Development Plan, which is stipulated in the Comprehensive National Land Development Act and approved by the Prime Minister's cabinet' (EDMS, 2007). Related to this, 'the Cabinet, under the Basic Environmental Law, approved the Basic Environmental Plan ... [which] clarifies long-term and comprehensive environmental policies related to water quality and quantity, including water conservation ... to secure an environmentally sound water cycle' (EDMS, 2007).

With regard to water for cities, water management is a function of the Tokyo Municipal Government. The TMG is governed through the Tokyo Metropolitan Assembly assisted by the Secretariat to the Assembly. Members of the Assembly are elected by Tokyo citizens and serve for four years. The President of the Assembly is elected among its members, supervises its affairs and appoints (or dismisses) staff members of the

Secretariat. Water management falls under the purview of the Executive Organs of governance, i.e. the Governor (elected by Tokyo citizens) and Vice Governors. Among the many Governor's Bureaus, water and sewerage constitute two of three Public Enterprise Bureaus (the Bureau of Transportation is the third).

According to the TMG (n.d.), the principal operations of the Bureau of Waterworks include suppling water to the 13.04 million residents living in the ward area and the 26 municipalities of the Tama area, an area totalling about 1,239 km^2. As of the end of March, 2015, the total volume of TMG's water sources is 6.30 million m^3/day, capacity of water purification facilities is 6.86 million m^3/day, and total length of distribution pipes is 26,774 km. An equally important function of the Bureau of Waterworks is to conduct the industrial-use water business that supplies industrial water to the eight wards along the Arakawa River and a portion of Nerima Ward.

The principle operations of the Bureau of Sewerage include:

- Responsibility for basic functions of the sewer system, i.e. sewage treatment, flood control through removal of rainwater and quality maintenance of public waters. In addition, based on the Management Plan 2016, formulated in February, 2016, the following initiatives are promoted:
- Implementation of reconstruction of facilities, flood control, earthquake measures and other policies that help the residents of Tokyo feel safe and secure
- Combined sewer system improvement, advanced treatment, global warming measures and other measures that contribute to the realization of a city with a good water environment and low environmental impact
- Stable provision of best services at minimum cost.

As illustrated in Table 9.1, there are a significant number of laws in place guiding water resource allocation, development and management in Japan, most of which directly impact Tokyo.

The stakeholders involved in water governance and management are also many and varied. These are summarized in Table 9.2.

Table 9.1 Major laws and/or regulations impacting water resources in Tokyo

Name of law or regulation	*Outline of law/regulation/relationship with operations of the bureau*
Waterworks Law	'The Waterworks Law' sets the basis for waterworks operations and states water quality standards, conditions for approval of operations, installation and management standards of waterworks and organized improvement for facilities, etc.
The Industrial Water Supply Business Law	'The Industrial Water Supply Business Law' specifies the principles for industrial waterworks operations and identifies notification of operations, obligation of water supply and standards of facilities, etc.
The Local Public Enterprise Law	'The Local Public Enterprise Law' stipulates fundamentals of operation management and specifies the management organization, finance and handling of the status of enterprise personnel, etc.
The Local Autonomy Law	'The Local Autonomy Law' lays out the installation, management and usage charges, etc., of waterworks facilities for public service
River Law	The 'River Law' defines parameters for occupancy of river water as a water source, approval for new construction, etc., of structures, management of dams, etc.
Basic Environment Law	The 'Basic Environment Law' sets water quality standards
Water Pollution Control Law	To prevent pollution of public waters, the 'Water Pollution Control Law' defines the regulations for the discharged water from business establishments and factories
Water Supply Ordinance of the Tokyo Metropolitan Government (TMG)	The 'Water Supply Ordinance of the Tokyo Metropolitan Government' stipulates water charges for Tokyo, allocation conditions of the cost of water supply equipment works, and the conditions required to maintain an appropriate water supply

(continued)

Table 9.1 (continued)

Name of law or regulation	*Outline of law/regulation/relationship with operations of the bureau*
Industrial Waterworks Ordinance of the Tokyo Metropolitan Government (TMG)	'Industrial Waterworks Ordinance of the Tokyo Metropolitan Government' stipulates the area of industrial waterworks in Tokyo, water charges for Tokyo, allocation conditions of the cost of water supply equipment works, and the conditions required to maintain an appropriate water supply

Source Adapted from Tokyo Municipal Government (2018)

Development of Water Resources

The Japanese government prepared a 'National Comprehensive Water Resources Plan' ('Water Plan No. 21') in June, 1999, which clarified the primary direction of Twenty-first Century water resources development, protection and utilization. The plan set goals to achieve three objectives between the years 2010 and 2015: (i) establish a sustainable water system, (ii) protect and improve the water environment and (iii) revive water-related culture. As per the Water Plan, a basic outline for water resources development was developed in major river basins across the country. The goal was to reach approximately 258 m^3/sec of water in the Yinchuan River and Arakawa River, and in 2001, 64% of this goal was achieved (MLIT, 2001). However, it was found that more resources were needed to meet the anticipated water demand, and dams were used as the main tool for developing water resources, as rivers and groundwater alone could not meet demand. The construction of dams allowed to meet demand for domestic water, industrial and agricultural water use, in addition to providing other uses such as power generation and flood control. In April, 2001, after the improvement of water resources development facilities, the total water storage reached approximately 2.5 billion m^3 (Takesada, 2009).

Table 9.2 Stakeholders in Tokyo water governance and management

Relevant government authorities and organizations	*Responsibilities*
Ministry of Internal Affairs and Communications	Participated in the preparation of overseas development strategies for the water industry, led by the Ministry of Economy, Trade and Industry (including the Ministry of Water Resources). The strategies were based on 'The Export Strategy for Infrastructure Systems'. Targets were revised in 2018 and aim to obtain orders for infrastructure projects with a total value of 30 trillion yen in 2020 (METI, 2018)
Kanto Bureau of Telecommunications, Ministry of Internal Affairs and Communications	- Community News Broadcasting; - Disaster countermeasure support (SOUMU, n.d.)
Ministry of Finance	Maintain and manage the nation's financial affairs
Kanto Regional Development Bureau (MLIT)	In the event of a disaster, the Kanto Regional Development Bureau is responsible for the early securing of emergency transportation roads and the early restoration of river embankments, port facilities, etc. (KTR, n.d.)
Ministry of Health, Labour and Welfare	Water supply for domestic use (Water Supply Law being a law to promote implementation of programmes which enable source water quality protection for public water supply (MLIT, 2008)
Kanto Bureau of Economy, Trade and Industry (Ministry of Economy, Trade and Industry)	Water supply for industrial use and hydroelectric power generation (Industrial Water Law, Industry Water Supply Business, etc.) (MLIT, 2008)

Relevant government authorities and organizations	*Responsibilities*
Ministry of Land, Infrastructure, Transport and Tourism (MLIT)	*Water Resources Department*: The department is responsible for overall coordination of adjusting measures for water supply and demand planning and reservoir area development (Water Resources Development Promotion Law, Japan Water Agency Law, Law Concerning Special Measures for reservoir Areas, etc.) *Sewerage and Waste Management Department*: Sewerage laws, etc *River Bureau*: Flood control, river water utilization and dam construction (River Law, Specified Multipurpose Dam Law, etc.) (MLIT, 2008)
Ministry of the Environment	Conservation of water quality and environmental preservation (Water Pollution Control Law, Water quality laws relating to conservation of headwaters for preserving quality of drinking water supply, etc.) (MLIT, 2008)
Japan Water Agency (JWA)	- Constructing dams and facilities - Flood control - Maintaining and improving normal functions of the river water, for example, conserving river environment or securing vested water - Securing water for domestic, industrial and agricultural use (APFM, n.d.)

(continued)

Table 9.2 (continued)

Relevant government authorities and organizations	*Responsibilities*
Japan Water Works Association (JWWA)	- Water Utility Management Advisory - Technical Research of water supply management, technologies and water quality - Publish water supply related books on management and technical subjects - Training: JWWA provides training to improve skills of employees working in water supply utilities Inspection Service: Based on objective inspection criteria, the organization conducts performance testing and product inspections of water supply equipment and materials - GLP Accreditation Service—Water Supply Service: In 2009, JWWA also developed 'Guidelines for Tap Water Quality Testing Good Laboratory Practice' (GLP). (JWWA, n.d.)
Japan Industrial Water Association	- Investigation and research on industrial water - Proposal and reporting on industrial water to the Parliament and Government - Conducting visits and inspection, and holding workshops, lectures, classes, meetings and exhibitions - Preparation and distribution of reference books and materials such as journals - Research and investigation of the standards of industrial waterworks - Activities necessary to achieve the purpose of the association (JST, 2009)
Public Utility Services Centre Co., Ltd	- Customer services at stations - Meter reading and billing—Providing computerized calculation of water charges - Collecting water charges

Relevant government authorities and organizations	*Responsibilities*
TSS Tokyo Water Co., Ltd	- Design, construction, operation and maintenance of waterworks and related facilities - Design, construction and supervision of water supply facilities - Operation and maintenance of water supply facilities—Services on customer connection affairs - Water quality assessment - Waterworks consultation and training - Management and sale of water supply equipment and materials - Research and development on waterworks - Worker dispatching undertaking (TSS, n.d.)

Compensation Measures for Upstream Residents

To meet the water demand of Tokyo through the construction of dams, government must work effectively with all stakeholders. Prior to undertaking large-scale water infrastructure development, such as dam building, government must reach agreement regarding compensation and resettlement with those residents to be displaced or somehow negatively affected by the activity (Kaigi, 2009). In addition to these measures, a 'Law Concerning Special Measures for Reservoir Areas' was created (MLIT, 2001).

Using Water Effectively

Midway through the first decade of the Twenty-first Century, average water use in Tokyo was estimated to be 361 L per capita per day (l/c/d). 'If we exclude heavy water users, such as hotels, public baths, and so forth, the average water consumption rate of households in Tokyo is estimated at around 244 [l/c/d]' (World Bank, 2008: 5). Data from various sources online suggests that consumption rates are similar today.

Effective use of water resources is not only about re/building large-scale facilities to alleviate the gap between supply and demand. It is also essential to reduce the impact of drought and to make more effective use of water in all its forms. In Japan, government has prioritized wastewater reuse through legislation and incentives for business and industry (Takeuchi & Tanaka, 2020). In the Greater Tokyo area effective wastewater reuse (such as treated sewage, recycled industrial wastewater), grey water and rainwater harvesting, and other types of non-standard water resource development and management have been ongoing since the 1980s. Although the water quality is low, this water is used for a variety of public and private purposes: for example, stream flow augmentation, green belt and private land irrigation, water sprinkling (*uchimizu*), toilet flushing and refrigeration (MLIT, 2001; Takeuchi & Tanaka, 2020). The Ministry of Construction (MOC) advocates actions such as building water-saving houses (MOC, 2000). According to the Bureau of Sewerage of the TMG, 'there are thirteen wastewater treatment plants in the 23 city wards and another seven in the regional sewerage system in the Tama district' (available at: https://www.narbo.jp/data/04_materials/ma_sewerage.pdf; see Table 9.3 for a selection). The effective deployment of these

Table 9.3 Wastewater Treatment Plants (WWTP) in Tokyo

Start Date	*WWTP*	*Capacity (m^3/day)*	*Process*	*Application*
1984	Ochiai	8,000	Sand filtration	Toilet flushing
1984	Tamagawa Johryu	n.a	Sand filtration/O_3	Stream flow augmentation
1993	Ochiai	8,000	MF/RO[a]	Recreational
1996	Ariake	30,000	Biofiltration/O_3	Toilet flushing
1997	Shibaura	5,000	Sand filtration/O_3	Toilet flushing, Train washing
1998	Shibaura	7,000	Ceramic filtration/O_3	Toilet flushing
2002	Shibaura	6,700	Sand filtration/O_3	Toilet flushing

[a]Micro-filtration process/Reverse osmosis membrane process
Source Adapted from Takeuchi and Tanaka (2020).

innovative practices has reduced the consumption of water resources while enhancing water security during extreme events such as drought, flood and earthquake (Takeuchi & Tanaka, 2020).

Key Issues and Challenges

Climate Change

Over the past 100 years, the average annual surface air temperature in Japan has increased by approximately 1 °C. Since 1970, in terms of precipitation, low rainfall years have become more frequent. The years (1973, 1978, 1984, 1994, and 1996) when water shortages caused damage, the precipitation amounts received were below average. Observations made also found an increasing trend between extremely high and low rainfall events. In addition to decreased precipitation and recurrent low rainfall years due to climate change, trends also showed decreased snowfall and increased early thaw events (MLIT, 2008). According to the Regional Climate Model (RCM), 'mean annual temperature in Japan could increase by 2–3 °C by 2100 (2081–2100) relative to the baseline (1981–2000) and that precipitation could increase in summer (June–September) and decrease in other seasons' (Ogawa-Onishi & Berry, 2013: 362).

Dry Spells

As per the Bureau of Waterworks, water shortages in Tokyo occur about once in every decade (Bureau of Waterworks, n.d.-b). Most recently in 2016, several river basins faced a shortage of reservoir water, which led to water users having to restrict their water intake. In the Tone River basin, a lack of winter snowfall combined with a dry May to create the shortage. In the upper Tone River basin, Ozenuma observation station recorded the lowest maximum snow depth in 62-years of 172 cm in 2015–2016, which is an amount that is only 60% of the annual average. The snowpack at the observation station melted one month earlier than the average at the end of April. In addition to this, the upper Tone River basin reported only 48% of the average monthly rainfall for the month of May in 2016. The deficit of river flow affected eight reservoirs in the area. The first drought coordination council was organized on June 14 by the Kanto Regional Development Bureau, when the total volume of the eight reservoirs reached 45% of the annual average. A 10% intake cut was maintained from June 16 to August 24 by domestic, agricultural and industrial water users, until the restriction was removed when Typhoon No. 9 brought adequate rainfall to the area (Priscoli & Hiroki, 2016). Given climate change forecasting, these events will present water managers with significant challenges in the coming years.

Natural Disasters

Tokyo is subject to earthquakes, floods (IWA, 2019) and weather-related natural disasters such as typhoons, heavy rains, windstorms and snow (MOFA, n.d.). These events cause damage to water supply and sewage networks, thereby disrupting water supply service provisions (IWA, 2018). For example, after the 2011 Japan Earthquake, it was reported that millions of Japanese residents faced the threat of no water resources. This is because the restoration of water supply infrastructure usually takes several weeks (Walton, 2011). A 2010 research survey found that TMG has polished its management skills in the comprehensive use of water resources through unified control of water levels and water quality, efficient water usage, reuse of sewage-treated water and protection of the ecosystem (Yoichi, 2010).

Pollution

Around 120 rivers are flowing through Tokyo, including the Tama and Sumida rivers. Although the water quality of these rivers declined significantly during the period of rapid economic growth, there has been remarkable improvement since the 1970s due to the control of pollutants from sources like factories and improvements made to sewage systems. Compared with the early 1970s, the water quality of Tokyo Bay has also improved (Bureau of Environment, 2018). However, the TMG still has some problems to overcome, such as algal bloom incidents (Anderson et al., 2019).

Water Privatization

Under Japan's increasingly ageing population, the revised Water Supply Act aims to strengthen the quality of municipal water supply services and to renovate ageing infrastructure to ensure water security. But some critics worry that the law paves the way for local governments to sell rights to manage water services for up to 20 years, which would lead to privatization, thereby limiting the government's capacity to make positive and timely reactions in the public interest. According to the TMG, one-third of the municipalities that manage water supply services are not able to pay water bills to cover operating costs, and the situation is expected to worsen as the country's population declines (Tomohiro, 2018).

Efforts Made to Achieve Water Security

Coordinated Drought Risk Management

Once every three years, restrictions are applied on water intake in the downstream of the Tone River basin (UNESCO, 2016). There is a tight supply of water in the capital area and in the past 10 years water restrictions have been imposed three times to ensure continuity of water resources and to stabilize water use in the Tone River basin. The restrictions help in increasing the supply of municipal and industrial water to the Tokyo area (Tournier et al., 2019).

Through real time telemeter systems, river runoff and water storage volume of dam reservoirs are continually monitored by river and dam administrators. A drought coordination council is initiated in an event of decrease in river runoff or reservoir levels, and when the entitled water use is forecasted to be impacted. The council comprises of the river and dam administrators (e.g. Japan Water Agency, the local government, Ministry of Land, Infrastructure, Transport and Tourism [MLIT], etc.), in addition to water users (e.g. irrigation organizations, domestic and industrial water supply agencies, hydraulic power companies, etc.). Drought coordination meetings are regularly organized to update entities on river and reservoir data, drought prediction based on data, and the associated impacts of a drought event on water users. In times of drought, council members come to an agreement on step-by-step water withdrawal restrictions, where members monitor drought impact and persuade end users and citizens to conserve water (Priscoli & Hiroki, 2016).

Article 53 of the River Law specifies all water right holders to coordinate among each other during drought conditions and also highlights the responsibility of the river administrator to provide the necessary information for proper coordination. In cases where an agreement cannot be reached it is the river administrator's duty to mediate negotiations. The purpose of water use (drinking water, agriculture, industry) does not affect who is given priority to access water, but it depends on the order the rights were granted. Generally, water rights are built on lowest river flow in ten years, in instances whereby river flow decreases below this threshold the entitled water amount may not be withdrawn. Therefore, the right to access river water depends on river flow, and water users cannot claim water rights against river administrators (Priscoli & Hiroki, 2016).

During severe drought situations, the government arranges a drought response meeting with eleven water relevant ministries and agencies, with the goal being to respond to the drought event with suitable measures. Generally, each water-related ministry and prefectural government is held accountable to have its drought response headquarters. In the past, to respond to droughts a range of measures have been applied, which include: (i) converting reservoir water allocated for hydraulic power to water supply, (ii) temporarily using water from private wells, (iii) delivering drinking water by water tanks, (iv) conducting a public campaign on water saving and (v) putting a hold on water that is used for public and school swimming pools (Priscoli & Hiroki, 2016). This suite of activities is tantamount to standard practice across all drought-prone megacities, with Cape Town's recent experience being instructive in this regard (Swatuk et al., 2021).

Stakeholder Participation in Water Resources Management

In 1997, the River Law was amended to plan for flood control, water use and environmental conservation for formulating a river improvement plan for all rivers in Japan. The law required public participation to be a part of the planning process (MOC, 2018). Another example is when the Tama River Plan was established by conducting roundtables which actively involved local residents, municipalities, industry, academic experts and administrators. A total of 26,600 people from the basin were involved in river basin seminars, river inspection tours and civil action, organized by the residents and administrations. Plan development was completed within two years, which was much quicker than anticipated because of effective stakeholder participation from the beginning of the planning stage (MLIT, n.d.-a).

IWRM at River Basin Level

Japan's integrated water resource management (IWRM) programme encourages sustainable water use and water cycle governance by implementing relevant policies and frameworks that involve appropriate sectors and stakeholders (MLIT, n.d.-a). The IWRM guidelines set at the River Basin Level have been developed by UNESCO/IHP in partnership with the Network of Asian River Basin Organizations (NARBO), to contribute to the World Water Assessment Programme (WWAP) (Nakajo, 2010). By 2020, Japan was 95% of the way toward reaching Sustainable Development Goal (SDG) Target 6.5.1 which measures the degree of implementation of IWRM. Also by 2020, 99% of the population were using a safely managed drinking water service (SDG 60.1.1), and 81% had access to safe sanitation (SDG 6.2.1). (See https://www.sdg6data.org/country-or-area/Japan#anchor_6.5.1.) Given Japan's small landmass, narrow rivers and coastal urban settlement patterns, the integrated management of water for humans and nature has a long history. The experience of the Tama and Tone rivers provides some background in this regard.

Tama River

From the 1960's, the Tama River basin was being rapidly urbanized, whereby environmental conservation and the use of riparian buffers by communities became major issues. In the beginning of the 1970's, civil society became concerned with the disappearing of natural areas by the

Tama River. The public opposed the development of ecologically rich riparian zones into sports areas. In support of river preservation many public activities began to spring up. This encouraged the government to establish the 1980 Tama River Environmental Management Plan. This plan was the first of its kind in Japan, developed through direct dialogue with local residents. In 1987, to promote awareness on measures that improve the Tama River environment, the Tama River Basin Council held a 'Tama River Week' for residents and administrative agencies. To further continuous knowledge exchange to build a collaborative framework on Tama River improvement, in 1988, a Tama River Basin Roundtable involving residents, river managers, academic experts, basin municipalities and other relevant stakeholders was held. This was done to build trust among stakeholders and aid in consensus-building to establish a 'good river/good city' management approach. In 2001, to further river improvement the 'Tama River Improvement Plan' for the next 30 years was developed by collaborating with all relevant stakeholders. In terms of NGO and civil society volunteer activities, there are at least 200 existing organizations that provide networks for a range of civil groups to exchange knowledge (UNESCO, 2009).

Tone River

Since 1958, restrictions on water supply have been common in Tokyo, particularly during summer months, when water demand of local residents is met by transporting water by trucks carrying water tanks. Even though Ogochi Dam completed construction in 1957, the dam could not meet the demand of the Tokyo region. Impacts were further compounded by land subsidence as a result of excess ground-water pumping for industrial use, and riverbed degradation of Tone River which caused water levels to sink. In this situation, the Tokyo Metropolitan Government (TMG) sought a new water source. In 1958, it was declared by the government that water in the upstream dams would be conveyed via a pipeline upstream of the river area to an existing purification plant. In 1961, the Water Resources Development Promotion Law and the Water Resources Public Corporation Law were both developed, in addition to an implementation body established by the government to develop an integrated plan for water use and flood control for the river basin. With the Water Resources Development Promotion Law in place, for the first time, the Tone River was designated as a river system on the basis of the law. It was decided that intake facilities would be unified (barrage construction) and a 14 km long canal would be developed to connect Tone and Ara River. In 1963, the government also announced a plan to develop Tone River canal. The construction of this canal was completed in 1968; this measure along with the intake unification barrage helped stabilize not only water intake, but also water supply (UNESCO, 2009).

Water Conservation

Water Conservation Forest

The water conservation forest located upstream in the Tama River has been managed by the Bureau of Waterworks, TMG for over a century. It is the largest forest managed by a water-supply corporation in Japan. The total area covered by the water conservation forest is 23,000 hectares, stretching nearly 20 kilometres north and south and 31 kilometres east and west. The rain that falls in the forest infiltrates into the spongy soil and the runoff flows slowly toward the river, this aids in stabilizing the volume of water in the river, preventing extreme events like droughts or floods. Due to this function of the forest, it is popularly known as the 'green dam'. Another purpose that is served by the forest is that it acts as a natural water filtering plant, in addition to preventing soil from flowing into the river (Bureau of Waterworks, n.d.-c).

The Ogouchi Dam developed on the main stem of the Tama River displays low volumes of sediments because of the maintenance of the conservation forest. Generally, with the ongoing usage of a dam significant sediment is built up over time. However, because of proper maintenance of the forest by the Bureau, this issue has been avoided for over 50 years, and the amount of sediment in proportion to the volume of water has been maintained at a low rate of 3.2% (Bureau of Waterworks, n.d.-c).

Rainwater Harvesting

To expand water storage capacity, rooftops in Tokyo have been transformed to rainwater catchments (Furumai, 2008). This has been done to preserve water resources (Furumai, 2016). As of March, 2002, within the Tokyo Metropolitan Area there were at least 850 rainwater harvesting facilities of which 284 were private buildings and 566 were public buildings.

There has been much interest in Tokyo and other regions in Japan in the use of household rainwater storage systems so that in times of emergencies, these reserved water sources can be used for firefighting or as emergency water supplies during disaster events. In the Mukojima district of Tokyo, collected rainwater from rooftops is being used for garden watering, firefighting and as drinking water during emergencies. Although rainwater harvesting is being utilized in Tokyo as a water preservation strategy, it has a greater potential to flourish and play a major role as a water supply source, flood preservation measure, and as a disaster mitigation strategy (Chen et al., 2021; Khanal et al., 2020).

Water Efficiency—Reclaimed Wastewater Use

Tokyo Metropolitan Government (TMG) manages the 'wastewater reuse' business to use water resources effectively. In this business, wastewater from sewers is highly treated and then used in various urban non-potable ways. Since 1984, this business includes a regional recycling system of recyclable wastewater for toilet flushing. As of 2008, an average of 8400 m^3/day of recycled water had been supplied to 129 facilities. As indicated in Table 9.3, the scale is expanding. Another use of reclaimed sewer wastewater is that it is discharged into urban rivers, which have low flow rates as a result of climate change and urbanization. Besides this use, secondary wastewater or highly treated wastewater can also be used for washing, firefighting, road spraying, entertainment in the park and so on (Furumai, 2008).

In March, 2011, a seismic intensity of 'upper 5' was recorded in Tokyo, as a result of the Great East Japan Earthquake so-called epicentral earthquake. According to the Tokyo Government Disaster Prevention Council's projection, epicentral earthquakes in some regions can cause seismic intensity of 7 at maximum and an average of 'upper 6' in a large number of regions. As a result, Tokyo Waterworks has enhanced their backup functions and established a water supply system that is earthquake-resistant so that in case of occurrence of serious seismic events, water supply is secured. Some of the measures under backup functions include: (i) duplexing water conveyance facilities and (ii) duplexing and reinforcement of water transmission networks. Major measures in support of earthquake-resistance of waterworks facilities include: (i) reinforcement of earthquake-resistance of purification plants and water supply (distribution) stations and (ii) set up of independent electricity (reinforcement of non-utility power generation facilities) (TMG, 2018).

Emergency Services

Emergency water supply stations have been set up in case of water shortages or other types of accidents that can occur during earthquakes. Over 200 water supply bases (water purification plants, water supply stations and emergency water supply tanks) have been established, so that, there is one water supply base within a radius of two kilometres from any place. Water supply tanks connected to distribution pipes, maintain stores of freshwater which comes from pumped water recycling systems. To complement emergency water supply points, temporary taps have been installed by fire hydrants which are near evacuation sites. This is done as part of restorative work in case there is need to temporarily halt water supply. Additionally, an all year round, around the clock emergency water services squad has also been established to handle water shortage emergencies (TMG, 2018).

Flood Risk Reduction

Significant measures have been taken to reduce flood risk, from inexpensive, small scale, nature-based solutions such as parks and playgrounds to massive expensive and technologically sophisticated built infrastructure such as the Loop Road No. 7 Underground Regulating reservoir built under the Kandagawa area of Tokyo. This structure has the capacity to store 540,000 m^3 of flood water drawn from three different rivers, the Kanda, Zenpukuji and Miaofa Temple (Plaza Homes Ltd., 2019). Most dramatic of all, perhaps, is the Metropolitan Area Outer Discharge Channel Facility. This massive underground facility consists of five 70 metre tall cylindrical water storage tanks interconnected over its 6.3 kilometre length by tunnels built approximately 50 metres below ground. The Facility collects run-off from five waterways and rivers before discharging the water into the Edogawa River and from there into the sea (Ortiz, 2018). It has a maximum holding capacity of 670,000 m^3 and drained an estimated 10 Mm^3 over a three-day period during Typhoon Hagibis (Typhoon No. 9) in October 2019 (Plaza Homes Ltd., 2019).

Pollution Control

According to the MLIT, an effective method for dealing with water pollution is to establish water quality standards, regulate the treatment of industrial wastewater, construct sewage treatment systems, dredge contaminated sediments and formulate sewage discharge standards (MLIT, n.d.-b). In two successful cases in Tokyo, it was found that with the progress of sewage construction, the water quality of the Tama River improved, creating a good water environment for Tokyo residents. The Sumida River also became a representative landscape of Tokyo through sewage regulations, sewage construction, dredging of contaminated sediments and water purification (Kitamura, 2012). With the improvement in river water, clean water supplies are now widely available, and deaths from infectious diseases caused by contaminated water sources have declined significantly (MLIT, n.d.-b).

Privatizing Some Water Supplies as a Means to Ensuring Sufficient Funds

In future, Tokyo could face the monetary burden of its ageing water infrastructure. Therefore, to deal with this problem, some water supply projects have already been entrusted to be operated and managed by private entities. As indicated above, Japan as a whole is well on the way to reaching its SDG 6 water and sanitation targets. In recent years, however, water supply systems across the country are approaching the end of useful life as facilities deteriorate. The need for renovations and renewals is expected to increase significantly. The Tokyo government estimated that if the amount of investment continues to decline year by year, the demand for upgrading facilities will exceed the amount of investment set by the government of Japan by 2020 (the government of Japan has strict limits and requirements on fiscal expenditure) (METI, 2008). According to Leckie et al. (2021: 24), the estimated annual investment cost for water and sanitation in Japan is 2.47 billion USD. For riverine flood protection it is 10.89 billion USD and for coastal flood protection, 5.18 billion USD.

The scale of the emerging problem as well as the anticipated cost to address it successfully has led the government to focus on programmes to revise investment in water facilities to make better use of private sector funds. For example, the 2002 amendment to the Water Supply

Act indicated that the technical operation of some water supply systems was entrusted to third parties (including private entities). This was done so that enough funding is available to renovate water facilities. In projects assigned to third parties, only a small percentage of the projects are delegated to private entities. Therefore, it is still not possible for private water service providers to take control of the entire value chain in future to replace municipalities (METI, 2008). Moreover, in the context of Tokyo's vulnerability to extreme events, its highly effective governance and management capacity, and the built-in tendency toward citizen engagement, public-private-community partnerships seem to stand a better chance of success than in many of the other megacities featured in this collection.

Conclusion

More than a decade ago, Tortajada (2010) identified water utilities in Tokyo as an example of good water governance. It is evident from this chapter that different actors have been working diligently for decades to achieve water security in Tokyo by building resilient water supplies, expanding sewer system coverage, implementing efficient and effective conservation measures and adapting to new challenges with creative solutions. Different levels of government have implemented policies and regulations that safeguard water quality and quantity, in addition to involving multiple local public and private stakeholders who help implement regulations at the local level, as well as bring specialized knowledge in support of water security.

Enhanced technical capacity has contributed to further development and sustainability of water and sanitation. Today, Japan is a world-class leader in water technologies; for example, producing 60% of membranes used in water treatment in the world. Japanese membrane technology is used in seawater desalination and advanced treatment, including wastewater recovery worldwide (MLIT, n.d.-a). Advanced technologies have brought about profits to the Japanese and Tokyo governments, allowing TMG to continue upgrading its technology and equipment while expanding its overseas operations.

Japan has one of the highest GDPs per capita, despite water shortages, compared with international standards. A high industrial wastewater recycling rate (about 80%) combined with a dramatically reduced water leakage rate (also referred to as non-revenue or unaccounted-for water rate) (METI, 2008) enables Japanese cities to make more and better use of the water they already have. Not only does this reduce the need for new sources of supply, it also reduces budgetary expenditures. The average non-revenue water rate in Asia is 34%, compared with 3% in Tokyo and 7% in Osaka, suggesting that water systems in Japan are highly efficient (TMG, 2018).

Moving forward, in terms of water security during water shortages or disasters, to supplement each other, both large-scale water systems and locally distributed water supply systems should be expanded within the context of an overall water-sensitive urban design (Yamashita, 2018). Additionally, with climate change, as extreme weather events become more frequent and severe, city-to-city knowledge exchanges will also play a vital role in developing best practices to adapt to risks (IWA, 2018).

References

Anderson, C. R., Berdalet, E., Kudela, R. M., Cusack, C. K., Silke, J., O'Rourke, E., Dugan, D., McCammon, M., Newton, J. A., Moore, S. K. Paige, K., Ruberg, S., Morrison, J. R., Kirkpatrick, B., Hubbard, K., & Morell, J. (2019, May 22). Scaling up from regional case studies to a global harmful algal bloom observing system. *Frontiers in Marine Science*. https://doi.org/10.3389/fmars.2019.00250

APFM (Associated Programme on Flood Management). (n.d.). *Japan Water Agency*. APFM.

Bureau of Environment. (2018). Water quality control. *Bureau of environment—TMG*. https://www.kankyo.metro.tokyo.lg.jp/en/pollution/quality.html. Accessed 6 April 2022.

Bureau of Waterworks. (n.d.-a). *Questions in regard to water charges*. Bureau of Waterworks, TMG. https://www.waterworks.metro.tokyo.lg.jp/eng/charge/charge-list.html. Accessed 6 April 2022.

Bureau of Waterworks. (n.d.-b). *In order to deliver tap water in stable fashion*. Bureau of Waterworks, TMG. https://www.waterworks.metro.tokyo.jp/eng/news/archive-46/. Accessed 6 April 2022.

Bureau of Waterworks. (n.d.-c). *Potable delicious water obtained from rich forests*. Bureau of Waterworks, TMG. https://www.waterworks.metro.tokyo.jp/eng/news/archive-47/. Accessed 6 April 2022.

Chen, W., Gao, W., Jiang, J., Wei, X., & Wang, R. (2021). Feasibility analysis of decentralized hybrid rainwater-graywater systems in a public building in Japan. *Sustainable Cities and Society, 69*, 102870.

EDMS. (2007). *Review of the international water resources management policies and actions and the latest practice in their environmental evaluation and strategic environmental assessment final report. chapter 3: Japan*. EDMS.

Furumai, H. (2008). Rainwater and reclaimed wastewater for sustainable urban water use. *Physics and Chemistry of the Earth, 33*(5), 340–346.

Furumai, H. (2016, June). Evaluation of rainwater harvesting and use potential considering climate change in Arakawa watershed. *Novatech 2016: 9th International Conference on Planning and Technologies for Sustainable Management of Water in the City*. Lyon, France: International Water Association. Hal-03322113.

IWA (International Water Association). (2018). *Tokyo endorses the International Water Association's principles for water-wise cities*. International Water Association (IWA). https://iwa-network.org/news/tokyo-endorses-the-international-water-associations-principles-for-water-wise-cities/. Accessed 6 April 2022.

IWA (International Water Association). (2019). *Tokyo report—Conclusions, key messages and outcomes. World Water Congress and Exhibition 2018*. International Water Association (IWA). https://iwa-network.org/wp-content/uploads/2019/10/2018_IWA_WWCE-Tokyo_Report.pdf. Accessed 6 April 2022.

JST. (2009). *Introduction of Japan Industrial Water Association*. Japan Science and Technology Agency (JST). https://jglobal.jst.go.jp/en/detail?JGLOBAL_ID=200905074363695694. Accessed 6 April 2022.

JWWA. (n.d.). *Profile: Japan Water Works Association*. JWWA.

Kaigi, N. D. D. (2009). *Dams in Japan: Past, present, and future*. CRC Press.

Khanal, G., Thapa, A., Devkota, N., & Paudel, U. R. (2020). A review of harvesting and harnessing rainwater: An alternative strategy to cope with drinking water scarcity. *Water Supply, 20*(8), 2951.

Kitamura, T. (2012). *Water Environment Management in Japan. WEPA Dialogue in Sri Lanka*. Ministry of the Environment.

KTR. (n.d.). *About*. Kanto Regional Development Bureau, MLIT. https://www.ktr.mlit.go.jp/index.htm. Accessed 6 April 2022.

Leckie, H., Smythe, H., & Leflaive, X. (2021). *Financing water security for sustainable growth in the Asia-Pacific region* (Environment Working Paper No. 171*)*. OECD. https://www.oecd.org/officialdocuments/publicdisplaydocumentpdf/?cote=ENV/WKP(2021)3&docLanguage=En. Accessed 23 March 2022.

McDonald, R. I., Weber, K., Padowski, J., Flörke, M., Schneider, C., Green, P. A., Gleeson, T., Eckman, S., Lehner, B., Balk, D., Boucher, T., Grill, G., & Montgomery, M. (2014). Water on an urban planet: Urbanization and the reach of urban water infrastructure. *Global Environmental Change, 27*, 96–105.

METI. (2008). *White paper report*. Ministry of Economy, Trade, and Industry (METI). https://www.meti.go.jp/english/report/downloadfiles/2008WhitePaper/3-4.pdf. Accessed 6 April 2022.

METI. (2018). *METI releases overseas development strategy of water industry*. https://www.meti.go.jp/english/press/2018/0727_001.html. Accessed 6 April 2022.

MLIT. (2001). *Shutoken Hakusyo (Metropolitan area white paper)*. Ministry of Finance.

MLIT. (2008). *Water resources in Japan*. Ministry of Land, Infrastructure, Transport and Tourism (MLIT). https://www.mlit.go.jp/tochimizushigen/mizsei/water_resources/index.html. Accessed 6 April 2022.

MLIT. (n.d.-a). *Achieving water security in Japan and worldwide*. Ministry of Land, Infrastructure, Transport and Tourism (MLIT).

MLIT. (n.d.-b). *Japan's experience and technology regarding water resources management*. Ministry of Land, Infrastructure, Transport and Tourism (MLIT).

MOC. (2000). *Kensetsu Hakusyo (Construction white paper)*. Infrastructure Development Institute.

MOC. (2018). *The river law with commentary by article: Legal framework for river and water management in Japan*. River Bureau, Ministry of Construction, Infrastructure Development Institute.

MOFA. (n.d.). *Disaster and disaster prevention in Japan*. https://www.mofa.go.jp/policy/disaster/21st/2.html. Accessed 6 April 2022.

Nakajo, Y. (2010, July). A spiral approach to IWRM: The IWRM guidelines at river basin level. *Hydrocomplexity: New tools for solving wicked water problems* (IAHS Publ. 338). Kovacs Colloquium.

Ogawa-Onishi, Y., & Berry, P. M. (2013). Ecological impacts of climate change in Japan: The importance of integrating local and international publications. *Biological Conservation, 157*, 361–371.

Ortiz, D. A. (2018). *An intricate systems of dams, levees and tunnels defends Japan's capital. Will it be able to cope with climate change?* BBC Future. https://www.bbc.com/future/article/20181129-the-underground-cathedral-protecting-tokyo-from-floods. Accessed 23 March 2022.

Petersen-Perlman, J. D., Veilleux, J. C., Zentner, M., & Wolf, A. T. (2012). Case studies on water security: Analysis of system complexity and the role of institutions. *Journal of Contemporary Water Research and Education, 149*(1), 4–12.

Plaza Homes Ltd. (2019). *Preventative measures against flooding in the Tokyo metropolitan area*. Plaza Homes Ltd. https://www.realestate-tokyo.com/news/tokyo-flood-prevention/. Accessed 1 April 2022.

Priscoli, J. D., & Hiroki, K. (2016). Introduction. *Water Policy, 18*(S2), 1–5.

Sato, C., Haga, M., & Nishino, J. (2006). Land subsidence and groundwater management in Tokyo. *International Review for Environmental Strategies, 6*(2), 403–424.

SOUMU. (n.d.). *Introduction of Kanto General Communication Bureau.* Ministry of Internal Affairs and Communications. https://www.soumu.go.jp/soutsu/kanto/. Accessed 6 April 2022.

Swatuk, L. A., Brill, G., Buchner-Marais, C., Carden, C., Conradie, E., Day, J., Fatch, J., Fell, J., Hara, M., & Ncube, B. (2021). *Towards the blue-green city: Building urban water resilience.* South African Water Research Commission.

Takesada, N. (2009). Japanese experience of involuntary resettlement: Long-term consequences of resettlement for the construction of the Ikawa Dam. *International Journal of Water Resources Development, 25*(3), 419–430.

Takeuchi, H., & Tanaka, H. (2020). Water reuse and recycling in Japan—History, current situation, and future perspectives. *Water Cycle, 1*, 1–12.

TMG. (2018). *Water supply in Tokyo.* Tokyo Metropolitan Government (TMG). http://www.waterprofessionals.metro.tokyo.jp/tmwb-7.html. Accessed 6 April 2022.

TMG. (n.d.). *The structure of the Tokyo Metropolitan Government (TMG).* https://www.metro.tokyo.lg.jp/ENGLISH/ABOUT/STRUCTURE/structure04.htm. Accessed 6 April 2022.

Tomohiro, O. (2018, December 17). With water privatization, Japan faces crossroads in battling its aging pipes. *The Japan Times.*

Tortajada, C. (2010). Water governance: Some critical issues. *International Journal of Water Resources Development, 26*(2), 297–307.

Tournier, J. P., Bennett, T., & Bibeau, J. (2019, June 9–14). *Sustainable and safe dams around the world: Proceedings of the ICOLD 2019 Symposium, (ICOLD 2019).* Ottawa, Canada, CRC Press.

TSS Tokyo Water. (n.d.a). *Leak detection and prevention.* TSS Tokyo Water Co., Ltd.

TSS Tokyo Water. (n.d.b). *Profile. Tokyo Water Co., Ltd. (TSS).* TSS Tokyo Water Co., Ltd.

UN. (2015). *Sustainable development goals knowledge platform.* United Nations. https://sustainabledevelopment.un.org/sdg6. Accessed 6 April 2022.

UNESCO. (2009). *IWRM guidelines at river basin level. Part 2–1: The guidelines for IWRM coordination.* UNESCO.

UNESCO. (2016). *Water, megacities and global change. Portraits of 15 emblematic cities of the world.* UNESCO.

UN FAO. (2017). *Water for sustainable food and agriculture. A report produced for the G20 presidency of Germany.* FAO.

UN-Water. (2013). *2030 water secure: Developing capacity to secure the 21st century water risk.* UNU-INWEH.

Walton, B. (2011). *After earthquake, millions in Japan without water—Extent of damage to water infrastructure unknown*. Circle of Blue. https://www.circleofblue.org/2011/world/after-earthquake-millions-in-japan-without-water%E2%80%94extent-of-damage-to-water-infrastructure-unknown/. Accessed 6 April 2022.

World Bank. (2006). *Water resources management in Japan policy, institutional and legal issues. World Bank Analytical and Advisory Assistance (AAA) program* (China: Addressing Water Scarcity Background Paper No. 1). The World Bank.

World Bank. (2008). *Japanese water and wastewater utility management. Accountability and performance management for better results* (MNSSD Learning Series 1). The World Bank.

Yamashita, A. (2018). History of urban water use in Tokyo with focusing on surface and subsurface water as water sources. In T. Kikuchi & T. Sugai (Eds.), *Tokyo as a global city* (pp. 115–135). Springer.

Yoichi, F. (2010, September 15). Global water security: Japan should play a key role. *Asahi Shimbun*.

CHAPTER 10

Toward Sustainability, Away from Collapse: Challenges for Twenty-First Century Megacities

Corrine Cash and Larry Swatuk

Introduction

This collection was conceived fully in light of the global climate crisis, but slightly predated the onset of the global health pandemic. What does this juxtaposition of immediate (COVID-19) and imminent (GHG-induced climate change) disaster tell us about the prospects for achieving water security in the megacities of the world? First there are the facts, that is, the things that are well-known. Secondly there are the prospects, that is, the things that might come to pass given different scenarios. The latter

C. Cash
Mount Allison University, Sackville, NB, Canada
e-mail: ccash@mta.ca

L. Swatuk (✉)
University of Waterloo, Waterloo, ON, Canada
e-mail: lswatuk@uwaterloo.ca

L. Swatuk and C. Cash (eds.), *The Political Economy of Urban Water Security under Climate Change*, International Political Economy Series,
https://doi.org/10.1007/978-3-031-08108-8_10

not only reflects the former, but as told in this collection, clearly reflects the positions, interests and needs of the people telling the story.

Aside from the editors, this collection displays the perspective of primarily young generalists, not seasoned specialists, almost all of whom have educational backgrounds and lived experiences firmly grounded in the Global South, mostly in community-based action. All but one identifies as female. Their interests lie in social justice, equity, diversity and inclusion. They identify ecological sustainability as the foundation for all action. They are not easily persuaded by big shiny expensive things. They are also not naïve. They know that water falls free from the sky but pipes and pumps and filtration systems cost money. What does their research tell us about the prospects for avoiding day zero in select megacities around the world? Do current events alter their conclusions or reinforce them?

Density and Death

With the onslaught of the pandemic, there were more than a few pundits willing to declare the densified, public-transport oriented city dead and buried. As the wealthy raced off to less densely populated places, the less well off were forced to navigate the COVID-19 infused urban world. While some thought that the virus would draw us toward a new, transformational order, reality proved otherwise: in a highly unequal world, the pandemic struck highly unequally. In the early months of the pandemic, where hand-washing and counter-top wiping became the new obsession, many people across the Global South were being forced to choose between fetching water for household chores or for incessant hand washing. Understandably, many women chose to risk the virus in support of everyday household activities. In dense urban spaces, social distancing was not an option. Where electricity was always undependable, people had to 'shop for the pot' on a meal-by-meal or day-by-day basis, forcing them into densely populated public spaces. In light of these well-known but Covid-highlighted realities, a new emphasis was placed on WASH activities. Would the finance be forthcoming for improved water and sanitation across the Global South? According to the World Health Organisation and UNICEF (2020: 1), 'The provision of safe water, sanitation and hygienic conditions is essential to protecting human health during all infectious disease outbreaks, including the Covid-19 pandemic'.

UN-Water paints a rather dismal picture of global performance regarding key SDG 6 targets (see https://www.sdg6data.org/):

- 74% of the world's population uses a safely managed drinking water source (SDG indicator 6.1.1, 2020)
- 54% of the world's population uses a safely managed sanitation service (SDG indicator 6.2.1a, 2020)
- 56% of the world's domestic wastewater is safely treated (SDG indicator 6.3.1, 2020)
- USD 9.3 billion is the amount of water and sanitation-related official development assistance received in 2019 (SDG indicator 6.a.1).

Considering that the World Bank estimates that approximately USD 114 billion/year until 2030 is necessary to build (let alone operate, manage and maintain) the infrastructure related to reaching targets SDG 60.1 and 6.2, the total finance highlighted above illustrates the scale of the finance challenge. Moreover, the global averages mask the true extent of the water, sanitation and hygiene challenges facing countries, cities and communities across the Global South.

While those most vulnerable to water borne disease, water-related disability affected life years and water-related extreme events are the urban poor crowded into ill-serviced, inadequate housing, the evidence amassed in this collection shows that policymakers, while acutely aware of socio-economic inequality in their cities, are more inclined to place scarce resources behind projects with the greatest (hypothesized) society-wide impact. This means large-scale, high-tech, expensive infrastructure such as desalination plants, water transfer schemes, dams and inter-linked systems of delivery. In line with the Dublin Principle that water should be considered an economic good, decisions increasingly reflect return-on-investment, and in some cases both water supply and wastewater management have been turned over to the private sector.

If the poor feature positively in decision-making it is as an indirect beneficiary of these 'society-wide' projects. Water, like economic growth, is expected to 'trickle down' to the base of the social pyramid. Pandemic or no pandemic, this generally means that community-based WASH efforts (even though the community may be several hundred thousand people) are left to the not-for-profits, foundations, and community-based-organizations. Some, like Water.org operate in the context of markets and micro-finance, following in the footsteps of initiatives such as the Grameen Bank. COVID-19 reinforces the fact that every city's story, no matter its size, is a tale of two cities: the wealthy, well-watered and -sewered on one side of the tracks; and the poor, ill-watered and non-sewered on the other side.

Citizen Action and 'Stakeholder Participation'

All cases illustrate this tale of two cities, with China's South North Water Diversion Project, Tokyo's Metropolitan Area Outer Discharge Channel Facility and Melbourne's desalination plant developing alongside of direct citizen action in support of lake rejuvenation, tree planting in catchment areas, groundwater mapping and stream clean up campaigns. Sometimes the two cities meet in common cause, such as joint City-Community efforts at slum upgrading and City-School initiatives in support of environmental education. At other times, however, the two cities clash as in Cochabamba where unilateral decisions in support of privatization met with sustained protest.

The Right to the City

All chapters place an emphasis on sustainabililty, generally filtered through the lens of the Sustainable Development Goals (SDGs), in particular SDG 6 on water and sanitation for all. Granted the SDGs are a crude indicator of performance on the ground, but they do provide a useful means for comparison, at least as a starting point for a deeper dive into a particular aspect of development.

Most of the chapters go beyond SDG 6, and even beyond water, to inquire into the very quality and character of urban design. C-40 cities advocate for a space where people 'live work and play', so scaling down from suburban car culture to a blue-green city shaped around principles of water-sensitive urban design. This raises questions of the very materiality of the city, how it's constructed, and how its construction shapes the day-to-day lives of its inhabitants. Clearly, there is the financial aspect, the city as an economic machine, a post-industrial place of hard surfaces full of people deploying soft skills. Yet, as opposed to a finished entity, immovable in time and space, a city is a living, breathing organism that supports human beings. Even ancient walled cities were penetrated socio-economic spaces. The European mediaeval Hanseatic League operated for more than five hundred years in support of the trade and commercial interests of towns and merchant associations. Across much of the world, rivers themselves served as conduits for the people, goods and services flowing to and through towns, villages and cities.

Sustainability, therefore, is more than metrics. It is about livability, and in the urban context, it is about spaces where people are respected irrespective of their class, race, caste and gender. The papers in this collection only skirt around these difficult issues. Pitched at the level of policy and performance in light of abiding current and future challenges, they do not delve into the difficult questions regarding the modalities of ensuring a socially just city. What they do is make a series of recommendations that are remarkably similar:

- improved governance through inclusive, transparent and accountable decision processes and practices;
- green design leading to the use of appropriate and affordable technology;
- a preference for nature-based solutions that can be jointly undertaken by all stakeholders in order to not only build sustainably but to also build trust and social capital.
- Fairness in pricing and the use of market forces
- Specific actions taken in clear sight of complex and integrated systems.

Complexity, Complex Systems and Integrated Management

In the context of climate change, most cities have chosen to focus their efforts on moving to low carbon economies. Aside from coastal cities' worries about sea level rise, water has been an after-thought in climate change action plans. Given water's indispensability in all human endeavour, approaches to ensuring water security have been largely reductive (see Morales and Swatuk in Chapter 3): find it, access it, deliver it, dispose of it. Almost all chapters highlight a key problem with this approach: mimicking temperate zone water management practices has locked-in arid, semi-arid and tropical zone countries and cities to processes ill-suited to their hydro-ecological environments. At the heart of water-sensitive urban design (WSUD) is an attempt to recover socio-ecological complexity in planning and decision-making. Some elements of WSUD have had great uptake in the decision-making corridors of cities and states: improved forest management in upper catchment areas (Cape Town, Sao Paulo, Tokyo); green infrastructure to manage stormwater runoff and recharge aquifers (Beijing, Cape Town); rainwater harvesting (Bangalore, Chennai); demand management (Melbourne, Cape Town); wastewater reuse (all cases); reduction in water losses and unaccounted-for water (all cases). As noted above, some of these efforts draw states and civil societies together in a mutually supportive way.

However, the scale, complexity and variety of the challenges regarding urban water security simply outrun a city's capacity to live within its 'water budget'. The goal of managing water resources through empowered river basin organizations is simply not possible when it comes to megacities. As shown in every case in this collection, policymakers are uniformly driven toward supply-side solutions beyond the basin within which they are located. As cities grow, projects grow in scale and complexity. Green infrastructure undertaken at various scales can make a meaningful difference, but it cannot substitute for new supply.

Megacities' resource footprints are global, extending far beyond their immediate watersheds, and so constitute what J. A. Allan (2005) describes as 'problemsheds'. Water shortage in Beijing cannot be solved through local water endowment; it can only be solved by bringing water from elsewhere. This can be in the form of food imports (e.g. the water embedded 'virtually' in rice production) or direct water imports via a large-scale project such as the SNWDP. Decisions were taken to assure water security come with trade-offs. Each decision taken rules out a different decision. To commit to a multi-billion dollar project carries with it great responsibilities and turns a watershed into a problemshed. Most of the case studies placed significant emphasis on city's commitments to some form of integrated resource management, be it IWRM or integrated urban water management (IUWM), or integrated water management. Theoretically, most of the cities could operate within an IWRM framework as articulated in SDG 60.5.1. Only Beijing, Cape Town, Istanbul and Sao Paulo draw significant amounts of water from outside of their primary watershed. Importantly, all chapters emphasize the need for an 'IWRM-oriented' planning sensibility, as opposed to slavishly adhering to some sort of technical formula.

Complex systems analysis requires decision-makers to consider the interrelationships of numerous variables operating within socio-ecological systems. IWRM is one possible approach. The water-energy-food-ecosystems (WEFE) nexus is another. Little considered in any of the chapters is the role of virtual water in urban water security. If the pandemic has taught us about the vulnerability of supply chains within neoliberal globalization, the war in Ukraine has reinforced how vulnerable all cities are to disruptions of staple food supplies (Kemmerling et al., 2022). This is somewhat surprising given how impactful food price hikes were in 2008, leading to a series of riots in urban areas around the world (Berazneva & Lee, 2013; Leach et al., 2020). Put differently, urban water security—indeed urban social sustainability—is food security. Few if any cities, however, have integrated systems of food supply into water security considerations. If they have, it has been in an ad hoc way through solid waste management (Adhikari et al., 2009).

Paying for Water

Reductionist approaches to achieving water security overwhelmingly concentrate on supply infrastructure (Zeitoun et al., 2016). As shown in the Tokyo case, even green approaches to stormwater management and wastewater reuse require extensive new infrastructure, which requires capital. This leads unavoidably to pricing and the important question, who must pay? All chapters reflect on the economic costs of water supply and sanitation. While there were some serious concerns raised regarding letting 'the market' decide who gets how much water at what cost, all contributors considered cities' moves toward block tariffs as a fair and reasonable approach. Applying a polluter pays principle was also seen as important, as were penalties for over-pumping groundwater. In all cases, paying for water was regarded as important but needed to be embedded in improved state-civil society relations through, for example, sustained consumer engagement, transparent and accurate reporting by utilities, and space made for citizens to directly participate in water governance. This could be through, for example, urban water forums and/or citizen science/participatory GIS in monitoring and reporting on leakages, flood events and so on.

Smart Cities/AI/Surveillance and Monitoring

There was little directly said in the chapters about 'smart cities', although much was implied. For example, managing Tokyo's stormwater or Beijing's drinking water is highly technical, deploying several 'fail safe' systems (World Bank, 2018). For Calvillo et al. (2016: 273), 'a *smart city* is a sustainable and efficient urban centre that provides a high quality of life to its inhabitants through optimal management of its resources'.

Climate change and COVID-19 have combined to bring the concept of the 'smart city' to the forefront of post-pandemic urban planning. Enhanced abilities to monitor systems of supply in real time offer possibilities for increased efficiencies of resource use and heightened citizen safety. However, apps for tracking person-to-person contact during COVID-19 now hold out the promise for governments to monitor citizen movements, carrying with it a fascist undertone of constant surveillance of 'outgroups'.

Part of the promise of AI is doing more with less effort, meaning that the technology does most of the work. For example, a computer chip placed on a community water pump can be calibrated to send a signal to the water utility if water has stopped flowing over a particular duration of time. While there is obvious value in such technologies, the 'surveillance' issue noted above raises the important question of governance arrangements. Most papers noted the poor level of state-citizen engagement, and highlighted that an important benchmark of successful IWRM is meaningful stakeholder participation. In the case of AI and 'smart cities', this means interrogating the ways and means decisions were taken regarding the deployment of certain technologies. Put differently, if decision-makers have never set foot into a slum, how do they know what water/sanitation technology is appropriate? While smart cities are primarily about the application of technologies in support of resource use efficiencies, decisions regarding what might work where and why is of equal importance. Too often, technologies have been a weak substitute for direct engagement with the citizenry. Put differently, for the authors of these chapters, a smart city is also one where public-private-community partnerships are well established in pursuit of a commonly agreed upon goal. In high density areas, public toilets and water kiosks have often been vandalized because they are emblematic of the gap between the 'two cities'. Bridging this gap is essential for sustainable resource management.

Ethics, Trade-Offs, Tipping Points and the End of Civilisation

The papers in this collection take governments at their word and assess their performance based on their published documents and public pronouncements. These documents uniformly express an ethic of care and a logic based on matching needs with capabilities. The authors cannot peer into the rooms where decisions are made, to observe the trade-offs, the benefit-cost analyses, the hard-bargaining that without doubt underlies actual practice. Assumptions are often made by analysts based on ideological positions. Performance in support of urban water security is often regarded as a reflection of elites who understand water as an economic good, and/or as a factor of production. Access to water and sanitation was declared a human right more than a decade ago, yet almost one billion people lack access to potable water and improved sanitation (see Chapter 1). Is the answer as simple as governments serve themselves and are generally corrupt? Based on the findings of the essays in this collection, one would have to say that no, it isn't so simple.

If it were so simple, then all cases would show the same results. Instead, what one finds from the evidence presented here as well as in the wider literature, is that sometimes things work very well despite expectations. The question being, what accounts for the different outcomes? While a full analysis is beyond the scope of this short conclusion, one can point to a variety of variables: colonial/imperial history, for example, plays an important role in all megacities of the Global South but the impact is not uniform. To be sure, Cape Town, Sao Paulo, Chennai and Jakarta all bear the heavy legacy of European urban design, but how these cities were embedded in the broader political economy of the region and the colonial world impacted them differently. Cultural factors no doubt play a role, with civil society activism across India, indeed a willingness to fight for what you believe in, providing different possibilities than in states such as Turkey where civil society has been deliberately oppressed or mobilized in the name of populist nationalism. Tokyo's difficult geography with its susceptibility to a variety of natural hazards naturally pulls states and civil society in a common direction of concern for disaster management and mitigation. Events often act as tipping points, such as South Africa's long struggle against apartheid leading to a post-apartheid dispensation making water supply a priority. Beyond this collection, Manila offers an interesting case where a social revolution resulted in a dramatic shift in the constellation of social forces to bring slum dwellers firmly into the urban governance framework (Cash, 2021).

Adaptation and resilience are buzzwords meant to galvanize thinking around the ways and means of ensuring that cities continue but have the capacity to change for the greater good. What is missing from much of the sustainable cities discourse is mobility. In the presence of populations on the move, displaced in the millions by conflicts throughout the Middle

East, North Africa and now Ukraine, human 'mobility' is regarded as a threat to be contained. Yet people have always moved, just as societies and civilizations have always collapsed (Diamond, 2005). The march to the cities will continue. Whereas, from a critical political ecologist's point of view, the Indonesian government's decision to abandon Jakarta and build an entirely new capital city feels like failure, perhaps it is simply the best of a series of very bad options. To reiterate, mobility is the hallmark of human settlement. If we are serious about sustainability, and avoiding collapse, it seems important to us that we pay careful attention to what works, where and why, and to critically ask ourselves, is this fungible? The essays in this collection offer some interesting ideas along these lines, but there is much more work to be done.

References

Adhikari, B., Barrington, S., & Martinez, J. (2009). Urban food waste generation: Challenges and opportunities. *International Journal of Environment and Waste Management, 3*(1/2), 4–21.

Allan, J. A. (2005). Water in the environment/socio-economic development discourse: Sustainability, changing management paradigms and policy responses in a global system. *Government and Opposition, 40*(2), 181–199.

Berazneva, J., & Lee, D. R. (2013). Explaining the African food riots of 2007–2008: An empirical analysis. *Food Policy, 39*, 28–39.

Calvillo, C., Sanchez, A., & Villar, J. (2016). Energy management and planning in smart cities. *Renewable & Sustainable Energy Reviews, 55*, 273–287.

Cash, C. (2021). Creating the conditions for climate resilience: A community-based approach in Canumay East, Philippines. *Urban Planning, 6*(4), 298–308.

Diamond, J. (2005). *Collapse: How societies choose to fail or succeed*. Penguin Books.

Kemmerling, B., Schetter, C., & Wirkus, L. (2022). The logics of war and food (in)security. *Global Food Security, 33*, 100634.

Leach, M., Nisbett, N., Cabral, L., Harris, J., Hossain, N., & Thompson, J. (2020). Food politics and development. *World Development, 134*, 105024.

World Bank. (2018). *Resilient water supply and sanitation services*. The World Bank.

World Health Organization (WHO)., and UNICEF. (2020 July 29). *Water, sanitation, hygiene, and waste management for SARS-CoV-2, the virus that causes COVID-19*. https://www.who.int/teams/environment-climate-change-and-health/water-sanitation-and-health/burden-of-disease/wash-and-covid19. Accessed 8 April 2022.

Zeitoun, M., Lankford, B., Krueger, T., Forsyth, T., Carter, R., Hoekstra, A. Y., Taylor, R., Varis, O., Cleaver, F., Boelens, R., Swatuk, L., Tickner, D., Scott, C. A., Mirumachi N., & Matthews N. (2016). 'Reductionist and integrative research approaches to complex water security policy challenges'. *Global Environmental Change, 39*, 143–154.

Index

L. Swatuk and C. Cash (eds.), *The Political Economy of Urban Water Security under Climate Change*, International Political Economy Series,
https://doi.org/10.1007/978-3-031-08108-8

W

www.ingramcontent.com/pod-product-compliance
Ingram Content Group UK Ltd.
Pitfield, Milton Keynes, MK11 3LW, UK
UKHW020835290926
15470UKWH00004B/1354
* 9 7 8 3 0 3 1 0 8 1 0 7 1 *